AL QAEDA DECLARES WAR

AL QAEDA

THE AFRICAN EMBASSY

BOMBINGS AND AMERICA'S

SEARCH FOR JUSTICE

TOD HOFFMAN

DECLARES WAR

ForeEdge

ForeEdge

An imprint of University Press of New England

www.upne.com

© 2014 Tod Hoffman

All rights reserved

Manufactured in the United States of America

Designed by Mindy Basinger Hill

Typeset in Minion Pro

University Press of New England is a member of the Green
Press Initiative. The paper used in this book meets their
minimum requirement for recycled paper.

ISBN 978-1-61168-546-6 (cloth: alk. paper)
ISBN 978-1-61168-565-7 (ebook)
Library of Congress Control Number: 2013954867

5   4   3   2   1

To Sally for accompanying me

Hold tight to your anger
And don't fall to your fears
—Bruce Springsteen, "Wrecking Ball"

CONTENTS

Illustrations follow page 156.

AL QAEDA DECLARES WAR

Everything is touched by the holy when in the presence of death.
—Karl Marlantes, *What It Is Like to Go to War*

[1] DARK DAY IN AFRICA

There comes no warning.

No ominous music rises up. No shadow passes across the flawless blue sky. The man who has been preparing himself to kill and to die doesn't smell of sulfur, nor do his eyes glint red. He could scrape right by you without raising a goose bump.

The unsuspecting victim has no peace to reflect, no comfort of farewell. No last opportunity to seek grace. Solid and sentient, preoccupied by hopes for the future and disappointments of the past. The present barely remarked upon. The unlikely miracle of passing across this earth never paid sufficient awe.

Nobody wakes up conceding, today is the day the world goes on without me. Yet, one day, that is exactly what happens. You'd go mad behaving as if life or death hinges on whether you walk along this side of the street or that; whether your office is on this floor of the building or another, your desk facing the window or the wall. Even though your fate can turn on nothing more momentous.

Until this suffering force erupts. Swallowing the world in an all-engulfing roar. A flash of white and orange and black charged with energy that rips and twists and sizzles and melts. Agonizing, disemboweling, dismembering, liquefying. In a fraction of an instant, between one blink and the one never to follow.

This is the apocalypse writ small; misery by misery, anguish upon anguish.

August 7, 1998, marked exactly eight years to the day since American troops had arrived in Saudi Arabia to take part in Operation Desert Shield, the first phase of a massive response to Iraq's invasion of Kuwait. They had been invited to defend the kingdom against the threat that Saddam Hussein would continue his march of conquest across the Arabian Peninsula. Hardly anyone in East Africa—or anywhere else, for that matter—was wary of the anniversary. That war had been won, Iraq expelled from Kuwait, and the Saudi kingdom preserved. The world had moved on. But not Osama bin Laden.

While he brooded and plotted vengeance over the presence of foreign troops on his native soil, the citizens of Nairobi, Kenya, and Dar es Salaam, Tanzania, were preparing for the frantic hustle that begins with every dawn.

Poor people can't afford to be lazy.

Those lucky enough to have office jobs downtown rise before the sun. They dress in clothes still damp from the previous night's hand-rinse, their bodies already sweaty in the stifled air of the shanty. Many will spend more than an hour commuting, bleary-eyed, on dangerously overcrowded buses and minivans. Street peddlers gather their wares and lay claim to the prime spots before the traffic converges along main arteries and clogs up at the roundabouts that punctuate the city like full stops. They rush among the impatient cars and trucks, pushing soft drinks and snacks, newspapers and, when they spy tourists—prized for their ready cash and shame for their plenty—small trinkets. At the same time, the peddlers are vigilant for a whiff of police, who threaten them with summary fines for obstructing the unmoving traffic or lash out with their long canes. Baksheesh can buy some peace, but, oh, the cost. When every thin shilling is dear. When you are spurned on a hundred approaches for every sale.

The rewards for hard work are so meager. The fires of ambition easily snuffed out by disappointment. The prospects for comfort in this life slip over the horizon with each setting sun. The temptation to give up is a tender caress. That most don't succumb is a testament to Africa's strength. People rising day upon day with no greater expectation than to see tomorrow. To do one's best under circumstances that are weighted down by the worst is true courage.

Along Daniel arap Moi Avenue, one of Nairobi's main thoroughfares, vehicle and foot traffic is a thick, writhing serpent uncoiling the entire day. The U.S. Embassy—a five-story structure, with two stories underground, including a parking garage—sat on a half-acre lot at the confluence of Moi and Haile Selassie Avenues.

The suicide bomber doesn't agonize over life's most disturbing question: How and when will I die? That answer he is given.

He isn't trying to sidestep the moment. He doesn't negotiate with his deity for any more days. He isn't anxious over an uncertain future. He doesn't admit doubt. He believes fervently in all that eternity promises: the fertile garden, the succulent virgins.

One conundrum he faces is this: how to hurry on to paradise without violating Islam's injunction against suicide, a grave sin punishable by eternal damnation, the very antithesis of what the martyr seeks. And this paradox: since God forbids suicide, must He not place some value on this life?

The distinction between suicide and martyrdom is no trivial issue in the thinking of an al Qaeda jihadi. Bin Laden went to great lengths to provide religious sanction for his group's actions. It was critical to his efforts to win hearts and minds and to maintain the loyalty of his troops that he imbue his exhortations to kill with moral authority. He was adamant, therefore, that his murderous invocations were Islamically correct and, thus, blessed by God.

The idea of committing a sin in furtherance of a righteous cause is theologically untenable. Osama's trick was to twist the sin of suicide into the virtuous act of martyrdom. As well, he had to convince his disciples that their innocent victims constituted reasonable and necessary sacrifices to a greater good, that the truly innocent would share the rewards of paradise with their killers, while only the wicked would suffer.

Mohamed Rashed Daoud al-'Owhali was only twenty-one when he intended to die a martyr—along with as many others as he could possibly kill. He had trained in al Qaeda camps and steeled himself for that day. He was in the passenger seat of a cream-colored Toyota Dyna truck. Its covered cargo bay was packed with a volatile mix of TNT, aluminum nitrate, and aluminum powder, along with gas cylinders to amplify the force of the explosion. The driver was a fellow Saudi known as Azzam (whose real name was Jihad Mohammed Ali al-Harazi, aka Abu Obeydah al-Maki).

Al-'Owhali's job was to force the guards at the American Embassy to allow Azzam to drive the truck into the garage. He had a pistol in his jacket pocket and four stun grenades tucked into his belt. In his pants pocket were keys that would enable him to open padlocks at the rear of the truck and manually detonate the bomb in the event that the button Azzam was to push in the cab should malfunction.

They pulled out of 43 New Runda Estates, the residential compound shared by the conspirators, around 9:45 am Azzam followed a pickup truck driven by Fazul Abdullah Mohammed, known as Harun, the "key al-Qa'ida operative who coordinated the planning, logistics, preparation of explosives."[1] The two trucks threaded through the congested streets of downtown Nairobi. Harun leading them in the direction of the embassy, as far as the closest roundabout, at which point he turned off, leaving the bombers to proceed on their own to carry out their mission.

Al-'Owhali was sweating profusely. Azzam suggested he remove his jacket.

Azzam circled around Haile Selassie and turned the wrong way down an alley that ran between the embassy and the Cooperative Bank Building. At that same moment a white sedan pulled out of the garage opposite, from beneath the bank. This momentary bottleneck brought the truck to a stop and drew the attention of security guard Benson Okuku Bwaku. He lowered the manual drop bar that controlled access onto the grounds. He said later, "I just feel something in my blood that the van was unusual."[2]

The car pulled back, ceding right of way, and, gingerly, the truck edged forward to the bar. Flustered, Azzam couldn't maneuver any closer to the embassy garage. Al-'Owhali sprang out of the truck and ran at the gate, yelling at the guard to raise the bar. Though armed only with a staff, Bwaku refused.

Too late, al-'Owhali realized that he'd left his jacket with the pistol behind. Having no other weapon, he pulled out the stun grenades and flung them in the direction of the embassy. They caused a shocking ruckus, but no damage. Azzam pulled out his own gun and began firing wildly. Bwaku fled toward the main building while desperately trying to summon help on his radio, "Base! Base! Terrorism! Terrorism!"[3] Another guard, Joash Okindo, pulled down and locked the steel gate to secure the underground parking garage.

Seconds later, at around 10:30, Azzam, concluding that they had been thwarted from advancing any closer to their objective, ignited the truck. He was extinguished in the first spark.

Was his last conscious thought of the agonies of hell or the anticipation of paradise?

Al-'Owhali was knocked flat on his stomach by the shock waves emanating from the blast. His shirt was shredded and he was bloodied, but, miraculously, he had only minor wounds to his forehead, hands, and back. Telltale wounds that would lead investigators to suspect he had turned away from the explosion, indicating foreknowledge.

He looked around at the carnage and confusion, heard the screams and wails through the smoky haze, saw people lying in the streets, writhing in pain and shock. He might have noticed body parts strewn about, arms and legs dangling from trees, dripping like putrefying fruit.

Al-'Owhali was supposed to be consumed in the conflagration. However, he rationalized, there was nothing more he could do. If he just stayed there, to no other purpose than to die, it would not be a heroic act of martyrdom, but a forbidden suicide. He quickly made the theological decision to flee, and found his way to Nairobi's MP Shah Hospital for care.

He has never conceded that his zeal for death wavered. FBI Special Agent Steve Gaudin, who would interview him, said, "Al-'Owhali explained to me that he was fully prepared to die in carrying out the mission and that that would equate to being a martyr. . . . But to die after your mission had already been completed . . . is not martyrdom, it's suicide, and he explains that suicide is not acceptable in his religion and that that wasn't what his mission was. To die a martyr carrying out the mission was fine, but there was no reason for him to commit suicide."

The bomb was so powerful that buildings five hundred feet from the epicenter suffered damage and debris from the blast was tossed over a ten-block radius.

The nearby Ufundi Cooperative House, which was home to a secretarial college, collapsed in a heap, crushing scores of people under the rubble.

The Cooperative Bank Building was heavily damaged—every single window of its twenty-two stories was blown out—though it remained standing. U.S. Ambassador Prudence Bushnell was on its top floor meeting with the minister of commerce. Tea had just been served when they heard what sounded like small explosions. Those closest to the window went to see what had happened. Here was the insidious thing about the stun grenades: the uproar drew people to windows and caused passers-by to slow out of curiosity, thereby exposing more people to the shards of splintered glass raining out in all directions, slicing flesh, ripping bone, and pulverizing eyes. Indiscriminately maiming there, killing here, miraculously sparing over there.

Bushnell was just rising from her chair to see for herself what was going on. Then came the enormous explosion. She was instantly thrown back and momentarily lost consciousness.

As she came to, in the vacuum of silence following the roar of the blast, she said, "I will never forget the rattling of a teacup, just kept rattling. I thought to myself that the building was going to collapse, that I was going to tumble down all those stories, and that I was going to die. . . .

"But it didn't. The teacup stopped rattling and there was quiet."[4]

One of her colleagues roused her and, together, they made a quick round of the floor, gathering up some other survivors and leading them to the stairwell. The ceiling had begun to cave in.

"I was struck by the almost eerie silence," she recounted. "It was a very hushed procession. As people joined us from different floors, sometimes you would hear somebody yell out welcome. You could also hear people who were praying. Some other people were singing hymns. Down we went. As we got to the lower floors, this huge procession of people, who were bleeding all over one another—there was blood everywhere, on the bannister, I could feel the person behind me bleeding on my hair and down my back."

When she reached the street to a scene of utter chaos, and with fears of a secondary explosion running high, she was rushed to a car and taken away. It was later ascertained that al Qaeda hoped, specifically, to kill her: firstly, because she was the ranking American at the mission, but also because she was a woman and they believed this would give the attack even greater resonance.

Inside the embassy, it was pandemonium. Frank Pressley, the information officer, had a piece of his jaw and his shoulder blown off in the explosion. "I looked around, I saw like chunks of blood or red, kind of meat, on the walls. Some of the walls were actually missing, too. It was pretty shocking."

He went on, "I saw some legs, a pair of just man's legs with the pants on."

George Mimba, a foreign service national, was the information systems manager. He was blown off his feet, blinded, and choking on smoke and debris. In desperation, he crawled in the direction from which he felt cool, breathable air. "I was shaking. When I opened my eyes, I saw the garden, a green garden. I said, 'Where am I?' As I was moving toward the window, I could feel people's—could feel bodies of the dead people."

Despite fears that the building would collapse, despite the horror of the dismembered bodies and the blood, Mimba ran back into the embassy to help others reach safety.

Tobias Otieno, who had worked at the embassy for thirty years, was pulled by rescuers from the wreckage. "My eyes were shattered by the exploding glass, I shattered my eyes, I lost my vision, and then I lost my left hand on the wrist was severed off. It was hanging by a thread, and my four upper teeth, and several wounds on my face and body."

Regional medical officer Dr. Gretchen Anne McCoy got out of the building after the blast, but returned several times to search for casualties. On one foray inside, she saw two of the victims. "Michelle [O'Connor] was basically decapitated from the jaw up and Jay Bartley was in the doorway and his legs were basically thrown over his shoulders. They were clearly dead. There was nothing more that could be done for them."

In all, the explosion unleashed by Azzam claimed 213 innocent people, some torn apart by the massive blast or consumed in its fire, some shredded by spears of glass and blades of metal propelled from the embassy and surrounding buildings. Others were crushed beneath tons of concrete and other debris loosed by the bomb. More than four thousand five hundred were wounded, many grievously, losing eyes and limbs. Skin melted in pools like wax, cartilage and muscle fused, bones crackled. Blood everywhere.

Ironically, Harun, one of al Qaeda's leading figures in East Africa, would go to great lengths to explain how the operation was carefully planned to minimize civilian casualties. The attacks were timed to follow closely one of the five daily calls to prayer, when all righteous Muslims ought to have been off the street, on the premise that this made it less likely to kill the observant. He also said that non-Muslims were more likely to be safe in their offices than, for example, at noon when they could be on the street for their lunch break. He also insisted that having al-'Owhali set off stun grenades was intended to cause people to flee the area before the bomb exploded.[5]

Ten minutes after the Nairobi explosion, a second suicide truck bomb was detonated, 415 miles to the southeast of the city, at the U.S. Embassy in Dar es Salaam (harbor of peace in English). More than two hundred people were wounded and eleven lives were taken. Gone, gruesomely gone.

Overlooking the Indian Ocean, Dar es Salaam is a less frenetic, less crime-ridden city than the Kenyan capital. The trade winds make for a more temperate climate. The diplomatic quarter is in the upscale Oyster Bay neighborhood not far, but still removed, from the downtown core. Traffic in the area is steady, but not as heavy as in Nairobi. The State Department designated the post threat level as low.

The embassy comprised two buildings in an enclosed compound on Laibon Road. The three-story chancery was originally built by Israel in the 1970s to house its mission. It had been constructed with the possibility of terrorist attacks in mind and, therefore, exceeded contemporary U.S. standards. The Americans leased it in 1980 and added a four-story annex. Though surrounded by a perimeter fence, at some points the embassy was as close as twenty-five feet from the street.

Because the tap water in Dar es Salaam is unsafe for consumption, the embassy's potable water supply was brought in by huge tankers. August 7 was delivery day. The truck pulled up a little past 10:30 am. The driver and his assistant began to fill the storage tanks at the side of the building. While they worked, their truck obstructed access to the grounds.

Meanwhile, a 1987 Nissan Atlas truck had left 213 Ilala Road about a half hour earlier. It was driven by an Egyptian, Hamdan Khalif Alal, known as Ahmed the German because of his light complexion and fair hair. Khalfan Khamis Mohamed, known as K. K., volunteered to accompany him because, unlike Ahmed, he spoke Swahili and English. Should Ahmed get lost in Dar's labyrinthine streets or have need for any reason to communicate with anyone, Khalfan would do the talking. He was not to be martyred.

K. K. got out of the truck when they reached Uhuru Road, within sight of the embassy, and returned to the Ilala residence, where he set about thoroughly cleaning the house and everything in it to eliminate all trace of explosives.

Ahmed continued down Laibon Road.

The driveway onto the embassy grounds was protected with a gate manned by a pair of unarmed Tanzanian guards. Ahmed pulled up, but, because of the water truck, he was forced to come to a stop about thirty-five feet from the outer wall of the chancery building. Having closely monitored embassy routines, the attackers most likely planned for their arrival to coincide with the departure of the water truck. However, for some reason, the timing was off on this day.[6]

Since he was incapable of talking his way past the guards, there was nothing for Ahmed to do except push the detonator. He could pause to decide which of several breaths was to be his last. At 10:39 he completed his mission.

The brunt of the explosive force was absorbed by the water truck, which was propelled three stories into the air and came to rest against the chancery. The driver was killed at the same instant as the bomber.

At first, it was presumed that the bomb had actually been contained in the water truck. That suspicion was reinforced by the disappearance of the driver's assistant. In truth, that unfortunate man had been absolutely obliterated, leaving no more trace of his existence than an ant crushed beneath a boot. Five Tanzanian security guards were also killed instantly, along with a gardener, a cleaner, a Somali visa applicant, and a Kenyan waiting in the courtyard for his American wife, who was inside cashing a check. Several Americans were among the hundreds wounded.

Acting Ambassador John Lange was in his top-floor office meeting with his

political-economic staff at the time of the explosion. He would recall, "Every room in the building was devastated. I was sitting with my back to the outside wall when glass blew in over my head—in what seemed like slow motion—and rained down on those in front of me. Thankfully, no one in our meeting was seriously injured."[7]

Marines and security officers moved quickly to secure the site. Ambulances and firefighters rushed to the scene. Lange described a situation that was initially confused, but over which control was quickly established. The injured were taken to the Muhimbili Hospital, Dar's main medical facility.

"And the Marines came, and it still rings in my ears," Lange testified in court, sounding as though he had been, understandably, overwhelmed by the extraordinary situation. "I still remember the regional security officer coming up to me on the street to say, 'Sir, the Marines have secured the building.' There was something comforting about the idea that in this chaos we still had been able to secure the building."

Staff assembled at Lange's nearby residence to coordinate activity, communicate with State Department headquarters at Foggy Bottom, and set up a makeshift first aid clinic. They quickly moved to account for all American and foreign service national personnel.

That the death toll was far lower in Dar than Nairobi had much to do with the fact that, while suffering major damage, no buildings collapsed. A number of neighboring diplomatic establishments were damaged, along with many American residences. The ceiling of the ambassador's home, about a thousand yards from the epicenter of the explosion, caved in. Since the ambassador's post was vacant at the time, it was unoccupied.

"The compression of the bomb blast was less," explained FBI Assistant Special Agent in Charge (ASAC) Ken Piernick, who initially led the investigation. "It blew up and out a lot more than in Nairobi, where it was contained by surrounding buildings."[8]

The FBI responded to the attacks with the largest overseas deployment in its history. Moreover, it was "not just the biggest joint counterterrorism investigation mounted overseas by American intelligence and law-enforcement agencies . . . [but also] the first in which they share[d] rules and roles."[9] It yielded spectacular results.

"Probably the finest investigation I was ever involved in," recalled Pat D'Amuro, an ASAC in the National Security Division at the FBI's New York field office, who was dispatched to Nairobi. "The reason it's important for this story to be told is that the East Africa investigation pulled together massive amounts of intelligence and can be credited with opening eyes around the world to the extent of the threat posed by al Qaeda."[10] And yet, little would be done to dismantle that threat until after 9/11.

Twenty-two suspects, including bin Laden, were indicted for nearly three hundred crimes by the U.S. Attorney's Office for the Southern District of New York, which was given jurisdiction over the case. Within months, perpetrators had been arrested in Kenya, Pakistan, the United States, South Africa, Germany, and the United Kingdom. In 2000, four defendants—al-'Owhali, Mohamed Saddiq Odeh, K. K. Mohamed, and Wadih el Hage—were brought before the federal court, the first al Qaeda terrorists to be tried. Said Mary Jo White, the U.S. attorney responsible for the Southern District, "We got to put the organization on trial alongside the individuals. We got to publicly lay out the hierarchy of al Qaeda. The entire blueprint for our military going after its leadership in Afghanistan [following 9/11] came out of this investigation."[11]

In the annals of terrorism, al-'Owhali stands alone as the only suicide bomber ever to both succeed in his mission and to survive. I wish I could have the opportunity to ask him about that. To ask, "At the instant you decided to live, seeing the hellish scene you'd caused, hearing the sounds that only excruciating agony can produce, smelling the noxious mixture fueling the raging inferno, did you—even for that instant—wish you could take it all back?"

I don't know what he might answer. Does fanaticism admit no compassion? Is he grateful for the second chance at life, or is he bitter to have been denied the pleasures of martyrdom? Did the panic that caused him to save himself open a wedge through which misgivings seep? Did his own fright not arouse empathy?

"He's not a monster," states Fredrick Cohn, one of the attorneys who defended him at trial.[12] Not in the sense of being some otherworldly creature, he isn't. But he is certainly a human being capable of monstrosity. We know he was prepared to indiscriminately take the lives of others. We can't be sure of his willingness to sacrifice his own, despite the apparent resolve.

Al-'Owhali would believe that the prescribed punishment for suicide is to repeat its torment for all eternity. Though having fled death, he is nonetheless cursed to an analogous fate. He currently spends twenty-three hours of every day isolated in a small cell in the Supermax Federal Detention Center at Florence, Colorado, the highest security facility in the U.S. Bureau of Prisons. The twenty-fourth hour he spends in solitary recreation in a slightly larger pen. He will pass the rest of his days like this, without variation. He has little to do with his time but think. About what he did. About who he is. And about the bigger questions concerning what it all meant.

And, oh yes, about how and when he will die.

History is where everything unexpected in its
own time is chronicled on the page as inevitable.
—Philip Roth, *The Plot against America*

[2] OSAMA'S WAR

Joe Billy, an ASAC in the National Security Division at the FBI's New York Field
Office, was in his Federal Plaza office in lower Manhattan watching the first
reports of the carnage as they were broadcast on CNN. His boss, John O'Neill,
poked his head in and stated, simply, "It's bin Laden."[1]

The leader of al Qaeda was already well known in terrorism and counterterrorism circles. Two years earlier, he had called attention to himself by issuing
a bombastic declaration of war against the United States. And only months
before the embassies were attacked, he'd called upon Muslims to kill Americans
whenever and wherever they could. If this was his handiwork, it was al Qaeda's
first direct strike against the United States, and he'd have demonstrated capability behind his bluster.

Osama began devoting himself full-time to jihad and the cause of liberating
Afghanistan from Soviet invaders in 1986, when he left the comfort of his af-
fluent life in Saudi Arabia and settled in Peshawar, Pakistan. He was welcomed
among the swarms of militants, recruiters, and arms dealers who were aiding,
and profiting from, the battles across the frontier. His deep pockets and the
renown of his family name made him a rock star in the jihadi world. While as-
siduously cultivating the image of a warrior, he was mostly a financier, paying
his way to prominence.

Bin Laden's father, Mohamed, lived a classic rags-to-riches fable that would
be familiar to any telling of the American dream. An impoverished Yemeni, he
immigrated to Saudi Arabia, where he worked as a laborer, eventually found-
ing a construction company that grew into a grand conglomerate. He amassed
fabulous wealth from public projects. His first major contract came in 1950, when
he built a paved road between Jeddah and Medina to accommodate the growing
traffic to the annual Hajj pilgrimage. He would go on to renovate Medina and, in

1956, to enlarge the mosque at Mecca. In 1958, he began refurbishing the Dome of the Rock and Al Aqsa Mosque in Jerusalem. Thus, in the course of a decade, Mohamed bin Laden had a direct hand in improving the three holiest sites in Islam. With his private aircraft to ferry him around, he boasted that he was able to pray at Mecca, Medina, and Jerusalem all in the same day. This connection to the sacred places was central to Osama's legendary piety.

The bin Laden family has flourished by hewing to the social contract of serving the al-Saud dynasty and explicitly keeping out of politics.[2] Even Osama's initial flirtations with the radical Muslim Brotherhood in the early 1970s while he was still in high school were not perceived as threatening to the regime. He wasn't, they thought, some unpredictable outsider, but a trustworthy member of the establishment.

The Brotherhood had been feared as a reactionary fringe in many Muslim countries, especially Egypt, where it was outlawed for decades because of the challenge it posed to the secular government. In Saudi Arabia, fraternizing with it "did not, then, carry him into a state of opposition toward the Saudi government; in some respects, it deepened his alignment with [King] Faisal's foreign policy." As Steve Coll explains, "The Muslim Brotherhood's revolutionary goals made the King uncomfortable because they challenged the authority of the Al-Saud family, yet Faisal's own vision of a politically conscious Islam echoed the Brotherhood's call for action against enemies of the faith."[3] The monarchy happily accommodated Islamists so long as their vitriol and violence were directed away from the kingdom. They have, after all, long supported the spread of their own puritanical Wahhabi school of Islamic practice, which fit comfortably with bin Laden's worldview of a perpetual conflict between believers and nonbelievers, and the responsibility upon the former to wage jihad against the latter. The tensions between the excesses indulged by the profligate royals and their minions (including most of the bin Ladens) and the austerity of the pious Wahhabis is a significant concern for the ruling elite, who are determined to placate the Islamists without surrendering their pleasures.

During the Cold War, the Americans had no quarrel with God-fearing theocrats. All they craved were stable regimes resistant to the pull of the Soviet orbit. Thankful that Islamists could never find common cause with atheists, the Americans believed they stood as an unwavering bulwark against Soviet ambitions in the Middle East and Central Asia.

Only much later would they regret how their single-minded fixation on the Communist threat left them so undiscriminating about those whom they befriended—and armed. Or, perhaps, history will ultimately judge that al Qaeda was a better alternative to sustaining a sullen nuclear armed standoff against a sometimes expansionist European empire.

The reasons the United States adopted the ferocious Islamist fighters as proxies to tie down Soviet forces that invaded Afghanistan in 1979 (contrary to persistent rumors, bin Laden was not among those with whom the Americans had a direct relationship) were the same for which the Cold War had been fought across the developing world for decades. The United States was not even necessarily op-posed to the Sunni Taliban when they first emerged and imposed long-absent, and much-needed, order after the fall of the Afghan Communists in 1991. That they considered the Shia rulers of neighboring Iran heretics and had no affinity for Iraq's profane Saddam Hussein seemed the basis for a nice regional balance. Their friendly relations with Pakistan's powerful Inter-Services Intelligence (ISI) suggested that they could be receptive to reason. All in all, the Americans did not anticipate any long-term crisis emanating from Afghanistan or brought about by the so-called Afghan Arabs who had fought there and subsequently found themselves with neither a purpose nor a place. On the contrary, they expected some lasting dividends from the assistance they'd rendered.

What the Americans ignored was that the Islamic extremists were even more cynical than the most hardened cold warrior. They made little distinction be-tween non-Muslims, whether atheist, Christian, or Jew. All were obstacles to the expansion and ascendancy of Islam. For the United States, the Afghan struggle was supposed to end with the Soviet withdrawal. For bin Laden, it was just the beginning; affirmation of Allah's favor and the righteous enormity of his power.

Osama carried himself with the peculiar arrogance of the fanatic. Using the outer trappings of a Spartan lifestyle—consuming only nibbles of food, forsaking comfort, and wearing the robes of a pauper—to pass for humble, yet convinced of his direct knowledge of God's will. Believing everything, including his own actions, were fated by God, he recognized no excess. With each bloody triumph, he became more certain of divine approval. As an agent of Allah's will, he absolved himself of any wrongdoing and felt justified in every ruthlessness.

Disregard for human life was one of bin Laden's key strategic advantages. Glorifying death was a hallmark of his zealotry. He encouraged his followers to think of this life as nothing but a brief opportunity to prove their worthiness for eternal paradise. The most certain way to earn God's favor, he insisted, was through martyrdom, to willingly sacrifice oneself in jihad on behalf of Islam. Ten days after American cruise missiles destroyed his training base at Khost in retaliation for the embassy bombings, bin Laden said, "I am fighting so I can die a martyr and go to heaven and meet God. Our fight is now against the Americans. I regret having lived this long. I have nothing to lose."[4]

There have always been conflicting stories about bin Laden's personal courage, with both sides, frankly, tinged by propaganda. His acolytes, the willing purveyors of his legend, insisting on his tranquillity under fire—to the point where he is reputed to have once dozed off under a heavy barrage of Soviet artillery—were the only eyewitnesses to his behavior. Equally biased were his enemies, who portrayed him as gun-shy, having rarely been in harm's way.

Referring to bin Laden's early mentor, Abdullah Azzam, a Palestinian with whom he created Mektab al Khidemet, the Services Bureau—forerunner of al Qaeda—Steve Coll notes, "Their conduct suggests that Osama and Azzam were less interested in becoming martyrs than in creating a movement based on the emotional power of other people's martyrdom."[5] Certainly, bin Laden would employ his charisma and wealth to convince many to sacrifice their lives in his service.

In November 1989, Osama returned to Saudi Arabia a conquering hero (in his own heart), righteously claiming victory over the mighty Soviets as if their withdrawal from Afghanistan were heavenly reward for his personal devotion and sacrifice. Swelled with self-importance, he cast about for another mission. In the Arab world, where war is always near, he wouldn't have to wait long for the next cause to present itself.

During the early morning hours of August 2, 1990, Saddam Hussein's forces invaded Kuwait. He rationalized this naked aggression by claiming it was rightfully Iraqi territory, a province severed by colonial interlopers, and declared his intention to annex it. This immediately sparked fears that he would march on Saudi Arabia in a gambit to seize control of its oil fields.

Bin Laden met with high-ranking Saudi defense officials and offered the services of his Afghan-hardened mujahideen to defend the Kingdom. He was rebuffed in favor of the United States and a coalition of other Western forces. He watched with horror as tens of thousands of American troops—men, women, Christians, and Jews—swarmed into the Arabian Peninsula—the land Mohammed specifically designated as off limits to infidels—for Operation Desert Shield beginning August 7, 1991. He was humiliated by the implication that Americans were better qualified to defend Muslim land than he was, lamenting that Saudi Arabia "has become an American colony,"[6] and declaring, "Never has Islam suffered a greater disaster than this invasion."[7]

For the first time, Osama dared to publicly question the royal family's legitimacy as custodians over Islam's holiest places. His family's influence probably saved him from suffering any apparent punishment. However, on May 1, 1991, he left the kingdom. "The circumstances surrounding his departure remain somewhat unclear," reported Coll, but one of his older brothers insisted he wasn't forced to leave.[8] According to former CIA agent Vince Cannistraro, who was a security advisor to the al-Sauds at the time, the Saudis told bin Laden that the CIA intended to kill him and they "staged a dramatic midnight 'escape'" to get him out of the country.[9]

He ended up back in Afghanistan, a brief stopover until he received an official invitation from the ruling National Islamic Front (NIF) to come to Sudan. Several Sudanese intelligence officers were sent to meet with him in Afghanistan: "Essentially, he was being offered an entire country in which to operate freely."[10]

Sudan promised a convivial environment. Though nominally led by a military officer, General Omar Bashir, the NIF was really controlled by Hassan al-Turabi, an Islamic scholar determined to establish a state governed strictly according to Islamic law and scripture.

Bin Laden purchased a farm north of Khartoum and, along with his four wives and growing brood of children, moved to the dusty North African city sometime between late 1991 and mid-1992.

With the NIF's support, bin Laden built up a diversified business portfolio. He owned the Al-Hijra Construction firm, which was given the contract to build a new highway linking Port Sudan, the main harbor on the Red Sea, with the capital. He ran two trading companies, Wadi al-Aqiq and Ladin International. Al Themar was an agricultural concern that managed a million-acre farm at Al-Damazin, where he grew peanuts and corn and manufactured sesame oil. His Thaba Investments was given a near monopoly on exporting gum, corn, sunflower, and sesame products, and traded in sugar, bananas, canned goods, and soap. The Blessed Fruit Company grew fruits and vegetables. Al-Ikhlas produced sweets and honey. Al-Qudurat was a trucking company. The Khartoum Tannery manufactured leather. He also owned a bakery and a furniture manufacturer. In addition, he invested $50 million of his own fortune in the Al-Shamal Islamic Bank in Khartoum.[11] "These companies were operated to provide income to support al Qaeda and to provide cover for the procurement of explosives, weapons and chemicals and for the travel of al Qaeda operatives," according to the indictment that the U.S. government would bring against him.[12]

Lawrence Wright suggested that bin Laden was content to run his businesses and live quietly in a functioning Islamic society, until the United States became engaged in Somalia: "Al-Qaeda as a terrorist organization was really born in the decisions that bin Laden and his *shura* council would make in this brief period when bin Laden was wavering—the lure of peace being as strong as the battle cry of jihad."[13]

The arrival of the Americans in Somalia in December 1992 gave credence to al Qaeda's suspicion over their broader motives in the Gulf, where they remained in force even after Saddam retreated. It seemed to them to be the second claw of a pincer movement to occupy the Arabian Peninsula. In fact, Operation Restore Hope was a United Nations–sanctioned humanitarian effort to bring order and relief to famine-stricken Somalis. Jamal al-Fadl, a senior al Qaeda member who defected to the United States in 1996, revealed that in late 1992 or early 1993 Abu Ubaydah, the organization's military commander at the time, "says the American army . . . already took off Gulf area and now they go to Somalia, and if they successful in Somalia, the next thing it could be south of Sudan and that's going—they going to take the Islamic countries." Bin Laden told al-Fadl, "We have to cut the head [of the snake] and stop them, what they doing now in Horn of Africa."[14]

On December 29, 1992, two people were killed when bombs exploded at two different hotels in Aden where U.S. troops en route to Somalia were housed. Intelligence revealed that the attacks were carried out by a Yemeni group whose leader sat on bin Laden's military council, and some of whose members had trained at an al Qaeda camp in Sudan.[15] Bin Laden stated that the attack was meant to discourage U.S. forces from using Yemen as a staging ground for its Somali operation. He said, "The United States received our warning and gave up the idea of setting up its military base in Yemen. This was the first al Qaeda victory scored against the Crusaders."[16]

U.S. troops landed at Mogadishu on December 9. In their efforts to ensure that international food aid was distributed to the population, they became progressively more embroiled in actions against Somali warlords, who fomented chaos to preserve their freedom to act with impunity and their control over the lucrative supplies pouring into the country. Americans were assigned to take some of the worst criminals into custody.

On October 3, 1993, an operation to apprehend senior lieutenants of an especially notorious warlord, Mohamed Farrah Aidid, in central Mogadishu—"the world capital of things-gone-completely-to-hell"[17]—went haywire. What was meant to be a simple snatch-and-go operation turned into a desperate and chaotic rescue mission when U.S. ground forces became pinned down by intense enemy fire and two Black Hawk helicopters were shot from the sky by Somali militiamen using rocket-propelled grenades (RPGs).

Images of American corpses being desecrated by frenzied crowds charged on bloodlust horrified the public and destroyed any sympathy for those starving Somalis it had been the mission's purpose to aid.

In the fateful confrontation to rescue trapped American soldiers and recover casualties, an estimated five hundred Somalis were killed and thousands were wounded. The United States suffered eighteen deaths. Had they chosen to do so, the Americans could have returned in force and inflicted even more catastrophic damage. Yet, the lasting perception has been that they were somehow defeated. In fact, there was just no political will (or reason) for the Americans to fully commit and no defined strategic objective to attain. As it was, the United States decided the time had come to withdraw. The warlords' victims would suffer further, as the international community lost interest in them, and ceded control to the worst of the thugs.

Somalia has remained in a condition of perpetual misery ever since, a tragically failed state caught up in anarchy. Pirates prey on merchant and private vessels far off its coast. To the extent that there is any central government, its capacity to assert sovereignty over its territory is severely constrained. It is fertile ground for al Qaeda and its affiliate, al Shabab, which has emerged as a regional threat in its own right, kidnapping westerners from neighboring Kenya and, in September 2013, staging an attack on a Nairobi shopping center that left more than sixty dead. In *Black Hawk Down*, his seminal account of the Mogadishu battle, written long before 9/11, Mark Bowden concluded, "The eight-hundred-pound gorilla's only weakness is his will. Routing Aidid would have, in the long run, saved American lives."[18]

In that book, Bowden only tacitly referred to an al Qaeda presence in Somalia: "Aidid's men received some expert guidance in shooting down helicopters from fundamentalist Islamic soldiers, smuggled in from Sudan, who had experience fighting Russian helicopters in Afghanistan."[19] Former FBI special agent Ali Soufan claims that it was actually an al Qaeda member who fired the rocket that took down one of the Black Hawks.[20]

Much of what bin Laden thought he knew about America he learned from Somalia. He mythologized the Mogadishu battle as a great Islamic victory and propagandized the American withdrawal as evidence of cowardice. He turned this incident into a decisive lesson in America's lack of resolve when even minimal casualties are inflicted. In an interview with *Al Jazeera* in December 1998, he said, "We believe that America is weaker than Russia, and from what we had heard from our brothers who waged *jihad* in Somalia, they found to their greatest surprise the weakness, frailty, and cowardliness of the American soldier. When only eight [bin Laden was mistaken because, as noted above, it was actually eighteen] of them were killed they packed up in the darkness of night and escaped without looking back."[21]

He was right that America's leaders were unprepared and unwilling to become embroiled in a major commitment to Somalia, but he badly miscalculated the courage and skill of American soldiers. He was also sorely ignorant about America's objectives in Somalia: "The dispatch of forces to Somalia was a move uniquely devoid of geopolitical concerns and expressed only the nation's desire to fulfill a humanitarian obligation,"[22] wrote Daniel Benjamin and Steven Simon, both counterterrorism directors with the National Security Council during the Bill Clinton administration. For their part, "Al-Qaeda's decision makers were convinced that Somalia was only the beginning of American efforts in the region and that they needed a long-term strategy. The radicals were certain that the United States would come to the aid of Christians in southern Sudan, who had been embroiled in a civil war with the northern Muslims of the Khartoum government for a decade. This would pose a direct threat to Sudan's Islamist regime."[23]

Bin Laden would inflame his followers with claims that Operation Restore Hope had resulted in the death of thirty-thousand Muslims. According to Abu Jandal, his one-time bodyguard who provided a great deal of information to American investigators following his arrest in Yemen in the wake of al Qaeda's suicide attack against the destroyer USS *Cole* in 2000, it gave him his excuse for attacking America's embassies in East Africa.[24]

There's an AK 47 on the dashboard
And mercy's left this town
—Johnny Clegg, "Africa (What Made You So Strong)"

[3] THE EAST AFRICA CELL

It was 1992 when al Qaeda began assembling the East Africa cell that would carry out the plot against the American embassies. Osama sent his number three, Abu Ubaydah al Banshiri, chair of the military council, to Kenya to run it. Upon arriving in Nairobi, he adopted a new identity, married a local woman, and sought out business opportunities in order to be self-sufficient and have legitimate cover.

A former Egyptian police officer, he was among Osama's most trusted lieutenants: "Some said that if [his second in command, Ayman al-] Zawahiri had taken over bin Laden's brain, Abu Ubaydah had his heart."[1] According to bin Laden's brother-in-law, Jamal Khalifa, Osama was deeply impressed with Ubaydah's devoutness, saying he "is memorizing all the Koran, and when you see him most of the time, he is fasting, and in the night, he is praying the night prayer, which is very difficult. He is really a very good religious Muslim."[2]

Harun, a key member of the cell, said it was Abu Ubaydah's idea to stake a claim in East Africa. He properly assessed the region's remoteness as a source of vulnerability. In Somalia, he foresaw the potential for another Afghanistan: a place where a tottering government might give way to insurgent Islamists. He believed the time had come for al Qaeda to distinguish itself. During the Afghan jihad, it had merely been one of many groups, and was noted more for its financing than its fighting. In East Africa, Abu Ubaydah thought, he had found an environment where they could make a unique mark for themselves.[3] Abu Jandal, bin Laden's former bodyguard, explained, "He [bin Laden] would always say that we must hit America on a front it never expects."[4]

"Where East Africa was a wake-up call for us," said FBI agent Joe Billy, "was seeing an al Qaeda operation unfold completely removed from traditional areas where you'd anticipate attacks. That was the most startling thing: their ability to have operatives establish bona fides in-country and stay under the radar while planning their deeds."[5]

Meanwhile, bin Laden was developing alliances with Islamic extremist groups around the globe. Most were in the Middle East and North Africa, but he was also becoming well connected in Southeast Asia and across Africa, in Somalia, Eritrea, Chad, Mali, Niger, Nigeria, Uganda, and Kenya.[6] Benjamin and Simon report, "Al-Qaeda's operational focus in the early 1990s was on anti-American attacks in Africa."[7] Michael Scheuer, a former CIA analyst who headed the first operational unit tasked to investigate bin Laden, wrote, "Africa has remained a high-interest locale for bin Laden since the 1994 withdrawal of UN and U.S. forces from Somalia."[8]

Abu Ubaydah was in charge of relations with Somali rebels. He sent his deputy—and eventual replacement as head of al Qaeda's military council—Mohammed Atef, widely known as Abu Hafs, to Somalia to liaise with local warlords, reconnoiter potential targets, and coordinate training. Mohammed Odeh, a conspirator in the embassy bombings, was sent to train al-Ittihad al-Islamiyya fighters in southeast Somalia. Harun went to Mogadishu to work on a plot to attack a U.N. building with a truck bomb. Scheuer says that bin Laden sent 250 fighters to Somalia to help Aidid and other anti-American warlords.[9]

Among the key players in al Qaeda's East Africa cell was Wadih el Hage. He was one of the operatives sent from bin Laden's base in Khartoum to Nairobi.

Wadih was born on July 25, 1960, into a Christian family in Lebanon. When he was two, the family moved to Kuwait, where his father worked for an oil company. As a teen, he converted to Islam, but didn't tell his parents, fearing their disapproval. In 1978, he arrived in the United States to study at the University of Southwest Louisiana in Lafayette, and eventually became a naturalized American citizen.

"In many ways, he's very Americanized," said Sam Schmidt, one of his defense attorneys. "He expressed himself in a very American fashion. He feels he's entitled to his opinions. And he expected the best of America; there's a little naiveté there.

"He obviously has many elements of the Middle East in him, but he has a more pluralist attitude for having been raised in a Christian household, marrying an American, also a convert to Islam. He was not of the belief that you kill non-believers. He was strict with his family, but tolerant. He has too much American in him to be otherwise.

"He's an educated man, but it was hard for him to find a good job in the U.S. because of his appearance and faith. He found it hard to raise his family in a conservative environment. When he went to Sudan, he thought it was an opportunity to live a more simple and respectful Muslim life."[10]

Five years after arriving in the United States, inspired by stories of the heroic struggle of Muslims fighting off Soviet invaders, he went to Peshawar, gateway to the Afghan jihad. Having been born with a withered right arm, he couldn't be a soldier, so he toiled as a relief worker. Though he always denied receiving any firearms training, he did carry a gun, a pretty common accessory in that heavily armed frontier city.

During this period, Schmidt would remind the jury at his trial, "Wadih el Hage was not solely on the Afghani side. He was on the American side, helping against Russian aggression."

After about a year, he returned to his studies in Louisiana. Upon graduating in 1986, he went back to Pakistan, this time to Quetta, where he spent a year with bin Laden's Services Bureau. Over the years, he traveled frequently between the United States and Pakistan, where he continued his relief efforts.

Eventually, el Hage got to know bin Laden well and accepted his offer to move to Khartoum and become his personal secretary. Schmidt argued, "There was no reason . . . for Mr. el Hage to believe that going to work for Mr. bin Laden in the Sudan had anything to do with any worldwide terrorist conspiracy." Their relationship, he insisted, was strictly business.

In July 1994, Wadih went to Nairobi to replace Khalid al-Fawwaz, whose cover was running an Islamic charity called Mercy International. As well, he opened a business called Tanzanite King, which dealt in gems, and set up a new nonprofit called Help Africa People, where Harun was placed as his deputy. He met regularly with the leader of the East Africa cell and ranking al Qaeda member, Abu Ubaydah.[11]

While both Mercy International—in supporting orphanages, hospitals, and schools in Somalia—and Help Africa People—which was behind an antimalaria project—did engage in charitable endeavors, the al Qaeda defector source L'Houssaine Kherchtou identified Help Africa People as an al Qaeda front. Taps placed on its telephone lines by the Americans revealed frequent calls with bin Laden.

Fawwaz, meanwhile, moved to London, where he established the Advice and Reformation Committee (ARC), through which he served as a conduit for bin Laden's messages to the world. Among his responsibilities was to provide satellite telephones and other sophisticated communications gear so that Osama could stay in touch with his ever-farther-flung operations. The ARC was used to exert pressure on the Saudi regime to reform. It published and distributed communiqués, written by bin Laden, criticizing all aspects of the al-Sauds' rule, including, of course, their failure to adhere to Islamic law.

When bin Laden was formally stripped of his Saudi citizenship in March 1994, thus rendering him stateless, he felt free of any obligation to restrain his contempt for the kingdom. His purpose, he said in an interview, was "to promote virtue and repudiate vice" in the kingdom.[12] ARC communiqués were also used to condemn the United States, illustrating his growing obsession with what al Qaeda referred to as the far enemy (as distinct from the near enemy, which was the insufficiently pious regimes presiding over Muslim countries).

Africa proved hard on Wadih and his family. In search of a more comfortable life, they returned to the United States in late 1996 and settled in Arlington, Texas, where, notwithstanding his physical disability, he took a job in a tire shop. That's where he was when the embassies were bombed.

Investigators at the Counter-Terrorism Center (CTC), a joint FBI/CIA unit, first came across el Hage in 1991 in connection with the murder of Mustafa Shalabi, who ran Brooklyn's Alkifah Refugee Center, a popular gathering place for recent Muslim immigrants, where money was raised and fighters recruited for the Afghan jihad. According to court papers, "tens of thousands of dollars flowed through its bank accounts in its heyday in the late 1980s and early 1990s." It "evolved into the American outpost of Mr. bin Laden's international terrorist organization."[13] It was also a hub for followers of Omar Abdul Rahman, the fiery Egyptian cleric known as the Blind Sheikh.

Shalabi had summoned el Hage from Texas to run Alkifah while he traveled to Egypt in an effort to resolve a leadership dispute. The day after Wadih arrived in New York, on February 26, Shalabi was killed. Rumors were rife and conflicting. Anybody from Mossad or CIA agents to followers of the Blind Sheikh was alleged to be responsible. In his study of jihadis operating in the United States, Steven Emerson asserted that "federal officials believe that Shalabi was killed pursuant to a *fatwa* issued by Sheikh Omar Abdul Rahman."[14] The murder remains unsolved.

Federal officials learned that Wadih had been of interest to local police in Tucson, Arizona, in connection with the 1989 murder of Rashid Khalifa, a local black Muslim cleric. El Hage was linked to an individual who had conducted surveillance on Khalifa prior to the killing.

No evidence against him was produced, and the FBI lost track of him by

1992.[15] At his trial, the government stipulated that it did not contend that el Hage participated in or had any prior knowledge of Shalabi's murder.

Omar Abdul Rahman, the Blind Sheikh, had been among Egypt's most influential Islamists. In 1980, he'd issued a fatwa declaring that heretical leaders deserved to be killed by the faithful. He was jailed following the assassination of President Anwar Sadat in 1981, but released after six months. He fled Cairo for Khartoum in 1990. An Egyptian court sentenced him in absentia for the 1989 murder of a police officer and for conspiring to overthrow the government. Despite being placed on a terrorist watch list by the State Department, he obtained a U.S. visa, thanks, Simon Reeve reported, to the intercession of the CIA, which was trying to recruit him.[16]

The Agency was not to be rewarded for its favor. When he settled in Jersey City, across from Manhattan, he continued to preach violence and spouted anti-American and anti-Semitic vitriol. He urged Muslims to attack the West, to "cut the transportation of their countries, tear it apart, destroy their economy, burn their companies, eliminate their interests, sink their ships, shoot down their planes, kill them on the sea, air, or land."[17]

The first attack against the World Trade Center on February 26, 1993, master-minded by Ramzi Yousef, was carried out by a rag-tag group of Egyptian jihadis connected to the Alkifah Refugee Center and under the spiritual guidance of the Blind Sheikh. Six people were killed and hundreds wounded when a truck bomb exploded in the underground parking garage. Though bin Laden's involvement in the plot has never been proven, Richard Clarke, who was National Coordinator for Security and Counterterrorism in the Clinton and George W. Bush administrations, called it "an al Qaeda operation."[18]

One of the participants in the plot, Mahmud Abouhalima, revealed to investigators that he'd met el Hage at an Islamic conference in Oklahoma City around 1990. On two subsequent occasions he'd purchased weapons from him: the first, in 1990, when he bought a 9 mm handgun to be used by the Blind Sheikh's bodyguard; on the other, he gave el Hage $4,000 to buy handguns and AK-47s to defend against the Jewish Defense League, led by right-wing Rabbi Meir Kahane. However, el Hage was unable to get them and "returned most of the money." He admitted his dealings with Abouhalima to prosecutors: "His claim is that, after purchasing the firearms, Mr. Abouhalima failed to pick them up."[19] The U.S. Attorney argued in court that el Hage also had a relationship with El Sayyid Nosair, another Alkifah hanger-on, who was convicted for the murder of Kahane in 1990. El Hage went to visit him in jail days after the Shalabi murder.[20]

The Blind Sheikh was hatching an even more ambitious scheme than bringing down the World Trade Center. In a single, grand day of terror across New York, he intended for his followers to bomb the George Washington Bridge, the Lincoln and Holland Tunnels, Federal Plaza, which houses the FBI field office, and the U.N. Headquarters. In 1996, he was convicted and jailed for life for his role in that conspiracy.

In 1996, al Qaeda suffered a major blow when Abu Ubaydah, its military chief and leader of the East Africa cell, drowned in a ferry accident on Lake Victoria. Called several years later by the prosecution to testify in a New York City courtroom, his unwitting brother-in-law, Ashif Mohamed Juma, would provide valuable insight into how the secret operative successfully built his cover.[21]

Using the alias Jalal Adel Habib, Abu Ubaydah married Juma's sister, Tahera, who was from Tanzania, in Nairobi in 1993. None of her family attended the wedding. Juma never knew his brother-in-law as Abu Ubaydah al Banshiri, had never heard of al Qaeda or bin Laden, and had no idea that the man he knew as Jalal Habib was connected to either.

Abu Ubaydah and his new bride moved to Mwanza, Tanzania, where he opened a diamond and gold mining business in partnership with Juma. They were together aboard the ill-fated ferry on May 21, returning to Mwanza from Bukova, where they had gone to mediate a dispute between another of Juma's sisters and her husband. There were more than twelve hundred passengers jammed onto a boat meant to carry less than five hundred. They shared a second-class cabin with seven others.

The ship had almost reached its destination at around 7:00 am when it suddenly listed heavily to the left. The captain overcompensated hard to the right, rocking the ship violently back the other way, causing it to capsize. Juma made it to the door of the cabin and tried to pull Abu Ubaydah after him, but lost his grip in the crush of people and rush of water.

Juma rose to the surface; Abu Ubaydah slipped back into the sinking ship.

"By the time I came out the ship had already gone about half of it is already under the water from the sidewards, and I climbed up on top. Now, I was on the side of the ship, and it was going this way, from straight it was going upside down, and I was walking on top and climbing up until I reached on the belly of the ferry," Juma recalled. As the ship slipped beneath the water, he clung to a float with about ten other survivors. They waited two hours before the first rescue ships arrived. Only 114 people survived the disaster.

Upon learning of her husband's death, Juma's sister called a number he'd given her for one of his friends. Three or four days later, Harun showed up in Mwanza to investigate. About two weeks after that, el Hage joined him and they shared a hotel room. They were hoping to recover Abu Ubaydah's body, but it was never found.

In his testimony before a grand jury the following year, el Hage admitted going to Tanzania following the sinking in order to discover the fate of a man named Adel Habib, whom he described as an Egyptian merchant and member of the board of his charity, Help Africa People. He denied knowing anyone by the name of Abu Ubaydah al Banshiri, or knowing that any such individual had died aboard the ferry. An important part of the perjury case brought against him by the government centered on this point.

"Did you look for Abu Ubaidah al Banshiri when you went to Lake Victoria in summer of 1996?" he was asked at the grand jury.

"No."

"Did anyone tell you Abu Ubaidah had drowned in that ferry accident?"

"No."

"And you were not sent to that lake to try to find Abu Ubaidah al Banshiri?"

"No, I went looking for Adel Habib," el Hage insisted.

L'Houssaine Kherchtou, the al Qaeda defector, testified that he knew Abu Ubaydah used the alias Jalal.

Assistant U.S. Attorney Pat Fitzgerald, the lead prosecutor against the Embassy bombers, asked Kherchtou, "Did you observe anything about Wadih el Hage's behavior or appearance at or about the time that Abu Ubaidah al Banshiri . . . had died?"

"Abu Ubaidah al Banshiri was loved by everybody," Kherchtou replied. "He was a very good person, and everybody was upset. Wadih, I saw him cry."

Abu Ubaydah was replaced as head of the East Africa cell by Abdullah Ahmed Abdullah (aka Abu Mohammed al Masri), better known as Saleh, who was identified by al-'Owhali, the erstwhile suicide bomber, as the leader behind both the Nairobi and Dar attacks.

By the time the CIA learned that el Hage was in Kenya, they were concerned enough with al Qaeda that an American citizen with ties to bin Laden—not to mention one whose name had come up in two separate homicide investigations—certainly caught its attention. Between July 1996 and September 1997 it was tapping the phone at his Nairobi residence. They picked up several exchanges with bin Laden's lines in Khartoum.[22]

On August 21, 1997, FBI Special Agent Daniel Coleman, accompanied by two CIA agents and a Kenyan policeman, served a search warrant at Wadih's home. They were satisfied to let him know they were aware of him, perhaps hoping he would infer that they had a deeper knowledge of his activities than was the case, and that alone might disrupt al Qaeda's plans, whatever they were.

His computer files were found to contain oblique references to sensitive documents that had apparently once been in his home, but had been moved elsewhere for safekeeping. There were suspicions at the time that these documents may have held clues to a terrorist plot. Among the items seized were a laptop computer, address books, notebooks, a day planner, and a phone index, along with printers and assorted diskettes and micro-cassettes. Everything was taken to the police post at Kenyatta International Airport. Documents retrieved from the computer confirmed much of what the defector Jamal al-Fadl had revealed about al Qaeda's organization, which reinforced the FBI's confidence in their primary source on the group. It was also discovered that el Hage had purchased guns for bin Laden in Eastern Europe and that he traveled frequently to Tanzania. There was, however, no evidence of any crime or impending terrorist attack. The agents interviewed him, but Wadih gave up nothing. He denied knowledge of bin Laden's activities in Kenya,[23] and spent most of the hour that they were in his home trying to convert them to Islam.[24]

By his own admission, el Hage returned to the United States not long after this search because he feared further harassment, saying he was afraid of the Egyptian, Pakistani, and Kenyan authorities. "He sort of felt outed as a bin Laden associate by the Americans, and thought they had put his security in jeopardy," explained his attorney, Josh Dratel. "He worried that the Kenyans might make life very difficult for him."[25]

FBI agent Pat D'Amuro interpreted the move differently: "When it started to get hot, he came back to the U.S."[26]

Over in the Southern District of New York, U.S. Attorney Mary Jo White "admits that the feeling in her office was that the East Africa cell had been largely dismantled and its remnants no longer posed a greater threat than countless other pockets of anti-American militants around the world."[27]

However, as it came closer to going operational, the East Africa cell was becoming increasingly anxious over its security. In a document found on a computer seized in the el Hage raid, Harun wrote that "an important man . . . seems to have fallen into the enemy's hands." "The cell is at 100 percent danger," he added.[28] He was likely referring to al-Fadl's defection.

With el Hage gone, Harun moved to the forefront of the cell's structure. He worried, "The American forces carry kidnapping operations against anyone who threatens its national security and its citizens." He referenced the arrest of Mir Aimal Kansi.[29] On January 25, 1993, Kansi had opened fire on cars waiting in traffic to pull onto the grounds of CIA headquarters in Langley, Virginia, killing two CIA employees and injuring three others. Kansi escaped the scene and fled to Pakistan, where he was apprehended in 1997 and rendered back to the United States to stand trial. (He was sentenced to death on February 4, 1998, and executed in 2002.)

Harun warned of joint American-Kenyan-Egyptian intelligence efforts to identify bin Laden's associates in Nairobi, "since America knows well that the youth who lived in Somalia and were members of the sheikh's [bin Laden] cell are the ones who killed the Americans in Somalia." He went on, "They know that since Kenya was the main gateway for those members, there must be a center in Kenya. . . . We are really in danger."[30] He overestimated the Americans' certainty, but, absolutely, they had a growing interest in the role al Qaeda played in its Somali debacle. And on June 10, 1998, the grand jury in Manhattan handed down a sealed indictment against bin Laden for conspiracy to kill U.S. soldiers in Somalia. It was granted based on documents found on el Hage's computer that implicated al Qaeda in the killings. While enough to support an indictment, the evidence was weak and a conviction was anything but certain.[31]

Then CIA Director George Tenet dismissed the effectiveness of an indictment, quipping, "At the agency, we believed that the terrorists sitting around campfires in Afghanistan were probably not losing much sleep over the doings of some U.S. district court—unless, that is, they were planning how to bomb the courthouse itself."[32]

Somalia would be a contentious issue at trial. Al Qaeda claiming credit for the "*Black Hawk Down*" incident did not rise to an evidentiary level of proof, and the prosecution never claimed that the defendants el Hage, al-'Owhali, Mohamed, or Odeh were directly responsible for the murder of American soldiers. It did, however, present evidence that Odeh had been an instructor at training camps in Somalia.

James Francis Yacone, who had been one of the Army Black Hawk helicopter pilots involved in the fateful raid in Mogadishu and went on to become an FBI agent, was called by the government to describe the operation. Yacone asserted that more than one hundred RPGs were fired at U.S. air support, indicating they had considerable firepower at their disposal. His own chopper was hit, forcing him to crash land, but far enough from the city that he was able to save himself and his crew from the mob that overran the other two Black Hawks that went down.

The defense objected to the introduction of this inflammatory story, arguing that it was prejudicial. Furthermore, Schmidt and Edward Wilford, an attorney for Mohamed Odeh, both argued that Somalia was a military action between two organized forces, not a criminal act. Their position was that training provided to Somali clans by al Qaeda was meant to prepare them for a possible battlefield contingency and, thus, was not relevant to the alleged al Qaeda conspiracy to attack Americans.

To implicate the defendants in a broad conspiracy to kill Americans anywhere, and to offer al Qaeda's interference in Somalia as an example, proving that some of them had been there and trained Somali militiamen was one thing. To hold them specifically responsible for the killing of American soldiers by others who may have benefited from their training was something quite different. The prosecution argued that this was, in fact, the case since training provided by al Qaeda was instrumental in the Somalis' capability to shoot down American aircraft. As well, al Qaeda's participation in Somalia, in whatever capacity, was illustrative of a pattern of anti-American agitation beginning long before, and culminating in, the embassy bombings.

After a great deal of debate, the presiding judge, Leonard B. Sand, ruled that, since none of the defendants, nor others indicted in the conspiracy who were not on trial, bore direct responsibility for those casualties about whom Yacone testified, it was not relevant to the overt acts being charged, and should be stricken from the record.

Knowing that the jury couldn't unhear the discussion about Somalia, attorney Anthony Ricco tried to frame Odeh's participation in a positive light to which jurors might relate: "Me and you, we watch it on the 6:00 news. It sounds terrible and we ask, 'Baby, what time's the Knicks coming on?' That's it. Other people, motivated by higher goals get involved. Some of them people, we often call them fools. And he left his hut and went to help somebody else out, and there's not a shred of evidence in this case to the contrary." Therein lay the nobility of the man with nothing taking the risk of going off to battle in comparison with those who have everything, but just let the great world spin.

In closing arguments, prosecutor Kenneth Karas tied Somalia to the American embassies, saying, "Because al Qaeda wanted to target Somalia, they decided they had to set up operations in Nairobi. Once they set up operations in Nairobi, they have a foundation in place that they are going to make use of five years later to attack the embassies in East Africa."

Fitzgerald would elaborate on how Somalia fit into the overall conspiracy: "What is important is if the people working in al Qaeda understood that in 1993 that the U.S. participating with the U.N. coming to Somalia was colonization, an enemy, and they are working to fight America. That puts the lie for the claim that years later they're surprised, surprised to learn America is the enemy, that this was something new. It only came out when bin Laden made that speech [the 1996 declaration of war]."

[4] FATWA

In May 1996, Osama left Sudan, returning to Afghanistan. The circumstances surrounding his departure remain murky, but he was evidently embittered to have, once again, been exiled, and he suspected that Sudan had succumbed to U.S. pressure. The ruling NIF was anxious to rehabilitate its deplorable image with the West, and the State Department had noted bin Laden's presence among the reasons for designating it a state sponsor of terrorism. As an impediment to normal diplomatic and economic relations, the designation was not without tangible cost. Generally, it made Sudan a pariah among nations.

In August 1994, the NIF turned the notorious terrorist Carlos the Jackal, to whom it had offered sanctuary since 1991, over to France to stand trial for the murder of two French police officers and an informant. Though Carlos had long outlived his usefulness to anyone, his extradition was a major symbolic initiative.

An enduring rumor is that Hassan al-Turabi, Sudan's de facto ruler, had offered to turn bin Laden over to American custody sometime in 1995. Richard Clarke denies this unequivocally: "The facts about the supposed Sudanese offer to give us bin Laden are that Turabi was not about to turn over his partner in terror to us and no real attempt to do so ever occurred."[1] The 9/11 Commission investigated and concluded there was no substance to the myth and, furthermore, the United States "had no legal basis . . . since, at the time, there was no indictment outstanding."[2] This is a critical factor: that without an indictment, there existed no grounds for detaining bin Laden simply on the basis of a suspected or professed threat.

Above and beyond whatever influence the United States may have exerted, the NIF was increasingly wary over Osama's growing assertiveness. John Prendergast, a former National Security Council official, was told by "a Sudanese who could only be identified as a Khartoum 'legal expert'" that "bin Laden was forced out because the Khartoum government felt he was becoming too powerful. With increasing influence over the Sudanese economy and a small private army at his disposal, bin Laden was determined to have his way. . . . 'Turabi wanted to guide and control bin Laden and other extremist elements. But bin Laden wanted to guide the Sudanese government, like he did the Taliban."[3]

Osama was linked to at least two terror plots during his time in Sudan. In November 1995, a car bomb exploded outside a facility in Riyadh where the United States trained members of the Saudi National Guard, killing five Americans and two Indians. The Saudis arrested four suspects who supposedly confessed. They were quickly executed before American officials ever had the opportunity to question them. They allegedly claimed to have been inspired by bin Laden. U.S. intelligence later learned that al Qaeda had shipped explosives to Saudi Arabia for use against American targets.[4] Perhaps even more disturbing to the NIF was an attempt to assassinate Egyptian President Hosni Mubarak while he was on a visit to Addis Ababa in 1995. He only narrowly escaped with his life.

Another attack immediately followed Osama's return to Afghanistan. In June 1996, a truck bomb exploded at the Khobar Towers in Dhahran, Saudi Arabia, where U.S. Air Force personnel were housed. Nineteen Americans were killed and more than three hundred and seventy wounded. Hezbollah, a terrorist group with ties to Iran, has been held responsible, but the 9/11 Commission found, "there are also signs that al Qaeda played some role, as yet unknown."[5]

The expulsion from Sudan cost bin Laden dearly. When he left, he supposedly lost investments worth as much as $150 million.[6]

Prior to returning to Afghanistan, al Qaeda "had concentrated on providing funds, training, and weapons for actions carried out by members of allied groups. The attacks on the U.S. embassies in East Africa in the summer of 1998 would take a different form—planned, directed, and executed by al Qaeda, under the direct supervision of Bin Ladin and his chief aides."[7]

On August 23, 1996, bin Laden declared war against the United States. The grandiosely titled "Message from Usamah Bin-Muhammad Bin-Laden to His Muslim Brothers in the Whole World and Especially in the Arabian Peninsula: Declaration of Jihad Against the Americans Occupying the Land of the Two Holy Mosques; Expel the Heretics from the Arabian Peninsula" was published in the London-based Arabic language newspaper, *al-Quds al-Arabi*. It was a furious diatribe, citing a litany of transgressions against Muslims, including the ongoing presence of American troops in Saudi Arabia, the killing of Abdullah Azzam, his old mentor and cofounder of the Services Bureau, and the jailing of Hamas leader Ahmad Yassin in Israel and the Blind Sheikh in the United States. He asserted, "The occupying American army is the principal and the main cause of the situation. Therefore efforts should be concentrated on destroying, fighting, and killing the enemy until, by the grace of Allah, it is completely defeated."[8]

Abdullah Azzam had been blown apart on November 24, 1989, along with two of his sons, by a powerful bomb as he arrived to lead Friday prayers at a Peshawar mosque. The list of suspects is long, including Israeli intelligence, Afghan security agents, one of a multitude of Afghan rebels or fellow jihadis jockeying for position among one another. Even bin Laden has been accused. You don't rise to prominence in the volatile world of fanatics without making mortal enemies. The case has never been solved.

Bin Laden taunted then–secretary of defense William Perry with the unwavering devotion of his minions: "These youths love death as you love life. . . . They have no intention except to enter paradise by killing you." This is the most unbridgeable chasm between conceptions of what it means to be human: their longing for a near and glorious death; our desire for a long life.

He went on to proclaim, "Terrorizing you, while you are carrying arms on our land, is a legitimate and morally demanded duty. It is a legitimate right well known to all humans and other creatures."[9]

CIA analyst Michael Scheuer took the threat very seriously, thinking, "It sounded like Thomas Jefferson. There was no ranting in it. . . . [It] read like our Declaration of Independence—it had that tone. It was a frighteningly reasoned document. There were substantive, tangible issues."[10] This was a serious person making a credible threat.

Following the Declaration's release, Richard Clarke claims, pressure exerted by the White House moved the CIA to create the unit dedicated to investigating bin Laden.[11] According to Clarke, the Clinton National Security Council had begun connecting the dots to bin Laden as early as 1993–94: "It just seemed unlikely to us that this man who had his hand in so many seemingly unconnected organizations was just a donor, a philanthropist of terror. There seemed to be some organizing force and maybe it was he. He was the one thing that we knew the various terrorist groups had in common."[12] Referring to the same time frame, the 9/11 Commission, however, reported, "By this time, Bin Ladin was well-known and a senior figure among Islamist extremists. . . . Still, he was just one among many diverse terrorist barons."[13] And an officer with the CTC said, "When we started this, we did not expect to find out bin Laden was who he was. The decision to focus on him was in some ways serendipitous."[14] As late as 1997, the CTC continued describing bin Laden as an "extremist financier."[15]

The unit that the CIA created to focus attention on bin Laden was initially known as Terrorist Financial Links, in recognition of terrorism's most celebrated financier. Scheuer, its chief from 1996 to 1999, dubbed it Alec Station after his son. It was unique for being a virtual station operating from a nondescript building in suburban Virginia, separate from the main Agency campus at Langley so that it could mimic a genuine overseas station. While a traditional station's responsibilities are parceled out geographically, Alec Station was innovative because jurisdiction was not defined or restricted by territory, but directed against an individual target wherever he might operate. As bin Laden's importance as a terrorist in his own right became evident, it was officially designated the Bin Laden Unit. Though it was a CIA installation, it was also staffed with FBI agents.

Alec Station was disbanded by the end of 2005, based on the "view that Al Qaeda is no longer as hierarchical as it once was" and a "belief that the agency can better deal with high-level threats by focusing on regional trends rather than on specific organizations or individuals."[16] In other words, the CIA has reverted to a geography-based outlook from one that acknowledged the transnational character of stateless terrorist actors.

Scheuer proposed several plans to disrupt bin Laden's finances as early as 1996–97, to no avail. He sought covert access to his bank accounts in Switzerland to ascertain how much money he had, but both the Treasury Department and CIA said no, lest such an operation undermine the international banking system. He proposed stealing the money Osama kept in accounts in Sudan and Dubai, but Treasury feared this would reveal that the United States had the capability to infiltrate foreign banks. There is often the temptation to keep intelligence capabilities stashed in reserve in the event that they are needed for some unforeseeable higher priority mission in the future. He proposed targeting the Islamic banks used by bin Laden, but Treasury pointed out that some of these institutions did business in New York, thus making them off-limits to CIA covert ops. Scheuer proposed a black op to burn down a bank in Sudan where bin Laden had an account, but his superiors turned it down because American citizens might have accounts there, as well. He proposed a sabotage attack against Osama's farm near the Ethiopian border, but this, too, was rejected.[17]

Meanwhile, in New York, the FBI had been preoccupied with Islamic terrorism since the 1993 World Trade Center attack. The I-49 squad was charged with building a prosecutable case against bin Laden and the rest of al Qaeda's leadership. Jack Cloonan, an investigator on the squad, bristles at the charge that bin Laden wasn't taken seriously enough early on. He insists, "We, in New York, were pushing the envelope pretty damn strongly, dealing with governments overseas, getting NSA intercepts. We were just a small group, but we picked up people in Sudan, in Morocco."[18] Those last references were to the successful recruitments of Jamal al-Fadl and L'Houssaine Kherchtou as sources early in the game.

In the spring of 1996, the CIA reportedly advised State about the active terrorist cell in Kenya connected with bin Laden.[19] At least three terrorist threats in Nairobi warranted investigation over the year leading up to the bombing. An unspecified allied intelligence service turned over an informant who advised that the Nairobi branch of the Islamic charity, the Al Haramain Foundation, was involved in a plot targeting the embassy. The CIA station chief advised the ambassador and other senior officials. While the CIA's preference was to allow the Foundation to operate as usual—but under surveillance—the diplomats preferred that the Kenyans step in and make arrests, which they did, taking nine Arabs into custody and seizing the organization's files on October 31, 1997. Agents read through the files, but found no evidence of a terrorist plot. The station chief declined to press his Kenyan counterparts to allow the CIA to question the suspects directly. He "said he did not want to strain his relations with the Kenyans," and headquarters went along, agreeing the decision was his.[20]

The CIA ended up dismissing the informant as not credible, and Kenya deported the arrestees. Some CTC team members were reportedly "furious" and "complained that their investigation had been dangerously short-circuited." They blamed the station chief, a career analyst on his first overseas assignment, for failing to press for access to the suspects. Embassy officials understood that the Kenyans had refused them access, not that there was an internal CIA dispute over whether it should be granted.[21]

In November 1997—fully nine months before the attack—Mustafa Mahmoud Said Ahmed, who worked for an al Qaeda front in Nairobi, walked in to the U.S. Embassy and offered specific details concerning a group planning to detonate a truck bomb inside its underground parking garage. He was administered a polygraph, which he failed. More damning to his credibility, he had made previous claims of impending doom at other embassies in Africa that came to naught.[22] The CIA was unable to confirm whether Ahmed genuinely had links to any terrorist group. Furthermore, it reported, a foreign intelligence service with which the CIA cooperates advised that Ahmed was an intelligence fabricator. In the forever double-dealing world of intelligence, the Agency was concerned that his approach was part of a sophisticated ploy on the part of terrorists to observe how the embassy would react to a threat so they could eventually circumvent its defenses.[23]

For all his trouble, Ahmed was ultimately taken into custody and interrogated by Kenyan security in the fall of 1997. He told them he had grown up in Zaire before attending Al Azhar University in Cairo. He had worked for Kuwait's minister of defense from 1980 until Iraq invaded in August 1990, at which time he returned to Zaire and set up a gem business that did deals for the brutal and corrupt President Mobutu Sese Seko. In 1994, he moved to Nairobi, where he established Taba International, a gem trading company. Bin Laden ran a company called Taba Investments in Sudan. Ahmed claimed to have met Osama in the mid-1980s.[24]

Ahmed reportedly told police he was acquainted with Islamic radicals and informed them of plots to blow up the American and Israeli embassies. He admitted that he and another man had taken photographs of both buildings on October 22, 1997. The Americans had dismissed his information as not being credible. A Tanzanian official was quoted saying that Ahmed has a "big criminal file" in Egypt, where he was wanted for terrorist activity.[25]

The State Department acknowledged that the CIA submitted two reports about Ahmed and that security at the embassy was elevated for several weeks as a result. However, when nothing materialized, things returned to normal.[26] As it happened, the embassy attack was carried out much as Ahmed predicted, though according to the *Nation*, Kenya's most influential newspaper, he'd said that three truck bombs were to be deployed.

The Kenyans soon deported him, and he turned up in Dar es Salaam, where the Americans believe he participated in that embassy plot.[27] Ahmed was among more than two dozen suspects—including Sudanese, Iraqis, Somalis, and a Turk—rounded up by Tanzanian police following the bombing. Most were released within a week, but he was one of two who were charged with eleven counts of murder on September 21.

According to Tanzania's Home Affairs Minister, Ali Amer Mohammed, Ahmed acknowledged knowing bin Laden, Odeh, and al-'Owhali.[28] He was in possession of Egyptian, Yemeni, and Zairian passports, as well as a supply of passport photos, some of which showed him with a beard, others without. Friends said that he was Iraqi.

Odeh would tell Pakistani investigators that he moved to Kenya at the invitation of a "Mustafa," who'd fought with U.S.-backed rebels in Afghanistan, and that the Dar bombing had been organized by Mustafa. Tanzanian law enforcement officers said there were references made to Ahmed, who was a regular at the Rawdah mosque in the Kisutu market area of Dar.[29]

The United States never sought his extradition, and Tanzanian authorities expressed an interest in prosecuting him. According to his Tanzanian lawyer, Abdul Mwengela, Ahmed's information came entirely from a conversation he overheard in a Nairobi hotel.[30] He was held in Tanzania until March 2000, when he was deported to Egypt.

A Clinton administration official acknowledged Ahmed's warning: "It is embarrassing. It is tragic." According to the *New York Times*, "Other officials defended the Government's handling of the case, noting that American intelligence is deluged with warnings about terrorist plots, most of which proved groundless."[31]

FBI Agent Ken Piernick, who headed up the Dar investigation, affirms that Ahmed was questioned by FBI agents, but they "concluded he didn't really know what was going on. His story was discounted as the ravings of a lunatic." He added, "You know, even a blind pig can find an acorn once in a while kind of thing."[32]

In a separate incident, Kenyan intelligence had advised the CIA about a forthcoming plot. The Agency consulted with the Israeli Mossad, which dismissed the information as unreliable, and CIA concurred with its assessment.[33] It was reported in the Israeli newspaper *Ha'aretz* on August 12 that Israeli authorities advised the United States to be skeptical about threats against their Nairobi embassy.

An anonymous American official confirmed that the United States had been told to be alert to individuals arriving in Nairobi from Pakistan. However, "like most such warnings, the information obtained by the foreign intelligence service was indefinite—too fuzzy for effective countermeasures. The embassy here never went on alert."[34]

Two days before the bombings, al-Zawahiri's Egyptian Islamic Jihad (EIJ), issued a fax saying America's "message has been received and that the response, which we hope they will read carefully, is being prepared."[35] The message referred to was the extradition in June of several EIJ members from Albania to Egypt, where they were allegedly tortured mercilessly and two were hanged.

Although "none of the warnings gathered by American intelligence in the year before the bombings pointed to a particular act of terrorism on a particular day, the United States had growing indications that the embassy was a target of terrorist plots, and that terrorists hostile to American interests were active in

Kenya." However, State said it was impossible to react to every threat, and the CIA advised that those it was reporting were either unfounded or being dealt with by Kenyan authorities.[36] Undersecretary of State for Political Affairs Thomas Pickering reported, "We get 30,000 warnings, threats per year. We take them all seriously. We look into them. We evaluate them."[37]

A State Department official claimed, "If we had known there was a significant bin Laden network in Kenya, we would have gotten our people the hell out of that building." However, intelligence and law enforcement sources strongly dispute the suggestion that State was uninformed. One intelligence official said that State received briefings about bin Laden's operatives "before, during and after" the August 1997 raid on el Hage's Nairobi residence. "Some of those reports referred to Osama bin Laden in the first paragraph," asserted an intelligence source.[38]

Were these examples of accurate intelligence poorly assessed or of vague intelligence taking on clarity after the fact? Until bin Laden did something, officials fell back to the default position on security, which is that nothing was likely to happen; precisely the opposite of how it has been since 9/11. In 1998 it still took a great deal to convince that an attack was imminent; today, it is presumed. In the aftermath of the unimaginable, the most far-fetched threat becomes credible. No analyst, no matter how experienced, is going to risk underreacting by assessing intelligence as incredible in a panic environment where anything, right up to a nuclear weapon, seems plausible.

"You're being flooded with some of the most dogshit, inaccurate threat reporting possible. And the obligation was to put it out there," marveled Roger Cressey, who headed the National Security Council's Terrorist Threats Sub-Group from 1999 to 2001, in reference to the post-9/11 atmosphere. "So, threat reporting that I would laugh out of my working group on threats was now making it directly into the White House. And making it directly into the Oval Office because God forbid the FBI or the CIA didn't tell the president or the White House of a threat and it became true."[39]

There is no compass to balance the course. Lack of analysis combined with the conviction that 9/11 was prelude to worse led the Bush administration to accept dogshit as gospel.

On February 23, 1998, bin Laden issued this chilling fatwa: "The ruling to kill the Americans and their allies—civilians and military—is an individual duty for every Muslim who can do it in any country in which it is possible to do it, in order to liberate the al-Aqsa mosque [Jerusalem] and the holy mosque [Mecca] from their grip, and in order for their armies to move out of all the lands of Islam, defeated and unable to threaten any Muslim."[40]

"This was a critical moment," asserted FBI Agent Pat D'Amuro. "That fatwa was a real shift in tone, in that he was no longer threatening the U.S. government and military, it was U.S. citizens globally, anybody."[41]

Mamdouh Mahmud Salim, also known as Abu Hajer al-Iraqi, was the author of the fatwa, as well as of the 1996 declaration of war.[42] Born in Sudan to Iraqi parents, Salim served in the Iraqi army as a communications officer from 1981 until 1983, when he defected to arch-enemy Iran. From there, he made his way to Peshawar, where he joined up with bin Laden in 1986. He was described as bin Laden's "religious advisor" and "close friend."[43] He considered himself bin Laden's equal, and was treated as such, never pledging *bayat*, an oath of personal loyalty, which would have implied subservience.

Salim was said to be able to bring the al Qaeda leader to tears when he sang verses from the Koran. He "had the greatest spiritual authority, by virtue of having memorized the Quran, but he was an electrical engineer, not a cleric. Nonetheless, bin Laden made him head of al-Qaeda's fatwa committee—a fateful choice. It was on Abu Hajer's authority that al-Qaeda turned from being the anti-communist Islamic army that bin Laden originally envisioned into a terrorist organization bent on attacking the United States."[44] He was also responsible for purchasing communications gear, and spearheaded efforts to procure chemical, biological, and nuclear weapons. Sometime between 1992 and 1996, Salim met an Iranian religious official in Khartoum as part of an effort to negotiate an agreement between al Qaeda, the NIF, and Iran to cooperate against Israel, the United States and other Western states. In late 1998, bin Laden referred to him as "one of the best men I have ever met."[45]

Salim had no compunction about killing innocents, saying, "If he's a good person, he'll go to Paradise, and if not, he'll go to hell."[46] Such was the order of the universe, according to al Qaeda theology. Whatever the suffering on this earth, faith is ultimately rewarded, infidelity punished.

Three months after issuing the fatwa, bin Laden granted an interview to ABC News (broadcast on June 10, 1996). He said, "We predict a black day for America and the end of the United States as united states, and will be separate states, and they will retreat from our land and collect the bodies of its sons back to America, Allah willing." He bemoaned the suffering of Palestinian and Iraqi children under the force of American sanctions: "We believe that the biggest thieves in the world and the terrorists are the Americans. The only way for us to fend off these assaults is to use similar means."[47]

How credible was the threat? As the 9/11 Commission conceded, "before 9/11, al Qaeda and its affiliates had killed fewer than 50 Americans, including the East Africa embassy bombings and the *Cole* attack. The U.S. government took it seriously, but not in the sense of mustering anything like the kind of effort that would be gathered to confront an enemy of the first, second, or even third rank."[48]

By that measure, the attention paid al Qaeda prior to the embassy attacks was quite impressive. As Lawrence Wright points out, "despite the bluster, the media, the lurid calls for jihad, al-Qaeda had really done nothing so far. There were grand plans, and there were claims of past successes that al-Qaeda had little or no part of. Although al-Qaeda had already existed for ten years, it was sill an obscure and unimportant organization; it didn't compare to Hamas or Hezbollah, for instance."[49]

FBI Special Agent Dan Coleman asked the U.S. Attorney's Office for the Southern District of New York whether it was even a crime to threaten the United States from the other side of the world without any demonstrated means for carrying out the threat. As Wright tells the story, "the lawyers puzzled over the language and found a rarely invoked seditious conspiracy statute from the Civil War era that forbids instigating violence and attempting to overthrow the U.S. government. It seemed a stretch to think that it might be applied to a stateless Saudi in a cave in Tora Bora, but on the basis of such meager precedent, Coleman opened a criminal file on the figure who would become the most wanted man in the FBI's history."[50]

Richard Clarke maintains that the fatwa "did not come as a shock to us. We had considered ourselves at war with al Qaeda even before we knew its name or its reach."[51] Who exactly "we" refers to is an open question. As the 9/11 Commission found, he certainly wasn't referring to either of the presidents he served, as "both President Clinton and President Bush chose not to seek a declaration of war on Bin Ladin after he had declared and begun to wage war on us, a declaration that they did not acknowledge publicly. Not until after 9/11 was a congressional authorization sought."[52]

Clarke went on, "We had been working with friendly governments for at least three years to identify and destroy sleeper cells in Europe, Africa, and the Middle East. We had arranged snatches of many al Qaeda operatives and had been planning to snatch bin Laden himself."[53] Yet, no move had been made against the most advanced cell at the time, the one in East Africa preparing to strike.

The CTC took note that Osama's ruling to kill American civilians was "the first religious ruling sanctifying such attacks."[54] On the other hand, since Osama lacked the formal religious standing to issue such an edict, it was unclear whether it would carry weight in the Muslim world. State issued an advisory, saying, "We take these threats seriously and the United States is increasing security at many U.S. government facilities in the Middle East and Asia."[55] Nothing was mentioned about Africa. This despite Ambassador Bushnell's urgent appeals to Washington for enhanced security at her embassy in Nairobi.

She sent cables to Foggy Bottom in December 1997 and in May 1998—the latter directly to Secretary of State Madeleine Albright—specifically noting how the embassy was left vulnerable by its close proximity to a very busy intersection. Assistant Secretary for Administration Patrick F. Kennedy described the tone of her memos as "concerned," saying she cited "multiple threats at the embassy. She talked about crime, she talked about administrative matters, and she talked about safety."[56] Her warnings went unheeded.

The embassy had been constructed in 1981, before the terrorist bombings of the U.S. Marine barracks (October 1983) and embassy (September 1984) in Beirut caused the government to reevaluate security at its missions overseas. The first line of defense was the Kenyan security guards contracted from a private firm. Their compensation was paltry, around $83 per month, and they'd recently seen health benefits for their families and daily meal allowances cut. Most of the guards lived in slums without running water or electricity.[57] After the fact, an anonymous administration official said, "If we [Americans] had had control of that outside parking lot and more guard posts, they [the terrorists] would have gone somewhere else."[58]

A team from Diplomatic Security and the Foreign Building Office visited Nairobi in March 1998 and concluded that the embassy was in compliance with security standards for a post deemed a medium terrorist threat. It suggested $500,000 in upgrades, including a new fence around the front parking lot, improved perimeter surveillance, and a special roll-down door for the parking garages. Of these, only the garage door had been installed at the time of the bombing.[59] General Anthony C. Zinni, then commander of U.S. Central Command, had visited Nairobi and warned that the embassy was an easy target. He offered the services of his specialists to review security, but was rebuffed by State.[60] The post was scheduled to undergo a $3 million security overhaul in January 1999.

Bushnell had her critics, and "was even seen by some at the State Department as a nuisance who was overly obsessed with security, according to one official."[61] However, *New York Times* reporters James Risen and Benjamin Weiser concluded, "a close examination of events in the year before the assaults, based on interviews with officials throughout the United States Government, shows her concerns were more intense, more well founded, more specific and more forcefully expressed than has previously been known."[62]

A review board convened after the bombing, chaired by Admiral William Crowe, former chair of the Joint Chiefs of Staff, determined that the embassy was in compliance with prescribed security standards, except for having the recommended set-back of at least one hundred feet from the closest street—it was only thirty feet from the main intersection. It did, however, conclude that State's system for assigning terrorism threat levels was "seriously flawed."[63]

In her memoir, Albright denied responsibility for any security shortcomings, writing, "It wasn't until the embassy bombings that I was able to get the full attention of those controlling the purse strings in Congress and the administration. Unfortunately, the only real solution in Kenya would have been to relocate the embassy to a less crowded site. That would have cost millions of dollars and could not even have been started before August 7."[64]

At this particular moment in history, the antagonists had very different perceptions of the world. "To us, Afghanistan seemed very far away. To members of al Qaeda, America seemed very close. In a sense, they were more globalized than we were," remarked the 9/11 Commission.[65] Each perception had some basis in truth. America's global influence makes it ubiquitous. For all that, America has a strong inclination toward isolationism, an attitude that suggests it is content to hunker down beyond the reach of its enemies and advocate from afar for freedom, peace, and democracy.

Michael Scheuer, who headed up the bin Laden Unit at the CIA, argues that understanding al Qaeda requires a familiarity with its worldview: "Western media and governments bemoan these attacks as 'terrorism,' and in this they are mistaken. Al Qaeda's victories, and those of its allies and supporters, are acts of war aimed at strategic objectives, motivated by faith, and conducted in a manner appropriate to the attackers' skills and resources. It is an arrogant and dangerous delusion to continue attaching the term 'terrorism' to these events, because the term clouds the fact that much of the Muslim world deems itself under attack by U.S. foreign policy."[66]

Prior to August 7, 1998, it is not hard to understand why few American officials had taken notice of Osama bin Laden. No American deaths had yet been attributed to him and his ambitious threats sounded like little more than crazed bombast.

Even for "many of those in the U.S. government who recognized the threat of jihadist terror *before* September 11, the pivotal event was the Africa embassy bombings," wrote Daniel Benjamin and Steven Simon, NSC staffers who counted themselves among that number. "Nothing before that coordinated attack had demonstrated such a combination of skill and murderousness. The indiscriminate violence of those bombings telegraphed al-Qaeda's desire to inflict mass casualties."[67]

Providentially, the embassy attacks had an important influence on Khalid Sheikh Mohammed, the mastermind behind 9/11, as they "convinced him that Bin Laden was truly committed to attacking the United States."[68] Thus came an important turning point, since K. S. M. was then a free-agent terrorist, dreaming up grandiose schemes that he lacked the organizational support or financial resources to bring to fruition. The success of the East Africa operation proved bin Laden was a worthy ally for his more ambitious aspirations.

K. S. M. came to the attention of American authorities in connection with the investigation into the first World Trade Center attack. He was the uncle of Ramzi Yousef, the leader of that conspiracy, and, it was learned, his collaborator. Together, they developed a scheme in 1994, code-named Bojinka, to simultaneously blow up a dozen U.S.-flagged commercial airliners on trans-Pacific routes. They conducted a test run, smuggling an explosive device aboard a Philippine Airlines flight from Manila to Tokyo. The bomb went off as planned in mid-air, killing a passenger and almost downing the plane. The two men also worked on plans to assassinate President Clinton and Pope John Paul II while they were visiting the Philippines.

Growing increasingly intrigued by K. S. M., the CIA succeeded in introducing a source to him after he relocated from Manila to Doha, Qatar in 1995.[69] He had a connection with a member of the Qatari ruling family who got him a job with the Ministry of Electricity and Water. In January 1996, a secret indictment was handed down against him in the Southern District of New York on the basis of evidence connected with Bojinka. Nonetheless, an NSC staffer said, "there was no U.S. agency advocating K. S. M.'s rendition. There was an NSC proposal that was shot down by every agency that had a jurisdiction and role. Why? Everyone thought terrorism was a joke and that the NSC staff dealing with this were a bunch of idiots."[70]

There would not be another opportunity to get him before 9/11. Someone tipped him off that the United States was on his trail and he left Qatar. He went to Afghanistan, where he met bin Laden and pitched his idea for what he called the "planes operation."[71]

[5] THE DEPLOYMENT

John O'Neill was convinced that the 1993 bombing of New York's World Trade Center was but a first blow in what was intended as a prolonged campaign. Indeed, he was certain that the destruction of the twin towers remained al Qaeda's prime objective. He was among the first senior FBI officials to appreciate that plots targeting the United States were being hatched in safe havens abroad, rendering the distinction between international and domestic terrorism moot. It was, he believed, self-defeating to try to sustain bureaucratic boundaries that ran counter to reality. Though constituted as a domestic law enforcement agency, the FBI has the mandate to investigate crimes against Americans wherever in the world they occur.

A legend in the Bureau, O'Neill was the G-man's G-man. He was a cop who dressed sharp like a gangster. Known in all of New York's best spots, he loved to entertain, and he cultivated friends in police and security services the world over. He was smart and independent enough not to be hamstrung by anyone else's conventional wisdom. He was also brash and difficult, even his close friends acknowledge. In early 1995, he was appointed section chief of counterterrorism at headquarters, and in December 1996 he moved to the New York Field Office as special agent in charge (SAC) of the National Security Division.

In a tragic twist of fate, O'Neill became the World Trade Center's chief of security upon retiring from the Bureau. September 11, 2001, was his first day on his new job. He died in the collapse of the south tower. To this day, when former colleagues invoke his name, their tone becomes hushed with emotion.

True to his nature, immediately upon learning of the embassy bombings, O'Neill took the initiative to deploy teams led by Pat D'Amuro to Nairobi and Joe Billy to Dar, notwithstanding Washington Field Office's jurisdiction over attacks in the Middle East and Africa. He argued that his New York investigators had an active interest in bin Laden and the background knowledge to pursue the case. Ultimately, agents from both Washington and New York descended on the two crime scenes.

It was O'Neill's Washington counterpart, Sheila Horan, who was assigned to command the investigation in Nairobi, while her number two, Ken Piernick, was put in charge in Dar. It wasn't easy on Horan to know that O'Neill was taking a direct interest in her investigation, and had sent over two of his most loyal soldiers. She was no stranger to Bureau politics or its old boys' network. She was among the earliest female special agents and the first to rise to a senior rank. Not the outsized personality that O'Neill was, she nonetheless carried her authority with confidence.

While the involvement of two separate field offices complicated the lines of command, it did not hinder the investigation. Once it was determined that bin Laden was responsible, NYFO was officially designated the office of origin and given jurisdiction for the case.

The deployment was a massive logistical undertaking for which the Bureau had no precedent. As Billy put it, "It wasn't like we were supposed to be ready and came up ill-prepared. This was a totally new thing."[1] It entailed hundreds of agents, crime scene technicians, evidence recovery specialists, forensic analysts, bomb techs, communications specialists, dog handlers, doctors, paramedics, and SWAT teams, all assembled at a moment's notice, along with all of their gear. Everyone was hurriedly vaccinated and began downing antimalaria pills, knowing full well that it takes time for the immunity to kick in.

Given that resources and facilities in Africa were limited or nonexistent, everything they could conceivably need had to be transported to the crime scene, including basics like food, water, medicine, and blood supply (because of the inadequacy of local stockpiles and concerns over the prevalence of AIDS) so as to ensure their self-sufficiency on the ground. Piernick, a former member of the Eighty-Second Airborne, had previous experience of such a large-scale operation: "Deploying is what the Airborne does, so I quickly concentrated on getting our people ready. I got a KC-10, which has a tremendous cargo capacity, loaded up at Andrews Air Force base."[2]

The New York contingent commandeered a city bus to drive them to Andrews. To everyone's immense frustration, the bus was fitted with a governor that kept it from exceeding fifty miles per hour. As it trundled down the highway, O'Neill kept calling, screaming at D'Amuro to disable the governor, but it was impossible. They ended up missing the first plane to Nairobi.

"The bus trip was worse than the seventeen-hour flight," D'Amuro said.[3]

Not that the flight was without incident. After landing to refuel in Rota, Spain, smoke filled the cabin and the aircraft had to be quickly evacuated. Nineteen hours passed before it was airborne again for the final leg of the trip.

There were still dismembered bodies and body parts strewn around the bomb site when the first contingent of agents arrived in Nairobi. It was a scene of greater carnage than any of them had ever encountered. "It was just horrible, very grue-some, total devastation, total confusion," Horan recalled.[4]

The agents' first priority was to secure the scene, a necessary precaution that would infuriate locals, who misinterpreted it as a lack of concern with rescuing Kenyans still trapped in the rubble. Marine guards did prevent civilians from rushing headlong onto the piles to dig willy-nilly for survivors because of a legitimate fear for the stability of the structure and that they could make the situation worse, getting themselves killed. Access control was also critical for the painstaking task of evidence recovery.

Ambassador Bushnell vehemently denied that the Americans were anything less than vigorous in their efforts to save locals, going on Kenyan TV to say, "We were shedding blood. Blood was blood. We were rescuing people. People are people. There was no determination as to race, religion, ethnic group. We were trying to get as many people out as we possibly could."[5]

And in the midst of so much death and destruction there were miraculous rescues. Thirty-five hours after the bombing, Gatili Nganya, a forty-five-year-old businessman, was pulled out of the rubble alive. Two days after the blast, a mother and her twelve-year-old son, who had been on the twentieth floor of the Cooperative Bank Building, were saved.

One of the most heart-wrenching tales was the effort to extract a woman named Roselyn Wanjiku Mwangi—Rosie—trapped beneath forty feet of debris in the Ufundi House. Rescue workers were guided by her plaintive voice. How-ever, because of the precarious jigsaw of debris over and around her, they had to move gingerly for fear of causing a shift that might crush her. As they dug, they were able to communicate, trying to keep her calm. We're coming, they assured her. Hold on. We know it hurts, it won't be much longer. We won't abandon you. We'll get to you, we will. But ultimately, they couldn't.

Death came hard to her, savoring the time it took to claim her, letting her strength leave her second by second. She probably had moments of near jubila-tion as she heard rescuers scrambling close by, followed by anguish at the weight of the rubble they could never remove in time. Slowly, one by one, her hopes and dreams fluttered away, as she came to accept there was no future. Rosie was the last victim to succumb.

Investigators were surprised and dismayed by the logistical sophistication evi-denced by al Qaeda's capacity to carry out almost simultaneous attacks four hundred miles apart. Said CIA veteran Milton Bearden, "Two at once is not twice as hard. Two at once is 100 times as hard."[6]

Of immediate concern was the dread question, what's next? Investigators on the scene were wary of the possibility that more attacks could be in store, perhaps timed to wreak maximum damage against American personnel.

Rumors circulating about the U.S. Embassy in Uganda being in danger seemed credible because Abu Hafs, al Qaeda's military head, was said to have connections at Kampala mosques.[7] According to Uganda's minister for security, Muruli Mukasa, "the attacks were planned to be more serious and devastating than those in Nairobi and Dar-es-Salaam." Eighteen people were rounded up by local police.[8] Piernick dispatched several agents to investigate. They were there for a couple of weeks looking into the threat, but didn't come up with anything tangible.[9]

Nerves remained jittery at America's African establishments for some time. On December 18 and 19, thirty-eight embassies and three consulates across sub-Saharan Africa were closed in response to threats uttered by bin Laden in support of the Iraqi people who were under American and British aerial bombardment.[10] In June 1999, U.S. embassies in Senegal, Gambia, Liberia, Togo, Namibia, and Mauritania and British embassies in Senegal, Gambia, Namibia, and Madagascar were temporarily closed after al Qaeda surveillance was detected around the facilities.[11]

In Nairobi, the FBI established a command post across Moi Avenue from the embassy on a field near the rail yards. It was here that evidence response teams brought millions of pieces of debris, large and minute, to be cataloged and examined by bomb specialists and forensic chemists in a valiant effort to sift out the tell-tale fragments that would reveal the components of the explosive device and the vehicle used to deliver it. Agents were sent to the morgue to observe autopsies and to retrieve any shrapnel that might help in piecing together the bomb.

"We tried to set up as discreet a work space as possible so we could control it. But picture the scene," SAC Sheila Horan recalls; "this is right in the middle of a very large city. People are walking all over the crime scene; people are walking all around where we're trying to work. The police were not stopping them. They were a bit lackadaisical. I remember walking up to them and saying, 'Please, guys, maintain a perimeter.' 'Oh, yes, ma'am,' and they lifted up their guns. Next thing I know, they're back to chit-chatting with their pals. So it was very, very difficult. Very difficult."[12]

All the while, investigators were coping with difficulties they never encountered in the States. One agent had to be assigned to attend to all the things that magically take care of themselves: supplying food, water, medicine, pencils and paper, communications equipment. SWAT members had to guard the hotel where the Americans were billeted. This necessitated a lot of extra manpower. In Nairobi, common street crime was a constant worry. One agent had his gun stolen. Thankfully, the local police succeeded in recovering it.

Over in Dar, the perimeter was more orderly because the command post could be set up directly on the embassy grounds, in the building that had housed the U.S. Agency for International Development. Once the fires were extinguished and the bodies removed, the collection of evidence began in earnest.

The American contingent was initially housed at the Sheraton Hotel in downtown Dar, but Piernick was dissatisfied with the security. Some staffers from the Iranian consulate were observed around the area, and Iran could not yet be conclusively discounted as a suspect. So everyone was moved to the Sea Cliffs, which backed onto the Indian Ocean and could be approached only by a single dirt road, which was easily controlled by SWAT members.[13]

Neither stricken embassy recorded images off their surveillance cameras, and thus had no video evidence of the moments before the explosions. Investigators set about interviewing everyone in the area to find anybody who might have seen anything on the day of the bombing. They went to the hospitals to interview victims, they talked to every embassy staffer, local and American. In the end, not much was gleaned from these efforts, but every base had to be covered.

"Eyewitnesses to events like that are most often in shock, so their recollections aren't usually very good," SAC Ken Piernick said.[14] In Nairobi, for example, interviews with two senior managers with the Cooperative Bank elicited very different accounts: one claimed to have heard gunfire and three blasts; the other insisted there were two blasts and no gunfire.[15] Both were sincere in their recollections. Both men were trying to be helpful. The discrepancies, however, could drive investigators mad. The problem highlights the importance of forensic evidence.

"I don't recall any significant leads coming out of interviews with witnesses," Piernick went on. "The people who saw what happened were the security guards, the men from the water truck, who were killed. There were no preliminary noises to draw people to pay attention before the sudden explosion, as there were in Nairobi."[16]

The most crucial pieces of evidence for which recovery specialists scoured the crime scenes in Nairobi and Dar were any fragments that could identify the composition of the explosive devices and the delivery vehicles. Speaking anonymously, an official involved in the investigation said, "Ideally, we want to match the eyewitness accounts to the physical evidence of the truck. If we can match it up, history shows that we're on our way to identifying the perpetrators."[17] The key to solving the 1993 attack against the World Trade Center had been a positive identification of the rental van that carried the bomb. In that case, one of the perpetrators not only rented the vehicle in his real name, but returned to the rental agency to reclaim his deposit, at which time he was arrested.

Because metal behaves predictably when subjected to stresses and absorbs explosive residue based on its proximity and position relative to an explosive force, forensic analysts are able, out of countless twisted fragments and piles of debris, to determine which pieces belong to the bomb delivery vehicle, and to identify its make and model. The most treasured piece of wreckage is that containing the vehicle identification number (VIN). The VIN is as unique to a car or truck as a fingerprint to a human. A senior law enforcement official said, "Get the car, get the VIN. It'll take you somewhere. Interview everybody. Somebody saw something. Somebody knows something."[18]

With suicide bombings, the vehicle is not usually registered to the actual bomber. Someone with responsibility for planning has gone about making the acquisition, which is a flaw in the organization. Were the vehicle connected to no one other than the bomber, it would lead to a dead end. This, however, is rarely the case. For example, Ahmed the German in Dar, who spoke neither Swahili nor English, couldn't perform the simple task of renting a car. The truck, therefore, is key to furthering the investigation.

Eight days into the investigation, Piernick was walking around the search grid at the end of the day when a blackened, greasy piece of metal caught his attention. He rolled it with his boot and saw numbers. He had it cleaned and, lo and behold, it was the VIN. It enabled the Bureau to determine that the bomb delivery vehicle was a 1987 Nissan Atlas.

Another critical discovery was made by bomb technicians combing the embassy's outer fence, which had been pelted with shrapnel. There, they found a piece of a gas cylinder stamped with a serial number. That led investigators to the welders who had, unwittingly, performed part of the fabrication of the bomb components.

Records checks revealed the Atlas was purchased by Ahmed Khalfan Ghailani along with Sheikh Ahmed Salim Swedan in July 1998. Swedan, in the company of Fahid Mohammed Ally Msalam (aka Usama al-Kini), also purchased oxygen and acetylene tanks to amplify the power of the blast. In court, Mohamed Zaidi identified a photo of Swedan as being the man to whom he sold his truck. Julius Kisingo Cam, a welder, testified that he modified the Atlas, adding a housing for an extra battery that Swedan, whose photo he identified, said was to power an air conditioning unit, as well as reinforcing the cargo box and adding a padlock to secure the rear door.

Three days into gathering evidence in Nairobi, a man found a scrap of metal with a number on it in the rubble of the secretarial college and turned it over to the FBI. It was among the more than six hundred fragments of metal retrieved from the vicinity of the blast that Supervisory Special Agent Donald Sachtleben, a senior bomb technician, showed to various automobile company representatives around Nairobi until someone from Toyota recognized crucial pieces as being from one of their trucks. In February 1999, he traveled to Nagoya, Japan, to have them analyzed by engineers and, on two occasions, Toyota officials flew to Washington. Based on their analysis, it was concluded that the pieces identified as belonging to the bomb truck came from a Toyota Dyna. Thus commenced the laborious though ultimately fruitful task of tracing local ownership records on this specific type of vehicle.

It was determined that Swedan and Msalam had acquired it from a Mombasa poultry farmer in late June or early July 1998. According to testimony in court from the vendor, Said Salim Omar, Swedan claimed to be in the transportation business. After turning over the keys, Omar never saw him again.

Swedan and Msalam remained at large until January 1, 2009, when they were killed in a safe house in Waziristan, northern Pakistan by an American drone-launched Hellfire missile. Swedan had risen to head al Qaeda's operations in Pakistan, and Msalam was his deputy. Both were under indictment for the embassy attacks.

For all the technical and operational expertise the FBI brought, it understood that it could get nowhere without strong support from the local police. Hence, establishing trust and credibility was a priority.

"We were the eight-hundred-pound gorilla in town," Horan acknowledged. "We just walked into the country, didn't have proper visas. We ran the investigation, but the Kenyan Police had to be intimately involved."[19]

Billy concurred: "Imagine a bunch of Tanzanian police showing up here, armed. It was very brazen of us, but we approached it as diplomatically as possible. At first, they didn't trust us and we didn't trust them. But, the Commissioner of Police and I quickly formed a bond. I'm not saying that extended to every officer, but certainly at the management level, we collaborated very well, and that was critical to the success of the investigation."[20]

Otieno Osur, director of police operations for Nairobi, lamented, "This is a real national disaster."[21] It was clearly beyond his department's capacity to handle such a complex investigation on its own. In both Kenya and Tanzania, authorities granted the Bureau unrestricted access to the crime scene, evidence, witnesses, and suspects.

"At first I was very unimpressed with their investigators," Piernick admits with regard to the Tanzanians. They looked shabby, their weapons were poorly maintained, they lacked supplies. "Frankly, they were impoverished. We gave them ammunition. We shared our MREs (military meals-ready-to-eat) with them."

Their comportment suggested lack of discipline and disinterest. First thing each morning, Piernick convened briefings for which the American agents arrived on time, raring to go. The Tanzanians would invariably arrive late, and frequently bleary eyed. "So I'm thinking they're pretty slack. After a while, I had my agents operating with them, and I started getting reports that, while we were sleeping, they're out all night in these shitbox cars, chasing down leads, watching suspects, going places we couldn't easily go. I really came to respect how they did so much with so little."[22]

Pat D'Amuro is similarly complimentary toward the Kenyans: "They were genuinely on board and wanted to work with us. CID had some capabilities. They were good with some interviews. The amount of evidence and intelligence we were able to collect directly correlates to the level of cooperation we got from them."[23]

In those places where white officers would draw unwanted attention, the Americans kept their profile low, allowing the Kenyans to do what they had to do on their own. As per protocol, when American agents went out, it was always in the company of CID officers.

Meanwhile, hundreds of calls were coming in to a tip line the Americans established in Nairobi. Calls of all kinds. Much of the information was sketchy at best. Some of it was nonsense. Some was downright crazy. But a very few held promise. One in particular that came in on the very first night.

The caller spoke of seeing a man, not too long after the explosion, who acted strangely. The caller witnessed the man entering a hotel in Eastleigh, a ramshackle part of town that would come to be known as Little Mogadishu for its concentration of Somalis, both refugees and Kenyan born. He had been wounded and his clothing was torn and bloodied in the back. The caller, further, saw him leaving the hotel to place calls at a pay phone across the street.

Why, out of all the calls, D'Amuro singled this one out, even he can't really explain, other than to say it was interesting and detailed enough, without embellishment, to sound credible. Years of listening to people spin stories imparts a feel for what's real, something like how an experienced physician can tell the composition of a tumor by touch. D'Amuro got a feeling from this one.

The caller didn't trust the Kenyan police and refused to meet with them. Because the FBI couldn't meet the caller alone, the agents emphasized that they would be present and appealed to the caller's moral outrage, noting that, in this circumstance, there was no ambiguity between right and wrong. This was not an act of petty crime to which one could turn a blind eye without troubling one's conscience. This was a grotesque act of mass murder. The worst Kenya had ever suffered.

Ultimately, the caller agreed to meet.

On August 12, Special Agents Steve Gaudin and Steve Bongardt, in the company of two Kenyan CID officers and a driver, went out to Eastleigh. The Americans stayed concealed in the vehicle while the Kenyans entered the Iftin Lodge.

The officers returned with a man whose head and hands were bandaged. This was al-'Owhali, who had been the passenger in the bomb truck. "We could have totally missed him if nobody had come forward with their suspicions," Horan stressed. "It was the first break."[24]

His only identification was an admissions card from the MP Shah Hospital. It gave his name as Khalid Saleh and indicated he had received treatment on August 7. The Kenyan police arrested him for failing to have any official identification. He was placed in the back of the truck where he got his first glimpse of the Americans.

Gaudin, along with Bongardt, an official with the Justice Department, two CID officers, and an FBI interpreter, first interviewed al-'Owhali on August 22 at CID headquarters. Gaudin treated him respectfully, ensuring that he had food when he asked for it, was given breaks when he needed them.

He made it clear: "Listen, you're the boss. You control what you say and what you don't say. If you want to continue to talk to us, you can. If you don't want to talk to us, you don't have to."[25]

Al-'Owhali held stubbornly to his original story: that he was Khalid Saleh, a businessman from Yemen. He had been wounded by the explosion, made his own way to the hospital for treatment, and then returned to his hotel.

Agents were dispatched to the MP Shah Hospital to see if they could dig up any information about their suspect. Nobody remembered him, but an orderly asked whether they were there to retrieve the keys and bullets he'd found. Surprised, they happily took the items.

When al-'Owhali was arrested, he claimed to be wearing the same clothes he'd had on the day of the bombing. He'd simply cleaned up, he said. There were no rips in his shirt or pants to suggest how close he'd really been to the explosion. His story began to break down on the simplest of oversights.

Noticing a pristine white sales sticker affixed to al-'Owhali's belt, Gaudin unhitched his own belt and mused about how he'd purchased it brand new for his trip to Africa. He had been in Kenya for only a couple of weeks. That's all the time it took, in the tortuous heat, for the leather to become visibly bent and sodden with moisture. Yet, here was al-'Owhali's belt, so unmarred despite having been worn continuously, with the sales sticker still attached, that it could be put back on the store shelf and sold as new.

Gaudin showed him the keys and bullets retrieved from the hospital and said he knew they belonged to him. When confronted with this evidence, al-'Owhali became extremely agitated, threatening that his "tribe" would "kill you and your whole family" and "said no embassies would be safe, not even the Kenyans', and that hostages would be taken."[26] He insisted that he wasn't properly advised of his rights, had been instructed to confess, and was threatened that he would be left with the Kenyans to "be hanged from your neck like a dog."[27]

This was an uncharacteristic outburst. For the most part, the interview had proceeded cordially to this point. He spoke calmly, even as the investigators posed extremely pointed and specific questions.

"Al-'Owhali's story really didn't hold up," Sheila Horan said. "He tried to stick to it, but kept having to change the details to fit our evidence. Our investigators didn't browbeat him. They just talked him through it, pointing out what didn't make sense. That's what won the day."[28]

He was shown pictures of mutilated corpses. They said, without recrimination, "You're a soldier. This is a war."

"Yes," he replied, the first hint of a confession.

He finally conceded the bullets and keys were his, and explained how, while leaving the hospital, he felt them in his pocket and turned back, slipping into a men's room. He rinsed the bullets and keys to erase his fingerprints and tried to flush them down the toilet, but they wouldn't go down. So he hid them under a ledge.

Eventually he agreed to talk, but attached one condition: "Mr. al-'Owhali explained that he would tell us his involvement in the bombing of the embassy if we would guarantee him that he would be tried in the United States because the United States was his enemy and not Kenya so he wanted a guarantee that he be tried in America to face his enemy," said Gaudin.

He was promised only that the Justice Department would do all that it could to fulfill this wish. With that, he agreed to talk and revealed his true identity.

This would come back to haunt al-'Owhali when his counsel challenged the admissibility of statements he gave while in Kenya. Judge Sand ruled that his statement "was a consequence of the strong desire he expressed to be tried in America so that he could confront his avowed enemy."[29] Therefore, he concluded, it was freely given.

During closing arguments, Fredrick Cohn, his lead attorney, would try to turn al-'Owhali's desire to be tried in the United States to advantage, saying, "Mohamed was kept in terrible conditions, in fear of his life from jailers, with jailers who had to hate him. It was clear that he wasn't going to get any trial in Kenya, and if he did, one so summary as not to be worthy of the name.

"To get a trial, he ultimately had to come to the United States, avowedly his enemy, but the only refuge that he had, and as the statements he made to Gaudin tell you, after begging for assurance that he would go to the United States for trial, he paid for the trip in the only coin he had, which was his statement." For the record, al-'Owhali never alleged mistreatment, whether by the Americans or Kenyans.

"The government depicted al-'Owhali as being extremely sophisticated, educated, aware of how the American judicial system worked, that he wanted to use it to his advantage and have a public platform to express his views," said Laura Gasiorowski, a member of his defense team. "But, I don't think anyone raised in that environment, in that culture, with an extremely insular religious upbringing, whose education is entirely in religious schools, has any notion about how the American judicial system truly works. Really, his education was religious indoctrination. He had no experience of cultures outside his own. How sophisticated can someone be when their upbringing is so stunted?"[30]

Al-'Owhali was born in 1977 in Liverpool, where his father was studying, and grew up in Saudi Arabia in a wealthy and prominent family. He was put into what attorney Fredrick Cohn refers to as a "religious nut school" by his mother who wanted him to become a cleric.

"I wanted to say that he was who he was because of his mother. Quite frankly," Cohn said, "that would have made a compelling defense, but he wouldn't attack his mother. He wouldn't let us do that."[31]

The defense would, however, harp on his youth, reminding the jury during summation that al-'Owhali would have been fourteen in 1991, the year in which the indictment alleged that al Qaeda embarked on its anti-American conspiracy. "How is he supposed to know about the scope of this conspiracy?" Cohn asked incredulously. "The government seeks to hold him criminally responsible for the activities of people long before he can be held to account for them."

After graduating, he made his way to the Khaldan camp in Afghanistan, where he received training in explosives, hijacking, kidnapping, assassination, and intelligence techniques. He joined the Northern Group of the mujahideen in 1996 and was sent to fight against the Soviets in Tajikistan. Though he made it to the front, the group ended up returning to Kabul without seeing any action. They did, however, have the opportunity to meet bin Laden, military chief Abu Hafs, and Saleh, a leader of the embassy plot. Bin Laden lectured them about al Qaeda's mission; they "were fighters bin Laden had privately marked as future key operatives," argued the prosecution. Al-'Owhali was selected for more advanced training, in security and intelligence, how to hijack buses and planes, kidnap, and seize and hold buildings. He decided not to pledge bayat to al Qaeda because it would commit him to absolute loyalty to the organization and he feared assignment to a noncombat role and being left with no alternative but to accept. By not swearing fidelity, he preserved the option to leave if not sent to fight.

Al-'Owhali told Special Agent Gaudin that he met bin Laden several times, "and had expressed to him interest in missions that he would like to do, and Mr. bin Laden told him, take your time. Your mission will come in time."

Ultimately, he was sent to join Afghani Taliban forces at the front, where he was stricken with tuberculosis. This was when he met the eventual suicide bomber Azzam, who treated him. Al-'Owhali shared his desire for a mission.

"So," Gaudin related, "Azzam told him, 'I'll be in contact when the mission starts to get ready. I'll let you know.'"

Upon recovering, al-'Owhali returned to the front, where he secured his reputation by distinguishing himself during a fierce battle near Kabul. Soon after, he was contacted by Azzam and told that the mission was to proceed. Al-'Owhali reiterated his interest and was sent to a specialized training center outside Kabul. When Gaudin showed al-'Owhali a photo of Azzam for identification purposes, "he called Azzam a hero and then he kissed the picture. . . . And as al-'Owhali was reflecting on his friendship with Azzam and [recited] this chanting poem, he started to cry."

Five months prior to the bombing, he was instructed to shave off his beard and travel to Yemen. Two months later, he returned to Pakistan where he was met by Azzam, who introduced him to a young Saudi named Khalid. Khalid explained to al-'Owhali that he has been selected for a "martyrdom mission" and was to die in a truck bombing against an American target in East Africa. As is the custom, al-'Owhali filmed a farewell video in which he claimed responsibility for the attack on behalf of the Liberation Army of the Islamic Sanctuaries.

He arrived in Nairobi on August 2 and was met by Harun and taken to his home. On August 3, Saleh gave him all the details of the attack and informed him that he would accompany Azzam in the truck that was to bomb the American embassy.

Al-'Owhali asked Saleh about attacking targets inside the United States. Gaudin reported, "Saleh had explained to him there were targets in the U.S. that we could hit, but things aren't ready yet. We don't have anything prepared to do that yet. First, Saleh explains to al-'Owhali, we have to have many attacks outside the United States and this will weaken the U.S. and make way for our ability to strike within the United States."

August 4 was the last time he ever saw Saleh.

\-\-\-

During his initial questioning, on an inspired hunch, al-'Owhali was handed a pen and paper and asked to write down the first number he called after the bombing. Surprisingly, he complied: 967–1-200578. This number, if not its significance, was already known to U.S. intelligence. The National Security Agency had picked up on it back in 1996 because it received a number of calls from bin Laden's satellite phone (including on August 10 and 11). They knew that phone rang in Yemen and belonged to Ahmed al-Hada. They knew it had received calls from Nairobi before the attacks, but, of course, didn't know why until later. Al-'Owhali's revelation confirmed al Qaeda's involvement in the attack.[32]

According to Lawrence Wright, "this Yemeni telephone number would prove to be one of the most important pieces of information the FBI would ever discover, allowing investigators to map the links of the al-Qaeda network all across the globe."[33] Al-Hada's name would surface again when it was learned that one of the 9/11 hijackers was his nephew.

Between August 4 and the 7, al-'Owhali placed a number of phone calls from Harun's house to al-Hada. The last was made about an hour before the attack.

Because it was never contemplated that he might survive, there were no provisions to extract him after the bombing. Upon leaving the hospital, he didn't know how to get to Harun's house, so he took a taxi to the Iftin Lodge in Eastleigh, with which he was familiar. He told the clerk he'd been wounded in the bombing which, by then, everyone had heard about, and lost all his documents and money. The clerk agreed to pay his taxi and extend him credit until he could contact people who would send him money. Al-'Owhali then went to a shop owned by a Yemeni, which is what he claimed to be, and replaced his bloodied clothes.

It was the following day that he called al-Hada, telling him he needed money and a passport with an entry stamp showing he'd arrived in Kenya after August 7. He was wired $1,000 and was awaiting the travel documents when he was arrested.

Al-'Owhali was interviewed over four consecutive days, for approximately four hours at a time. He answered questions in Arabic through an interpreter. When it was over, he had revealed the complete story of his involvement.

Moreover, at trial, Gaudin would testify that on August 25, "Mr. al-'Owhali had said to me that he had some information he called a 'blue chip.'" Gaudin responded with assurances that such information would not be used against him, but only for purposes of further investigation, offering him limited immunity if he disclosed it immediately.

He told investigators that, while staying at a guesthouse in Yemen, he'd overheard Abdul Rahim al-Nashiri, a fellow member of the Northern Group, discussing a plan to attack U.S. ships in Aden with missiles. It was al-Nashiri who had obtained the fraudulent passport that al-'Owhali used in Kenya.[34] Furthermore, he was the cousin of al-'Owhali's fellow Nairobi bomber, Azzam.[35] It was not revealed in court exactly how detailed al-'Owhali's information was about any forthcoming attack, nor whether it was followed up.[36] In January 2000 an attack against the USS *The Sullivans* in Aden was botched. On October 12, the *Cole* was successfully bombed by an explosives-laden skiff that sailed up to it virtually unopposed. The massive destroyer was nearly sunk. Seventeen crew members were killed and thirty-nine wounded. Al-'Owhali's offer became public through its inclusion in a defense brief that was never supposed to be entered into the public record.[37]

Al-Nashiri was behind the attack against the USS *Cole*. He went on to become al Qaeda's chief of operations in the Gulf. He was captured in November 2002 and detained at Guantánamo Bay.

Also staying at the guesthouse was another Northern Group alumnus and participant in the *Cole* operation, Tawfiq bin Attash, also known as Khallad. He, too, was involved in planning the embassy attacks. Khallad had lost a leg while fighting the Soviets in Afghanistan. He would be taken into American custody in April 2003 and subjected to enhanced interrogations, including very painful stress positions. His prosthesis was taken away and he was forced to balance for long periods on his one leg or to hang by his arms.[38]

On August 26, al-'Owhali was rendered to the United States, where Special Agent Coleman swore out the complaint against him.

Fredrick Cohn is a large, somewhat blustery man, with a thick Fu-Manchu moustache who brings a freight train's forward momentum to his interrogation of witnesses. He was pointed and aggressive in his cross-examination of Gaudin, who was formal and short in his replies.

Gaudin acknowledged that, although an interpreter was used for the interview, the advice of rights form provided al-'Owhali was only in English.

Cohn showed the jury close-up photos of al-'Owhali's injuries: "Did you get him to a doctor?"

"No, sir, I didn't," Gaudin said.

"You had no control over him at all, did you, when he wasn't being interrogated by you, is that right?"

"No, sir, I did not have any control."

"So he received, to your knowledge, no medical attention until finally he was seen by a doctor, I think an Embassy doctor around the eighteenth or within a week?"

"Within a week, yes, sir, I believe that's correct."

He went on to quiz him about conditions in Kenyan detention. "You don't know whether it was clean?"

"I've never been inside."

"You don't know if it was filthy?"

"I've never been inside," Gaudin repeated.

"You don't know if he had toilet facilities?"

"Sir, I don't."

"You don't know if he had a mattress?"

"I've never been there, sir."

"You don't know what happened? You don't know what was said to him? And you don't know the conditions of confinement?"

"Correct, sir."

With respect to the Tanzanian prisons, which couldn't be substantively different from those in Kenya, Piernick acknowledges conditions were "pretty abysmal. It was very tough, very raw. Prisoners depended on their families to purchase food and drink on their behalf, otherwise they didn't fare too well.

"One of the things we did when we went to interview anyone in custody," Piernick said, "was bring them food and water, for which they were very grateful. But, look, when in Rome. So, we didn't interfere with them, we didn't impose Western standards on them. But, we didn't see any abuse, other than the conditions, which were the result of poverty."[39]

Cohn intimated that al-'Owhali may have been mistreated by the Kenyans when Gaudin wasn't around, asking incredulously, "Never occurred to you to inquire as to whether or not they were threatening him and to make sure of his well-being?" Anything to imply that his incriminating statement was not given freely.

Gaudin related how on a day when he did not interview al-'Owhali, he went to the police station on his own initiative to bring him a container of milk he'd requested.

"Your visit with the milk was an act of pure friendship, is that right?" Cohn asked sarcastically.

"Yes, sir. Kindness, I guess."

In closing arguments, Cohn would make this incident sound ominous: "Why is that important? It is important for a couple of reasons. One is that it shows that Agent Gaudin had access. He told you at various times during the testimony that he was not in control, Kenyan authorities had control of the custody. But he had access. The other reason he went is because he wanted al-'Owhali to know that he only had one friend. He only had one friend. If anybody was going to save him from the Kenyans, it was Gaudin."

Al-'Owhali's direct defense consisted of entering into evidence a newspaper photo that security guard Charles Mwaka Mula identified as being of the man who exited the bomb truck and threw grenades at him, along with a composite sketch made by the FBI based on a description provided by Mwaka Mula. The two individuals did not resemble one another, thus calling into question his positive identification of al-'Owhali. With that, his defense rested.

[6] MOHAMED SADDIQ ODEH

On August 6, the day before the embassies were bombed, Mohamed Saddiq Odeh and Fahid Mohammed Ally Msalam boarded Pakistan International Airways flight 746 in Nairobi bound for Karachi. Odeh was traveling on a fake Yemeni passport under a false name.

At Karachi Airport, he caught the attention of an alert Pakistani immigration officer. Saleh, the one who provided him with the passport, had instructed him to shave his beard so as not to appear to be a devout Muslim. Notwithstanding this precaution, the initial screening officer took the time to scrutinize the passport and noticed that he looked significantly different from the face in the picture. Also, he noted how Odeh would not look him in the eye. "I was 100 percent sure it didn't belong to him," the officer would testify.

The Pakistani was already aware of the embassy bombings from media reports. Suspicious, he pulled Odeh aside for additional questioning. Msalam, the more senior of the two, walked into Karachi unimpeded.

According to a Pakistani source of Peter Bergen's, officers "asked him: 'Are you a terrorist?' Now, most people in that situation would say: 'Of course not,' but Odeh didn't say anything. When they asked him about the bombing, he said he had been involved and he started trying to persuade the immigration officer it was the right thing to do for Islam. To which the immigration officer replied, 'Not in my country.' At which point Odeh was handed over to intelligence officers, to whom he made a full confession."[1] Had he not been stopped then and there, he would have vanished without a trace.

"Pakistani officials said he had . . . voluntarily confessed there, and that he had identified several collaborators, calling Mr. bin Laden the driving force behind the bombing."[2]

Addressing the circumstances of Odeh's arrest, his attorney Anthony Ricco spun a story of how he hadn't fled Kenya of his own accord, but at the insistence of people that he knew were involved with the bomb plot. He would have preferred to travel on his own legitimate passport, but he didn't have time to apply for one, thus leaving him no alternative but to use the forgery. He did not shave his beard for the purpose of disguise, Ricco asserted, but only in an attempt to match the photo on the passport.

On August 1, just a week before the bombing, Odeh had run across Saleh, one of the conspiracy's organizers, in Mombasa. Saleh became very agitated, cursing at him that it was an emergency and he had to leave the country no later than the sixth. On the second, Odeh went to Malindi to attend to his furniture business, seemingly unperturbed by the gravity of the situation. On the third, he purchased a plane ticket for Karachi. On the fourth, he went to the Hilltop Hotel in Nairobi to see Saleh. Saleh commented that he had received news that al Qaeda people were evacuating their camps in Kandahar for fear of American retaliatory missile strikes, but Odeh said he never asked why. Also present was Abdel Rahman, who had been his explosives instructor in Afghanistan. Odeh told Special Agent John Anticev he wasn't expecting to see him, but wasn't particularly shocked because he knew that al Qaeda business was afoot. He learned that Abdel Rahman had been at the Hilltop for the past two months.

"Mohamed was asked to leave Kenya because Mohamed was a link," Ricco insisted, not because he was a participant. He was the smallest of small fish, while the real trophy swam free. Al Qaeda was anxious to get Odeh out of Kenya, Ricco went on, "because they recognized that if you ask Mohamed a question, you're going to get an answer." And that, he contended, was precisely what happened when he was interviewed by the FBI.

Joe Billy was dispatched from Dar to take him into U.S. custody. Initially, the intention was to bring him directly to New York, but they flew instead to Nairobi on August 14. When they put him on the plane, the Pakistanis told Odeh he was being flown to Afghanistan. According to Gary Berntsen, leader of the CIA's Emergency Deployment Team in Dar es Salaam who was part of the team that went to Karachi, when he discovered he was being returned to Nairobi, "Odeh's knees almost gave out. The FBI wanted immediate custody of Saddiq. But I didn't doubt that the Kenyans would get him to talk. . . . He would have a very bad time, and would share everything he knew about Osama bin Laden and the al-Qaeda organization."[3]

Pakistan, ever cautious about the sensitivities of Islamist sympathizers, felt compelled to don the fig leaf cover that Odeh had been returned to the scene of the crime, not into the hands of the Americans.

Billy is not without empathy for their situation. "A moment I'll never forget, we're standing on the tarmac, a Pakistani officer turns Odeh over to us. He gestures over his shoulder, in the direction of Afghanistan [and, thus, toward bin Laden], that they didn't want *him* to know about this." He shakes his head: "You think about this state living in fear of a terrorist organization."[4]

Only after 9/11 would America come to appreciate the anxious cast of al Qaeda's shadow. Yes, Pakistan has been a wavering ally and some senior people appear to have conflicted loyalty, but many of its officials have performed their duty with utmost courage.

There was never really any serious consideration given to having the accused face justice in Kenya. The attacks were perpetrated against American installations, the intended targets were Americans (notwithstanding the horrific loss of Kenyan life), and the United States was determined to take custody.

"I was in contact with the chief justice of Kenya, but he was procrastinating," Horan recalled. "He didn't want to outright tell us to take the case, but neither did any Kenyan authority imply they wanted to prosecute it. So, eventually, I just said, 'Take the evidence and the suspects, and send them back.' Huge risk on my part. But, never did anybody say anything. The Kenyans were totally relieved. I went to the justice and said, 'They're gone.' He just went, 'Okay, fine.' No repercussions, nothing. We just took them. The unspoken reality was that it was our investigation; we led it, we were the instigators."[5]

No doubt, the local authorities were profoundly rattled by the devastating incident. With Kenya's sizeable Muslim population, porous borders, and limited investigative and security resources, they appreciated—if without fully articulating it—that everybody was best served if the Americans pursued the matter. Moreover, they couldn't be sure how extensive was al Qaeda's infrastructure in their country and whether it was poised to carry out further attacks.

D'Amuro was caught in an unexpected quandary after the plane landed in Nairobi and Odeh was led away: "Mr. Pat! Mr. Pat!" Pakistan's high commissioner called for the man in charge, and informed him that it was the prime minister's jet that was sitting on the tarmac and it didn't have enough fuel for the return to Karachi.

"Now, the Bureau doesn't have a huge budget for jet fuel," D'Amuro laughs, "and they don't teach this at Quantico."

Concluding it was a relatively small price to pay for Odeh, he signed off on a $17,000 requisition to fill it up.[6]

At the time, *New York Times* intelligence correspondent Tim Weiner wrote pessimistically that early arrests "appear unpromising. And there are many reasons not to expect swift justice under American law. The intelligence agency, despite its best efforts, has few reliable sources in international terrorist networks."[7] Following Odeh's arrest, David Johnston wrote in the same paper, "A rapid end to the investigation would send a powerful message to terrorists, in contrast to the long list of cases that have remained open for years without the perpetrators being identified."[8]

Special Agent Anticev led the interrogation of Odeh at police headquarters between August 15 and 27, when he was remanded to the United States. During each session, two or three U.S. officials and between one and three Kenyans were present. The interviews were conducted in English and sometimes lasted the entire day.

From the very first, Odeh was advised of his rights under American law and voluntarily signed an advice of rights form. He was told, however, that he was actually in Kenya's custody and that Kenyan law did not provide for the right to counsel at this particular stage of the investigation. Therefore, the United States could not provide him with an attorney, which would be one of his fundamental rights were he in American custody. Anticev offered that, if he exercised his right to refuse to speak with American officials because of their inability to provide him an attorney, they would leave. Odeh consented to speak without benefit of counsel.

"He was the boss," Anticev testified, "he was in complete control of his own way of dealing with us. He could stop talking at any time. He could pick and choose to answer the questions, if he didn't like a question he didn't have to answer it."

Odeh's original court-appointed attorney, Jack Sachs,[9] claimed Pakistani authorities coerced his initial statement: "Three days and three nights without food and without water, under bright lights, no sleep—what would anybody say?"[10] He alleged that a Pakistani official told Odeh his confession would be exploited to improve relations with the United States, which had been strained since Pakistan tested a nuclear device the previous May. Officials at the Pakistani embassy in Washington denied the allegation.[11]

Later, Odeh filed an affidavit to suppress all statements he made to law enforcement officers in Pakistan and Kenya, claiming he had been "subjected to violence, threats of torture, psychological coercion, sleep deprivation, and other inhumane conditions." He claimed that a video of his interrogation in Pakistan was edited to remove evidence of improper questioning.[12] He asserted that when he was left alone with the Kenyans, they threatened torture or to take him into the city, tell people he was responsible for the bombing and allow them to "cut him to pieces." He further claimed the American agents threatened that, if he demanded an attorney, they would leave him to the Kenyans who, he believed, would torture him.[13]

Odeh was of Palestinian descent, born in Saudi Arabia and raised in Jordan. He attended university in the Philippines, studying architecture and engineering. During his student days, he listened to taped sermons by Adbullah Azzam, the cofounder of what became al Qaeda, which inspired him to abandon his studies and volunteer for the Afghan jihad in October 1990. He spent two months at the Farouq camp learning to use small arms, explosives, mortars, antiaircraft weapons, and rocket launchers. He was also trained as a medic and sent to the front at Jalalabad. While there, he was wounded and returned to Peshawar to recover. In early 1992, at the age of twenty-eight, he accepted an invitation to pledge bayat to bin Laden.

In March 1993, Odeh recounted, he was told that bin Laden wanted him to go to Nairobi, and from there, on to Somalia, where he would spend seven months, assisting a rebel tribe with links to the radical al-Ittihad al-Islamiyya group. Anticev said that Odeh explained, "As far as armed U.S. troops being in Somalia, al Qaeda thought . . . that it was wrong, and they considered it colonization."

In August 1994, Odeh returned to Kenya, settling in Mombasa. That October he entered into an arranged marriage with a local girl. Abu Hafs, al Qaeda's deputy military chief at the time, paid him a visit and bought him a boat with which Odeh was to start a fishing business. He was also provided with two employees, who were al Qaeda members, and was told his profits would be given over to the organization.

In February 1997, Odeh and his family moved to Witu, which is described as a "desolate area near the border with Somalia where banditry, gun-running, and smuggling are common," and opened a carpentry shop with his brother-in-law. He lived in poverty in a mud hut with thatch roofing.[14] There was no running water, nothing as basic as postal service, and just two telephones for the entire village.

"Mohamed fell in love with Kenya. Yes, Muslims fall in love, just like everybody else," Ricco tossed out, a clever little aside to chide the jury for any prejudices they may be harboring.

Foreshadowing evidence that would be presented about his participation in fighting in Somalia, Ricco went on, "Mohamed chose Kenya because of the involvement with Somalia, its proximity, but he chose the countryside of Kenya because it gave him solitude and a chance to think." Ricco spoke of how Odeh told the FBI that he was reluctant to participate in any operation in Kenya because he liked the country and the people.

Authorities searched Odeh's home following his arrest. Among the items seized was a diagram with two perpendicular lines radiating from a square. The prosecution said that it depicted a blast radius emanating from a bomb. The defense scoffed at this, saying nobody could tell what it was meant to illustrate. For all anyone knew, it could be a crude drawing of a snow cone. To which prosecutor Pat Fitzgerald retorted, "You don't go to Witu for a snow cone."

Anonymous police officials told the Kenyan daily—the *Nation*—that under interrogation, Odeh revealed that the bomb was assembled at the Hilltop Lodge. Consequently, a dozen FBI agents and six Kenyan detectives descended on the "low-cost hotel in a run-down neighbourhood" said to be popular with Muslim business travelers. They combed two rooms on the second floor for evidence. Hotel employees, however, said they noticed nothing unusual about the men who occupied those rooms in the days preceding the blast. And the janitors who cleaned up after them couldn't recall seeing anything suspicious in either room.[15]

Under questioning, Anticev said, Odeh "displayed knowledge of how explosives worked." He was able to discuss detonators and shape charges, a technique for directing the force of a blast for maximum destructive effect. As for an actual bombing, "the best place he said was to get the explosive charge inside the building." The next-best alternative? "Is to get the charge as close to the building as possible."

True to this, al-'Owhali had told Gaudin they never actually expected to get the truck inside the embassy garage. Saleh believed that would be impossible. He was expected only to force the guards to raise the drop bar so that Azzam could get up alongside the building.

"During the course of the interviews, is it fair to say that Odeh told you that he did not know in advance that the bombing would happen?" the prosecution asked Anticev.

"Yes, that's fair to say."

"Did he indicate during the course of the interview who he thought had bombed the American embassy?"

"His cell, Saleh and company."

"Did he indicate who he thought had built the bomb and where?"

"He thought that it was Harun and Abdel Rahman building the bomb at Harun's house."

"Did he indicate who he thought built the bomb for the embassy in Tanzania?"

"He made a statement that he believed that Abdel Rahman would have built that one, too."

"Did Odeh, during the interviews, make comments to you what he thought of the actual bombing and how it was carried out?"

"He thought it was a blunder. He blamed Saleh for making a big mistake. He didn't like the fact that so many civilians and Kenyans were killed. He said that the bombing of Khobar Towers was a hundred times better and that the individuals who drove the truck with the explosives should have got it into the building or died trying."

"During the time you interviewed Mr. Odeh, did he indicate to you why it was that he was talking to you?"

"Yes. He stated that the reason he was talking to us now was because the people that he was with were pushing him and pushing him and pushing him and they're all gone and he's left here facing big problems."

It is not necessary to win the war on the battlefield as well as in the media,
it is necessary only to win in the media. It is possible to lose on the battlefield,
win on television—and win. War is not partially a media event. It has become
completely a media event.
—Larry Beinhart, *American Hero*

[7] THE RETALIATION

The first claim of responsibility for the attack was received by the newspaper *Al
Hayat* from the previously unheard-of Liberation Army of the Islamic Sanctuaries. It said the Dar bombing had been carried out by Egyptian members of
the Abdallah Azzam Battalion. The statement demanded that the United States
withdraw its forces from Saudi Arabia, end its support for Israel, and free the
Blind Sheikh, who is in prison for trying to hatch the multi-site day of terror plot
in New York City.[1] It included a manifesto praising bin Laden.

President Clinton issued a predictable statement, calling the bombings "ab-
horrent; they are inhuman," and promising to "use all the means at our disposal
to bring those responsible to justice, no matter what or how long it takes."[2] The
United States posted a $2 million reward for information leading to the appre-
hension and conviction of the perpetrators.

Politicians thrust into such a situation are bedeviled by the irreconcilable
desires to strike back and to avoid unpredictable repercussions. It's a fine line
they balance between meaningful and symbolic action. Further complicating
matters in this case, the choice of where and what to strike at was far from obvious. It was challenging to devise a response that could both be proportionate to
the last attack and deter or degrade the perpetrator from carrying out the next.
A group with no obvious official ties to any state had committed an act of war
against the United States on the territory of other sovereign states that were, as
well, victims of the crime.

The president was determined that any measure undertaken on his authority in response to the attacks would be legal. For legality—however stretched or
bent—underscores the U.S. claim to the moral high ground. This would seem
to have ruled out targeting bin Laden directly, as assassination operations have
been prohibited since the Ford administration, a restriction that prompted Dewey
Claridge, director of the CTC from 1986 to 1988, to wonder, "Why is an expensive
military raid with heavy collateral damage to our allies and to innocent children

okay—more morally acceptable than a bullet to the head?"[3] The question raises an important philosophical issue, one that gets to the heart of counterterrorism policy, especially in the course of asymmetrical warfare against a stateless entity like al Qaeda.

"International law did not recognize revenge or punishment as justification for a military attack, but the customary laws of self-defense did sanction such strikes if they were designed to disrupt or pre-empt an enemy's ability to carry out future attacks. This principle helped shape the Pentagon's target list," Steve Coll explained.[4] The administration was not yet ready to reinterpret the no-assassination caveat within a broader framework. It was disinclined to acknowledge that bin Laden's leadership and personal determination to attack the United States was so integral to al Qaeda's capacity to endanger the United States and its citizens that he could be legally eliminated.

A variety of responses were considered, including deploying a contingent of American troops to engage al Qaeda militarily on its Afghan turf or coopting Afghan fighters, in partnership with Special Forces, to snatch bin Laden and take him into custody. Either option presented several problems that couldn't be resolved to everyone's satisfaction, including the reliability of intelligence coming in about Osama's whereabouts at any given time, the probability that the Afghans would purposely kill him and the fall-out that would provoke, the presence of women and children in bin Laden's compound and the likelihood of collateral deaths, and the probability of American casualties. Then, of course, there is the general propensity for military undertakings to behave like a drunk operating heavy machinery: it's impossible to foresee exactly what's going to go wrong, beyond the certainty that something will.

Hank Crumpton, a veteran operator of the CIA Clandestine Services who would command the Agency's paramilitary operations in Afghanistan following 9/11, wrote, "There was insufficient political will. The risk was too high, from a public political perspective. Imagine the pre-9/11 headlines "CIA Assassinates Saudi Militant in Afghanistan." I slowly began to understand that even if we had verifiable, pinpoint accuracy regarding Bin Laden's location, there was no assurance of a lethal strike."[5]

As much as Clinton wished he could keep attention focused on matters of substance at this critical time, the country was distracted by salacious reports of his affair with Monica Lewinsky, a young White House intern. It provided his political opponents with a headline-grabbing scandal to exploit in discrediting any of his policies and decisions. By coincidence, a movie called *Wag the Dog* was released during this period. It was about a president besieged by scandal who deflects criticism by launching a war—in this case against Albania. The film became a touchstone for Clinton's efforts to retaliate against al Qaeda for the embassy bombings. Whatever tack he chose to pursue, he would stand accused of "wagging the dog." The NSC staffers Benjamin and Simon wrote, disgustedly, "The bloodshed in East Africa had been eclipsed by a carnival."[6]

A Memorandum of Notification, crafted by lawyers and signed by Clinton, was issued to authorize the CIA to develop an operational plan targeting al Qaeda. White House staffers, whose battles are confined to verbal jousts in conference rooms, actually believed "they had written the document to provide the CIA with the maximum flexibility to kill bin Laden in the course of an arrest operation."[7] However, in the opinion of the agents out in the field, it was so ambiguous with regard to the use of deadly force in any attempt to apprehend him that they worried about their personal legal exposure should an operation go bad.[8] The CIA had the impression that they were supposed to capture bin Laden alive and render him to the FBI for arrest and trial—a far more complex undertaking than simply killing him.

Richard Clarke, Clinton's National Coordinator for Security and Counter-terrorism, is blunt on this debate: "The President's intent was very clear: kill bin Laden. I believe that those in the CIA who claim the authorizations were insufficient or unclear are throwing up that claim as an excuse to cover the fact that they were pathetically unable to accomplish the mission."[9] Notwithstanding his ex post facto assurance, pre-9/11, there was never an unequivocal statement authorizing any such action.

The 9/11 Commission reported, "Every official we questioned about the possibility of an invasion of Afghanistan said that it was almost unthinkable, absent a provocation such as 9/11, because of poor prospects for cooperation from Pakistan and other nations and because they believed the public would not support it."[10] And, let there be no mistake, public and bi-partisan political support for a full-on assault against bin Laden would not have been forthcoming on the basis of the losses suffered in Africa. Certainly nobody in the political sphere foresaw then that al Qaeda was capable of a 9/11-scale attack.

Ultimately, the government settled on launching sea-based Tomahawk cruise missiles against two targets: al Qaeda's training facility at Khost, Afghanistan, and the al Shifa pharmaceutical factory in Khartoum, where nerve gas was alleged to be manufactured.

August 20 was selected for the strike because, according to intelligence likely originating with Pakistan's ISI, bin Laden and his senior leadership were supposed to gather at Khost on that day for a meeting to plan future attacks.[11] Even in hindsight, CIA Director Tenet sounded excited: "We were accustomed to getting intelligence about where UBL [the CIA's designation for Osama bin Laden] *had been*. This was a rarity: intelligence predicting where he was *going to be*."[12]

Since it takes several hours to program and prepare cruise missiles for launch, it wasn't even enough to know where bin Laden was going to be, but whether he'd still be there when the payload arrived. Here was an opportunity to—best case scenario—wipe out al Qaeda or, at least, cripple it by destroying its command. Oddly, Tenet wrote, "I'm not certain at the time we fully comprehended the missiles' limitations."[13] Surely, those firing them were well acquainted with how they functioned and how long it took to deliver them to the target.

Unbeknownst in Washington, bin Laden interpreted the precautionary evacuation of U.S. diplomats from Pakistan and of American citizens from Kabul as indicators that retaliation was imminent. Khost was where he'd conducted his interview with ABC News the previous May. He may thus have anticipated the base was in America's crosshairs. Or, as has been reported more recently, it's possible he was "alerted by a former chief of Pakistan's intelligence service."[14]

"Bin Laden is a fairly shrewd operator, so after spending five years planning the attacks on the U.S. embassies, just about the last place he would be likely to hang his turban is the site from which he had told the world about his plans to attack Americans," Peter Bergen concluded. "Indeed, as early as May 16 he told a Pakistani journalist that he had 'information that Americans are planning to hit my bases so I am very careful.'"[15]

As it transpired, the strike on Khost killed as few as five al Qaeda militants (or as many as twenty[16]), and nobody of any stature in the organization. It also leveled the facility, but, as critics would point out, that amounted to little more than some barracks and jungle gyms in the desert, hardly representing much of a capital loss. It was literally an exercise in pounding sand. This, for an estimated $750 million worth of weaponry.

Adding insult to ineffectiveness, bin Laden reportedly recovered several unexploded Tomahawks that he sold to China for $10 million, and Pakistan recovered one that fell on its territory, well short of its target, which it used to reverse-engineer a cruise missile of its own.[17] Perhaps an even more far-reaching consequence, according to a pivotal Presidential Daily Brief given to President Bush just a month prior to 9/11, "after U.S. missile strikes on his base in Afghanistan in 1998, bin Laden told followers he wanted to retaliate in Washington."[18]

While taking out Khost had a negligible impact on al Qaeda and, on that basis, was a waste of very expensive, very sophisticated firepower, there was no denying its legitimacy as a target. Al Shifa remains a far more contentious choice. The attack occurred at night, so casualties were limited to the death of a single security guard, but the factory was destroyed.

Several pieces of intelligence put al Shifa on America's radar. It was owned by the unfortunately named Military Industrial Corporation, a Sudanese government enterprise in which bin Laden had a financial interest. The general manager of the plant resided in bin Laden's vacant villa in Khartoum. Most damningly, the CIA had obtained a soil sample from a human source who had reputedly taken it from the plant's grounds. The sample allegedly contained EMPTA, a chemical precursor whose only use is in the manufacture of VX nerve gas, the only application for which is as a chemical weapon. The reliability of that analysis has since been disputed by an independent review of thirteen soil samples at two separate laboratories by a Boston University chemist, which revealed no traces of EMPTA.[19] Benjamin and Simon, who were on the NSC at the time, go to considerable lengths to defend the strike, while conceding that officials did themselves a disservice by denying, for example, that al Shifa produced medicines, which it in fact did.[20]

The 9/11 Commission would conclude, "The failure of the strikes, the 'wag the dog' slur, the intense partisanship of the period, and the nature of the al Shifa evidence likely had a cumulative effect on future decisions about the use of force against bin Laden."[21]

The players continued to snipe among one another long after the fact about whether Clinton really intended to go after bin Laden. The president's testimony before the 9/11 Commission remains sealed. Clarke says that Clinton's authorization was clear, and adds, "I still to this day do not understand why it was impossible for the United States to find a competent group of Afghans, Americans, third-country nationals, or some combination who could locate bin Laden in Afghanistan and kill him."[22]

Aside from the inherent difficulty of such an operation, the sense of urgency regarding al Qaeda had not permeated the public conscience. Except for a few committed bin Laden hunters, nobody was pressing for such dramatic action. Given equal opportunity, inertia will out.

Even after 9/11, when bin Laden was cornered in Afghanistan's Tora Bora mountains, decision makers behaved tentatively. Gary Berntsen, who led a CIA covert operations team in the thick of the fight, urgently requested more U.S.

troops to prevent bin Laden from escaping across the Pakistani frontier. To his amazement, he was denied by generals who preferred that Afghans lead the fight, prompting him to exasperation: "Why was the U.S. military looking for excuses not to act decisively? Why would they want to leave something that was so important to an unreliable Afghan army that'd been cobbled together at the last minute? This was the opportunity we'd hoped for when we launched this mission. Our advantage was quickly slipping away."[23] And with it, bin Laden, who would survive another decade.

An unnamed Pentagon official told Peter Bergen that analysts were convinced that bin Laden was determined to make his final stand at Tora Bora and that he would never try to escape "because it would so damage his credibility with al-Qaeda and the wider jihadist movement."[24] The conviction that bin Laden was determined to die in battle seems a rather esoteric notion upon which to base strategic decisions. Surely nobody could be so confident in the quality of intelligence concerning his intensions as to arrive at such a conclusion.

In retrospect, CIA analyst Scheuer suggested that bin Laden was disappointed by the paltry American response to the embassy plot; that he had intended for the bombings to lure them into a toe-to-toe fight on his turf. He argues that leaving Sudan for Afghanistan in advance of the embassy bombings was a strategic decision based on the idea that he could better fight America on his familiar stomping grounds.[25] Scheuer quotes bin Laden's former bodyguard Abu Jandal: "He [bin Laden] kept saying that he wanted to fight America on a battlefield it cannot control."[26]

This is one perspective on the subject. In discussing 9/11 as a huge strategic blunder on bin Laden's part, Bergen argued that the consequence, when it finally did *lure* the United States into Afghanistan, was that it "lost the best base it ever had." In direct contrast to Scheuer's proposition, Bergen writes, "there is not a shred of evidence that in the weeks before 9/11, al-Qaeda's leaders made any plans for an American invasion of Afghanistan. They prepared instead only for possible U.S. cruise missile attacks or airstrikes by evacuating their training camps"[27] just as they had in 1998. This suggests that al Qaeda behaves like other organizations, extrapolating from the past to plan for the future.

Trying to read bin Laden's intentions was akin to the old practice of Kremlinology, which had observers scouring scraps of ephemera over years to glean hints at the innermost thoughts of the Soviet leadership. Clearly, bin Laden kept escalating his strikes at American targets. Given his low opinion of America's willingness to fight, it is difficult to fathom that he expected an attack so far on the periphery would lead to a full-on war. Nonetheless, he may have appreciated that, sooner or later, the United States would be left with no alternative but to unleash its might.

The FBI agents still in the field in East Africa were caught completely off-guard by the retaliatory strikes. They were given no advance notice and were, thus, left vulnerable to local outrage. Director Louis Freeh was in Nairobi at the time and even he was caught unaware.

"Freeh was dining with the agents that night," Horan recalls. "He called me out on the porch and said, 'Clinton has just launched.'" She laughs heartily, "I know he hated Freeh, but I was astounded he did that while we were on the ground."[28] The president and the director had a tense relationship because of the many ongoing investigations into Clinton's conduct, even going back to his days as governor of Arkansas, that the Bureau was pursuing.[29]

Piernick had a similar reaction when the news broke in Dar. "We saw it on CNN. I'm like, 'What the fuck?' I mean, here we are, in a Muslim country and he's attacked two Muslim countries. Next thing, I hear from HQ that we should reduce our personnel and that they're sending a plane over to pick up all nonessentials. Well, the only way to get these people to the airport was right through the city. Past the mosques. On a Friday. So, we assemble a SWAT escort, and we get out to the airport and we wait. And wait. And wait. No planes. So we go back through the city. Past the mosques. On a Friday night. I started planning overland routes to South Africa in case that proved necessary. But, a few days later, the planes came in and we shipped out some people. Ultimately, the Tanzanians didn't get all that worked up about the Sudan thing."[30]

The perception of Goliath will always suffer by comparison to David. The ferocious giant, with his appearance of invincibility is easily portrayed as the aggressive bully while David, resourceful and indomitable, is courageously assertive, standing up for all those who are too cowed to stand for themselves. In some quarters of the Islamic world, suicide bombers are respected as brave and self-sacrificing.

The nature of U.S. retaliation helped elevate Osama's status among some Muslims. The deployment of cruise missiles from ships thousands of miles out to sea was disdained as cowardly and arrogant. Maulana Sami ul-Haq, head of one of Pakistan's largest religious academies, from which at least eight members of Afghanistan's Taliban cabinet had graduated, said the missile strikes made bin Laden "a symbol for the whole Islamic world. Against all those outside powers who were trying to crush Muslims. He is the courageous one who raised his voice against them. He's a hero to us, but it is America that first made him a hero."[31]

Scheuer agreed, writing, "The event that greatly accelerated the growth of bin Laden's stature was the . . . U.S. cruise-missile raids on Sudan and Afghanistan. The East Africa bombings strengthened bin Laden's reputation for honesty—attack promised, attack delivered—but the failure of U.S. retaliation made him *the* hero of Islam. . . . U.S. retaliation also validated bin Laden as the foremost champion of Islamic struggle against what has been variously termed American: oppression, racism, hatred of Islam, double standards, barbarity, crusading, and support for the Zionist entity."[32] Simply surviving was enough to boost his image for defiance against all the might a superpower could muster. No matter, apparently, the savage and bloody act that provoked American enmity.

Improbably, Benjamin and Simon claim the missile attacks spooked bin Laden: "As intelligence services worked together around the world to dismantle al-Qaeda operations and arrest operatives, the network suffered serious blows. Were the losses offset by a surge in recruitment and donations from radical sympathizers pleased by the bombings? It is impossible to say."[33]

A consequence of the al Shifa strike was to further alienate Sudan, which was tentatively cultivating a reputation as a law-abiding state that discouraged terrorism. Ten days after the Nairobi and Dar bombings, FBI Agent Jack Cloonan was called by an intelligence contact in Sudan to tell him that two men involved in the plot had rented an apartment overlooking the American Embassy in Khartoum. John O'Neill called Richard Clarke seeking permission to collaborate with the Sudanese. Clarke summoned O'Neill to Washington, where he informed him that it would be impossible, given the imminent retaliation aimed at al Shifa. Following the missile strikes, nothing further was ever heard from the Sudanese about those presumed al Qaeda operatives.[34]

On two more occasions within fifteen months of the embassy attacks, cruise missiles were readied for launch against bin Laden, only to be stood down at the last minute. The first time was to target a temporary hunting camp in the middle of the Afghan desert where he was suspected to be staying. It turned out that a group from the United Arab Emirates was present. The death of several wealthy citizens of a Middle Eastern ally could have proved deeply embarrassing to the United States. The second opportunity was to be a strike against one of Osama's compounds, but his presence could not be confirmed, and the probability of civilian casualties was deemed too high. "Clinton was entirely ready to pull the trigger on the man responsible for the embassy bombings," insist Benjamin and Simon.[35]

Pursuing legal remedy at the same time, the administration had sufficient grounds for seeking bin Laden's arrest and extradition from Afghanistan after he was indicted by the federal grand jury in New York on November 8, 1998, for his role in the embassy conspiracy. It proceeded to exert pressure by freezing all of Afghanistan's assets in the United States, prohibiting all Afghan exports, as well as all imports, except food, medicine, and other humanitarian goods on July 4, 1999. After repeated refusals from the Taliban to turn bin Laden over, U.N. sanctions went into effect in November.

In January 2000, the U.S. Ambassador for Counterterrorism, Michael Sheehan delivered a strongly worded statement to the Taliban foreign minister: "We will hold the Taliban leadership responsible for any attacks against U.S. interests by al-Qaeda or any of its affiliated groups."[36] Holding to the Afghan custom of protecting invited guests, the Taliban stubbornly refused to yield all the way to the very end.

[8] KHALFAN KHAMIS MOHAMED

While all the other al Qaeda operatives scrambled to get out of Dar es Salaam before the bomb was detonated, K. K. Mohamed was abandoned to his fate. On August 8, all by himself, he slunk out of Dar on a bus for Mozambique. From there, he continued down to South Africa. When he reached the southernmost tip of the continent, he found a job flipping burgers in Cape Town, living in his boss's house, and tutoring the man's wife and son in the Koran.

Before leaving him, K. K.'s comrades had provided two phone numbers in Yemen and one in Pakistan for him to call in case of emergency. A few months after settling down, he called just to see who might answer. None were in service. He applied to the South African government for political asylum.

Jeremy Schneider would open K. K.'s defense by emphasizing that he was not—had never been—a member of al Qaeda, did not develop the plan to destroy the American Embassy, did not finance the plot, was by no interpretation a leader, had not recruited other participants, contributed no special technical expertise, and performed only the most menial functions. He claimed he was kept ignorant of the fact that the embassy was the target until five days before the attack.

"He was not a necessary element in any aspect of any mission whatsoever," the attorney told the jury. "What was he? He was a gofer. That's it. Do this. Okay. Get that. Okay. We need this. Okay. I'll obey. I'll listen. I'll do whatever you need me to do."

Schneider sighed. "He is not an evil person. . . . He was a fungible worker, someone who can easily be exchanged, interchanged with anybody else. That means a lot when you are discussing or evaluating the relative responsibilities of people involved in a mission, or when you're asked to evaluate in a death penalty case the relative culpability of people involved in a mission."

Twice during his presentation Judge Sand was compelled to intervene and remind the jury that the punishment that may be imposed upon a guilty verdict was not a pertinent consideration as to whether the evidence was sufficient to prove guilt beyond a reasonable doubt.

However, in a case where both convincing physical evidence and a confession implicated his client in the crimes for which he stood accused, and where twenty-two individuals were indicted—including the senior leadership of al Qaeda—but only four were standing trial, it was a reasonable tactic to show that K. K. was entrusted with only the most insignificant tasks, which virtually anyone could have performed. When experienced death penalty attorneys assess the likelihood of acquittal as slim, it is appropriate that they lay the foundation for mercy come the penalty phase rather than having to suddenly alter their premise from arguing innocence to acknowledging guilt.

K. K. was born in 1973 on the small island of Pemba off the coast of Tanzania. His father died when he was very young and he grew up with six siblings and several half-siblings. Around 1990 he moved to Dar to live with his brother and work in his small grocery store. He started spending more of his time around the local mosque, where he gained a strong sense of belonging to the wider Muslim community. He adopted its concerns—which included injustices against Muslims in places like Bosnia and Chechnya—as his own.

"My impression is that wherever people are very poor, and Islam is one of the few functioning institutions, people will congregate around it," said David Stern, another of his attorneys, who went to Tanzania and visited with K. K.'s family. "The brains behind this may be evil, but they are also very impressive and seductive. They're hard to resist when there is no viable alternative competing for allegiance."[1]

In 1994 K. K. went to Afghanistan, where he spent about a year undergoing religious and military training at an al Qaeda camp. He was among those selected for advanced training, which included explosives. K. K. had no idea what al Qaeda was, and had never even heard of bin Laden before arriving there, his attorneys would argue. He was motivated by the desire to become a soldier for Islam, not to join a particular al Qaeda conspiracy.

"He is from this little corner of Africa, uneducated, but clever," said Stern. "He is principled, in the manner the crusaders may have been principled, in that they believe so deeply that what they're doing is right, they can overlook those parts they know to be wrong."[2]

"K. K. Mohamed acted purely out of principle. He acted purely out of deep, deep religious beliefs, out of deep philosophical convictions, out of his understanding of the Koran," Schneider argued in court.

He wanted to fulfill his obligation to join the international struggle to help suffering Muslims. It was a grave disappointment when, upon completing months of rigorous training, there was nothing for him to do but return to Dar to be a grocery clerk. In 1997, he was happy to be summoned to Somalia on two occasions to help at a training base.

Finally, in March or April 1998 he was contacted by another militant, Mustafa Mohamed Fadhil, and asked whether he wanted a "jihad job." He responded affirmatively. On May 4, K. K. applied for a Tanzanian passport under the alias Zahran Nassor Maulid. In June he was told to purchase a Suzuki Samurai—but not why—which he did. He was accompanied in this task, according to the indictment, by Fahid Mohammed Ally Msalam, who was Sheikh Ahmed Salim Swedan's deputy, and registered the vehicle in his own name. At Fadhil's direction, he rented a residence at 213 Ilala Estates—also in his true name. He told the real estate agent that he liked the property because of the size of the house and the high walls surrounding it.

After accompanying Ahmed the German en route to bombing the U.S. Embassy, K. K. returned to the Ilala residence to clean up all traces of the bomb, which had been assembled there. He called his nephew to come collect some household items. Among them was the grinder he'd used to prepare the TNT. He asked the nephew to give it to his mother, but cautioned that she must "clean the grinder thoroughly because it was used for unclean things."

The prosecution focused on this detail as evidence of a dedicated terrorist following his orders and being so callous as to make a gift of an instrument that was directly tainted by death. For its part, the defense would point to the same incident and describe it as an act of a naïve man who was so poor that he couldn't bear to dispose of a commonplace appliance that his family desperately needed.

"That's the kind of simplistic man he is. That's where he came from, [the] island of Pemba. He's in this world of Islamic resistance, [but] what he thinks about . . . is giving some of these pieces of property to his family," defense attorney Schneider suggested.

The FBI knew to be on the lookout for K. K. because he'd bought the Suzuki and rented the Ilala house in his own name. They'd already questioned his family in Zanzibar and Dar. The Bureau's legal attaché in South Africa happened across his photo while reviewing the files of applicants for asylum. At the Americans' behest, the South Africans called K. K. in on the pretext that he needed to renew his status. When he arrived, he was taken into custody. He was first interviewed by FBI agents on October 5, 1999, in a holding cell at Cape Town International Airport.

K. K. acknowledged he was capable of answering questions in English. He was advised of his rights and affirmed that he understood. The agents showed him a printed advice of rights form in both English and Swahili. He signed both and agreed to answer questions. On that first day, Special Agents Abigail Perkins and Mike Forsee spoke to him from around 1:00 in the afternoon until after 10:00 that night. The next day, they spoke from noon until around 3:30 pm. That evening, they boarded a plane for the United States.

"Did Khalfan Khamis Mohamed indicate to you why he was willing to talk to you?" prosecutor Kenneth Karas asked Perkins.

"He said that basically because we had found him where he was in Cape Town, that we already knew everything, so there was no reason for him to tell us one thing when we knew that, in fact, another was true."

Stern followed up on that during cross-examination, asking, "So he just talked to you in spite of the fact that you had told him there was no real benefit, right?"

"That's right," said Perkins.

"You never told him the information you had from other interviews, did you?"

"I wouldn't tell him that information, no."

Stern continued by making the point that, without being aware of how much the FBI knew and without any promise of favor, K. K. was honest. Perkins did not catch him in a single lie, based on corroborating evidence gathered prior to his being interviewed. Thus did Stern try to give the jury the impression of an honorable man.

"Agent Perkins, did you ask Khalfan Khamis Mohamed if he participated in the bombing of the American Embassy in Dar es Salaam?" Karas inquired.

"He said that he was involved with a group of what he called brothers, and that they were involved in a jihad against America, including the bombing of the American Embassy in Dar es Salaam."

He provided incriminating details about how the bomb was constructed using TNT packed into more than twenty wooden boxes, with detonators, wiring, two heavy-duty truck batteries, and three or four bags of fertilizer. K. K. admitted that he and Fadhil had ground up the TNT, placed it in the boxes and nailed down the lids. Then, he and Ahmed Ghailani, loaded it all onto the delivery truck.

K. K. told the agents "that, based on his study of Islam, he felt it was his obligation and duty to kill Americans."

"Did he tell you when his views towards America began to form?" asked Karas.

"He said when he went to training camp in Afghanistan in 1994."

"Did you ask Khalfan Khamis Mohamed whether he considered the bombing of the Embassy a success?"

"He said that it was a success."

"Why?"

"He said because it sent a message to America, that bombings were the only way that America would listen and that it also kept the Americans busy investigating."

K. K. said that he was angry over U.S. policy in Palestine and the presence of American soldiers in Saudi Arabia. "He said he wanted America to understand that these Muslims weren't crazy, gun-wielding Muslims, but they were in fact working for a purpose." While he said he was sorry that Tanzanians died in the attack, "it was described as part of doing the job."

"What did he say he thought would happen to the Tanzanians that were killed in the bombing?"

"He stated that Allah would take care of them."

"Did he tell you how he felt when he saw the explosion had happened?" Karas asked.

"He did," she replied. "He said he was very happy."

Karas went on, "Did Khalfan Khamis Mohamed tell you what he would have done had you not caught him?"

"He said he would have continued in his efforts to kill Americans, including being involved in bombings," Perkins replied.

"Did you ask Khalfan Khamis Mohamed about what his hope was even after he had been caught?"

"He said that because he had been caught he hoped that others carried on and that he would carry on if he could."

On that chilling note, Karas concluded his examination of Agent Perkins.

"He never denied to you that he knew he was involved in building a bomb, did he?" Stern cross-examined Agent Perkins

"He did not."

"And he was aware that the things he said to you would be used against him in court, wasn't he?"

"He was told that."

Stern went on to paint a picture of him as a simple man, an obedient follower;

anything but an incisive leader. Moreover, that he was an expendable cog in the organization.

"When there came a time for everyone to go, he was the one who was told to stay, right?"

"He was asked to stay, yes," Perkins conceded.

Stern explained the defense's strategy: "We hoped the trial would reveal how minor a role he played. He was a really simple guy, a nobody. Everything would have happened exactly as it did with or without him. That can't be said about all the defendants."[3]

The defense rested without calling a witness on K. K.'s behalf.

[9] THE DEFECTORS

Those who generalize about people deny themselves the capacity to appreciate and exploit the particularities and peculiarities of an individual's character or situation. To wit, a *terrorist* is not some generic beast. The label *terrorist* does not convey a self-explanatory prescription for how to relate to such a person. Each terrorist chose the path of terrorism for his own reasons. The challenge for Western intelligence is to understand his personal motivation and offer an alternative life narrative that holds greater promise. Obviously there are the deeply devoted who can be moved by nothing outside their cause. But there are others who can accept the humanity of their rivals if given the opportunity to experience it. These people are potential sources.

JAMAL AL-FADL

In June 1996, Jamal Ahmed al-Fadl, who would come to be known as Junior by his handlers, walked in to the U.S. Embassy in Eritrea claiming to have information about people who "want to do something against your government." When he deserted al Qaeda, he took with him a treasure trove of knowledge that was crucial to the government's understanding of the organization. Al-Fadl was about as good a human source as an intelligence officer could wish to recruit.

"Even though he'd been out for more than two years and some of his information was dated, his great value lay in getting our noses under al Qaeda's tent for the first time and seeing its operational status, how they operated, some of the things they had done, what they were contemplating doing. This gave us an opportunity to assess the threat. He was an excellent source of information, great with photographs. As he got more comfortable, information came willingly. We were able to return to him for verification as we were developing our case. We became more confident that what he gave us was accurate," said Jack Cloonan, the FBI agent from the New York field office who helped to recruit and run him.[1]

Al-Fadl spent three solid weeks being debriefed, during which time it was made abundantly clear that his only hope for asylum came from being perfectly truthful. His every word was tested against intelligence acquired from other sources for signs of deception. He would be asked the same question multiple times on different occasions, with minor variations, to ensure consistency. His incentive to be honest and transparent came from leaving himself no other place to run. Moreover, contrary to the stereotype of the ascetic fundamentalist, Junior coveted life's material bounty.

Assessing Junior's importance, Ali Soufan, another of the FBI agents who handled him, wrote, "Before he arrived, we had little understanding of what exactly al-Qaeda was and how it operated. . . . It was information that Fadl told us that enabled the United States to credibly indict bin Laden in 1998."[2]

Whenever the government employs a cooperating witness, or CW, who has pled guilty to participating in the same conspiracy as the defendants, but who is not facing the same punishment, the defense does its best to muster rage at the inequity.

Why?

Why, for example, is the jury sitting in judgment of K. K. Mohamed while al-Fadl enjoys the protection of the American government and succor of the American taxpayer? Why is K. K. on trial for his life, while Junior looks forward to a life of ease? Moreover, why is Junior to be believed at K. K.'s expense?

Those very attributes that made al-Fadl a willing defector from al Qaeda's ranks could also impeach his credibility. For the altruistic informant is no less a chimera than the Loch Ness monster. When people are secure and satisfied in their circumstances, they do not defect. Without the promise of reward and protection, they would not inform. Hence, traitors are vulnerable to demonization, as much for their past loyalties as for the very act of betrayal.

It can be difficult for jurors to compartmentalize the apparent similarities between defendants and the CW and to shake the schoolyard taboo against snitching, notwithstanding that it is the lifeblood of successful law enforcement.

"Your hope is if you do everything the government wants you to do, you might never even go to jail at all, right?" K. K.'s attorney, David Stern, demanded of Junior.

"Yeah, I hope that."

"Even though you're a high-ranking member of al Qaeda, right?"

"Yes."

While the defense could belittle what al-Fadl had at stake, Cloonan recalled it as a moment of great solemnity when he looked over his charge sheet and pled guilty, knowing that he was surrendering to the mercy of the American government. Hanging over his head was the prospect of a long prison stint were he ever to fail to convince the authorities of his cooperativeness. Only someone who believes without reservation in the integrity of his handlers could look upon such a concession without trepidation. As Cloonan noted, "When he allocutes in a sealed courtroom, that's gut-check time."[3]

Under his agreement with the government, Junior pled guilty to conspiring with a group seeking to make war against the United States, as well as weapons and explosives charges for which he could be sentenced to fifteen years in prison. However, so long as he lived up to his promise to cooperate, he would face no jail time. In addition, he was resettled in the witness protection program along with his wife and children, and was paid close to $800,000.

Junior was called as the prosecution's first witness. He was to explain this mysterious entity, al Qaeda, and lay the foundation for its worldwide conspiracy to kill Americans whenever and wherever possible. He would demonstrate how and why it posed a threat to the United States, which, to that point, had culminated in the East African attacks.

Born in 1963 in Ruffa, just south of Khartoum, al-Fadl made his way to Brooklyn in 1986, finding work with Mustafa Shalabi, who ran the Alkifah Refugee Center until his mysterious murder in 1991. In late 1988 or early 1989, Shalabi directed him to go to Peshawar, where he took the pseudonym, Abu Bakr al-Sudani. It is common practice among jihadis to take multiple aliases, often, in the Arab tradition, based upon the name of one's eldest son and place of origin: hence, *abu*, or father of, Bakr, *al-Sudani*, from Sudan. He went on into Afghanistan, to the Khalid Ibn Walid camp, where he was trained to use the Kalashnikov rifle and RPGs.

At the Areen guesthouse, he met Salim, who headed al Qaeda's fatwa council, and bin Laden, himself. He saw action against the Soviets at Jaji and spent time at several other training camps, including Jihad Wal in Khost, where he learned how to use explosives, to set ambushes, and to plan assassinations.

Al-Fadl attended the meeting at which the creation of al Qaeda was first discussed and was invited to join. The group's purpose, he explained, was "to do the jihad." He became the third man to pledge bayat, which, he said, "means you swear you going to agree about the agenda and about jihad, listen to the emir . . .

whatever work they ask you in group, you have to do it." The emir, or leader, was bin Laden and the leaders granted themselves the authority to authorize whatever they pleased.

"The scholars in the group, they discuss that and they make the fatwa and they say it's okay," al-Fadl shrugged.

Just who has the authority to issue a fatwa—a pronouncement based upon an interpretation of the Koran and the teachings of the Prophet Mohammed—is a matter open to debate. It certainly requires a learned individual, but, since Islam does not have a priestly hierarchy in the Catholic tradition, a scholar may be qualified without having a formal title, while a man claiming a title may not have the required learning. What is essential is that the fatwa be Islamically correct; that is to say, that it be in accordance with the principles of Islam. Many Muslims rejected bin Laden's qualifications to issue fatwas because he was not an Islamic scholar and, of course, they rejected the legitimacy of his rulings that called for indiscriminate murder.

L'Houssaine Kherchtou, another defector, acknowledged that there could be disagreements even within al Qaeda as to whether bin Laden's fatwas were Islamically correct. For instance, there were those—and Kherchtou identified himself among them—who would not participate in the killing of women, children, or innocent civilians because they believed that it went against Islamic teachings. Edward Wilford, in defense of Mohamed Odeh, sought to establish that membership in al Qaeda did not signal abdication of moral judgment or blind obedience in the face of immorality. And that a member could exercise that moral judgment by dissociating himself from those actions with which he disagreed.

On Odeh's behalf, Anthony Ricco called Imam Siraj Wahhaj, spiritual leader of a Brooklyn mosque, to testify as an expert witness to address the rather esoteric question of Islamic correctness. Siraj explained that Islam is a religion of peace and that followers are duty-bound to question their leaders, not to follow blindly. Every Muslim is encouraged to study, to learn the Koran and the teachings of the Prophet Mohamed, to think for himself (or herself), and to debate openly what is proper conduct. Merely because someone issues a fatwa does not confer the authority to bind others to carry it out. The Imam emphasized that there is no Islamic authority that condones indiscriminate killing.

During cross-examination, Fitzgerald asked Siraj, "Did the Prophet Mohamed say anything or do anything in his lifetime to indicate that it was Islamically correct to bomb buildings?"

"If you study the life of Prophet Mohamed, peace and blessings be upon him, you will see the most gentle man. He would never allow innocent people to die, never. Never. Anyone who knows him, knows his life, would know that he would never allow such a thing, never." And in Siraj's voice, one heard the anguish of a decent, devout man who despairs at how his faith had been usurped by mad men.

Continuing on the theme of what was Islamically correct, Ricco asked FBI Agent Anticev, "Did Mohamed Odeh say to you when he took bayat that it was a promise to help Muslim people everywhere?"

"That plus pledging total allegiance to Usama bin Laden. That's part of bayat."

"As long as what he asked him to do was Islamically correct, right?"

"Yes."

"He told you that he would not follow anyone blindly like a cat."

"That he did," Anticev agreed.

"What Mohamed never said to you was that at the time he took bayat, that there was an agreement to kill Americans anywhere in the world, isn't that right?"

"Well, he took bayat in March of '92, right. No."

Trying to portray his client as a man of principle, Ricco asked, "Mr. Odeh said to you that he felt a sense of responsibility for the bombing because he was a member of al Qaeda, isn't that right?"

"Yes."

"But his sharing that with you was a moral sense of responsibility, isn't that right?"

"Yes."

"He never said to you that he was responsible because this was something that he did, isn't that correct?"

"Correct."

In 1990, al-Fadl helped to lay the groundwork for al Qaeda's relocation to Sudan, his birthplace, traveling there to rent farms and houses where the group would reside. For these tasks, he was entrusted with large sums of money. He paid out $250,000 to rent a farm north of Khartoum, and $180,000 for a salt farm at Port Sudan on the Red Sea coast.

Already at this time, he was involved in a double game, though one that appeared to benefit all concerned. He conceded that he collaborated with the Sudanese Intelligence Service. It only stood to reason that, notwithstanding its invitation to bin Laden, the NIF had niggling worries over the arrival of an armed and battle-tested force on its soil. Between 1992 and 1994, al-Fadl was present with Sudanese intelligence officers when they interviewed arriving al Qaeda members to assess whether they represented a threat.

Sam Schmidt, el Hage's lawyer, challenged, "You always reported to the NIF about what bin Laden was doing since bin Laden came to the Sudan, isn't that right?"

"I do both. I take from bin Laden to NIF, from NIF to bin Laden," al-Fadl replied innocently.

"So you play both sides, don't you?" Schmidt pressed.

"Yes."

"To your own advantage?"

"Yes."

Cloonan likens al-Fadl to a typically entrepreneurial immigrant who, regardless of any fetters that others may try to place on him, loved the horse-trading of the free enterprise system and was happy to trade what commodities he had in order to get ahead. He wasn't religious. He wasn't serving God. He was trying to make the best life for himself.[4] Now, you could—as the defense did—characterize that as downright vicious in its disregard for others, or you could appreciate that people of that mind-set represent the best prospects for penetrating al Qaeda.

Schmidt's contempt for al-Fadl is unqualified, "I think America really shamed itself by accepting al-Fadl's version of events. I have no respect for him. He started out for himself, he continued to be out for himself. He is willing to say anything to get what he wants. Was there some truth in what he described? Of course there was. He's not bright enough to recreate reality."[5]

U.S. Attorney Pat Fitzgerald acknowledged Junior's credibility problems head-on before the jury: "There is no doubt that al-Fadl looks out for number one. Number one is al-Fadl. There's no doubt that he has an interest in testifying. The question for you is, how does that interest affect what he says? Does it give him a motive to make things up, or does it give him a motive not to do that because he may lose something if he gets caught in a lie?"

Soufan conceded, "Sure, Junior was messed up. He had to be, to be al Qaeda. But, he was very significant to the investigation. And say whatever you will about him, he was right on the money."

He went on, "It's the nature of a CW that they committed some offense. That's why they become a CW; that's why they are in a position to be a CW. We must engrave on their mind and on their soul that they must tell the truth. If we catch them in a lie about one thing, it's all over. Because if they lie about one thing, their credibility is damaged on everything."[6]

Junior was sequestered in a safe house and placed under constant protection for three and a half years. During this period, he came to understand how the justice system worked and that, upon entering into a relationship, the FBI was obliged to live up to its promises. At the same time, he was represented by counsel, which gave him further confidence that his interests were being safeguarded.

"Junior was on an emotional roller coaster," Cloonan recalled. "He could be a bit hard to manage, unpredictable. He could be petulant and childlike. You'd have to sit and talk to him man-to-man and have several come-to-Jesus meetings with him. But, what we communicated to him, in terms of how we treated him, how we went about our business, got us a lot of information I don't think we would otherwise have gotten. It helped, on the one hand, to settle him down when he got his wife and kids out, but that raised other issues because now we're responsible for an entire family."[7]

For his work on behalf of bin Laden's legitimate companies, al-Fadl testified that he was paid $200 per month, plus another $300 for being a member of al Qaeda, which also entitled him to additional foodstuffs, including sugar, tea, and vegetable oil. Al Qaeda members would also be reimbursed for any medical expenses. However, even among terrorists-for-a-cause, petty jealousies could not be suppressed. Al-Fadl complained directly to bin Laden about some members being paid more than others, citing how, for example, Salim was paid $1,500 a month, and el Hage $800. The resentment caused by such disparities festered and, ultimately, precipitated his break from the group.

Come late 1993 or early 1994, a rumor circulated in Khartoum that a former Sudanese general and government minister, Moqadem Salah Abdel al Mobruk, was trying to sell a cache of black market uranium. The asking price was $1.5 million plus commissions. Bin Laden sent al-Fadl to negotiate a purchase.

Al-Fadl testified that he met with Mobruk and was shown a cylinder, approximately two to three feet in length with markings that indicated it originated in South Africa. Bin Laden paid al-Fadl a $10,000 commission for his efforts and, according to what Junior heard, intended to verify whether it was genuine. Eventually, it was determined that the cylinder was filled with red mercury, also known as cinnabar, which bears a resemblance to uranium, but has no use in nuclear weapons.[8]

Josh Dratel, el Hage's attorney, doubts the entire story: "I don't think anyone believes that he ever had access to uranium. I think it's a total bullshit story. Al-Fadl was a poseur, a boaster, someone who aggrandized his role as a means of making himself more valuable as a cooperator. He understood the game extremely well. Very manipulative."[9]

This episode came at a time when bin Laden was experiencing a personal financial crisis. After King Fahd officially revoked his citizenship, he found himself, supposedly at least, cut off from his Saudi sources of funding. His Sudanese businesses were failing. He was forced to reduce payroll. According to Lawrence Wright, "the camaraderie that sustained the men of al-Qaeda rested on the financial security that bin Laden provided. They had always seen him as a billionaire, an endless font of wealth, and bin Laden had never sought to correct this impression. Now the contrast between that exaggerated image of bin Laden's resources and the new destitute reality caused some of the men to begin looking out for themselves."[10] None more defiantly or shamelessly than al-Fadl, who, still upset that some members were paid more than he was, began siphoning off a personal—and unauthorized—commission whenever he sold produce, such as sugar or oil, to local companies. By this means, he managed to steal $110,000 from the group's coffers.

He used a portion of the money to purchase a car and some property in Sudan. The theft was discovered and he was confronted by bin Laden, who told him there could be no forgiveness until he repaid every dollar. "I don't care about the money, but I care about you because you start this [al Qaeda] from the beginning. You work hard in Afghanistan, you are one of the best people in al Qaeda," Osama told him. Nonetheless, he couldn't let people get the impression it was okay to steal from him.

"I didn't have any hope when I left the office," al-Fadl said. He knew he had no alternative but to leave al Qaeda and flee Sudan.

Schmidt painted al-Fadl as a mercenary offering himself to anyone and everyone once he realized he would never be able to repay what he'd stolen. He had approached the Syrians, Saudis, Eritreans, Lebanese, even the Israelis, before finding sanctuary with the Americans. In essence, al-Fadl was ready to give himself to anyone.

"You gave the Saudis a proposal to assassinate Mr. bin Laden, didn't you?" Schmidt asked.

"Well, any questions they ask me, I give them answers," Junior prevaricated.

"So when they asked you how the best way to murder or assassinate Mr. bin Laden, you came up with a plan and gave it to the Saudi government, isn't that right?"

"I don't have plan, but when they ask me that question, I give them what I know."

"It wasn't what you know, it was what you would do," Schmidt insisted.

"What I know, because I was in group before."

Unhappy with what the Saudis were willing to pay, Schmidt charged, al-Fadl turned to the United States: "Bottom line, there was no other place to go other than the Americans. The last place that you were going to try to get what you wanted was from the Americans, right?"

"Yes, I decide to go to America."

He first presented himself as an anti-NIF dissident, but quickly realized that the Americans were more interested in bin Laden than the government of Sudan. At that point, he claimed to have trained with Ramzi Yousef. "Isn't that what you said to the Americans, that you knew the mastermind of the World Trade Center bombing, Ramzi Yousef, on your first or second interview with the Americans? Isn't that correct?"

"Yes, I told them I saw the guy in Sada camp, the border of Pakistan and Afghanistan," al-Fadl said. In fact, he did not know Yousef.

"Isn't it a fact that the first time that the name of Wadih el Hage came up was when the FBI asked you what you know about Wadih el Hage on October 23, 1997?"

"I really don't remember."

"Mr. al-Fadl, you have told us that you remembered hundreds of names, Abu names, person's given names, and you told them all to the government, and it is your testimony here today that you don't remember when the first time you were asked about Wadih el Hage? Is that your testimony?"

"I don't remember when they asked me."

"It was more than one year after you started talking to the United States that the government asked you about Wadih el Hage, isn't that correct, Mr. al-Fadl?"

"I don't remember," al-Fadl insisted, sounding less than plausible.

Cross-examining on behalf of al-'Owhali, David Baugh questioned al-Fadl about his agreement with the prosecution, asking contemptuously, "Would you prefer to consider yourself an informant, a snitch, a turncoat, what?" Fitzgerald quickly objected, and Judge Sand sustained.

Tough words for Junior to hear. But probably nothing he hadn't wrestled with himself. However he might be caricatured, it wasn't easy to abandon the community to which he'd belonged for a very long time, to turn his back on a difficult way of life that he had once embraced. To actually leap into the arms of his onetime enemy.

"I do wonder, in my own mind, how committed to the cause Junior ever was,"

Jack Cloonan mused. "But, by word and by deed, I think he chose to side with us. Now, was he motivated solely because he was on the run? I don't know, but I will tell you that Junior liked money. He was a pragmatist and a deal-maker. If you have those two things, by and large, if we comport ourselves well, we're going to win."[11]

L'HOUSSAINE KHERCHTOU

L'Houssaine Kherchtou was a very different type than Junior. He was far more stable, a devoted family man. Born in Morocco in 1964, he spent several years in France and Italy, where he worked as a caterer. Inspired to join the Afghan mujahideen by a militant preacher, he left Milan for Pakistan in January 1991, and ended up at al Qaeda's Farouq camp, near Khost, Afghanistan. He was just one month shy of his twenty-seventh birthday when he pledged bayat to bin Laden in April.

Following his initial training, he was sent to the front for a couple of months to do battle against the Afghan Communists, after which he was selected to attend advanced training in surveillance. Classes were given by Ali Mohamed, a former Egyptian policeman and U.S. Army soldier who played a prominent role in preparing the embassy bombings. Kherchtou learned what to look for in assessing a target premise, for instance, to note ins-and-outs, guard positions and movements, access points, and where a bomb should be placed to achieve maximum destruction and loss of life. He went on to study electronics, covert photography and how to develop pictures. After this, he took time off to go to Mecca on the hajj, in fulfillment of one of a Muslim's primary obligations.

In October 1993, Kherchtou left Pakistan for Nairobi, where he enrolled in flight school. He would remain for two years, during which time he became aware that many al Qaeda members were passing through Kenya.

"They were going to Somalia to train people," he would testify. "They were against the United Nations in Somalia." Among those he was told went was Mohamed Odeh, whom he knew as Marwan from the Abu Bakr Sadeek training camp. He added that el Hage knew him, as well.

Upon earning his pilot's license in 1995, Kherchtou moved to bin Laden's base in Khartoum. In December, he was advised by his wife's doctor that she needed a C-section to safely deliver their baby. Like any large enterprise, al Qaeda promised its employees certain basic benefits, including health care. Confident that he would be given the $500 for the procedure, he booked a room at a Khartoum hospital.

However, al Qaeda was experiencing one of its periodic financial crises, and he was denied when he asked for the money. It was suggested that he take his wife to a Muslim hospital where he could get free care, but Kherchtou was convinced that she wouldn't survive the procedure at such a facility. Distraught and disgruntled, he refused to go along when bin Laden relocated to Afghanistan several months later.

"Did you consider yourself part of al Qaeda after you refused to go back to Afghanistan?" prosecutor Pat Fitzgerald asked Kherchtou on the stand.

"No."

On the day of the embassy bombings, Kherchtou just happened to find himself in Nairobi interviewing for a job as a pilot. As he was about to board a departing Kenya Airways flight on August 11, a security officer pulled him aside. Though assured he wasn't under arrest, he was, nonetheless, escorted to a police station and placed in a crowded, filthy cell where a communal bucket served as a toilet. There was no bedding and no place to wash.

While in custody, he was interviewed by an intelligence officer from a country that he was instructed by Fitzgerald in court not to identify. It was, however, specified that the officer was neither Kenyan nor American. It is probably a good guess that Moroccan intelligence was first to contact him.

"He [the officer] started talking about everything that he knew. He knew me very well, my wife, my kids and my life. So I started talking to him." Kherchtou said they spoke over four or five days. "I told him a lot of things, but not everything."

The officer promised to get him out of jail if he would provide information about al Qaeda. Kherchtou agreed that he would contact the officer in three months. On August 21, he was released and left for Sudan.

"After three months, what did you do?" Fitzgerald inquired.

"I didn't contact him."

Based on what Junior had told them about him, the Bureau was anxious to make contact with Kherchtou. However, without a functioning intelligence presence in Sudan and the Nairobi station having been devastated in the bombing (at least one CIA officer was reportedly among those killed, though his identity was never revealed),[12] the odds of mounting a successful clandestine recruitment operation in Khartoum were poor. Better to get L'Houssaine out than to put American agents in. Altogether, about a year and a half would pass before they would have an opportunity to pitch him.

The Americans needed a convincing pretext to lure him to what, for them, would be a more hospitable locale. At their behest, Moroccan intelligence passed a message to him that there was an immigration issue pertaining to his children that could be resolved only in Morocco.

Upon arriving in Rabat, he was picked up by intelligence officers, who brought him to a safe house where the FBI's Soufan, O'Neill, and Cloonan, and U.S. Attorney Fitzgerald were waiting.[13] Kherchtou spent two weeks being debriefed and, ultimately, agreed to a deal whereby he would come to the United States, which he did on September 21, 2000.

"He understood that he would have to get up and testify in court. He knew that his life was never going to be the same," Cloonan said. "Sitting in that safe house, explaining what we were prepared to offer and what he'd have to do, and the moment of decision came, I really didn't think he was going to take the deal. He withdrew to pray and, when he returned to the room, he accepted."[14]

He pled guilty to conspiracy, fully aware of the potential for a life sentence if found guilty. In exchange for his testimony, however, he could receive no prison time and be admitted to the Witness Protection Program. Because his wife's health was the underlying reason for his betrayal of al Qaeda, Kherchtou promised to be a more sympathetic witness than Junior.

David Ruhnke, another of K. K.'s attorney, pursued this on cross-examination, asking, "You pleaded guilty yourself to a conspiracy that included the killing of Americans, is that correct?"

"Correct."

"You have been now admitted into the United States to live, correct?"

"Correct."

"How many members of your family has the government moved to this country?"

"My wife and three daughters."

"It is your hope that you will not spend a single day in jail, isn't that true?"

"Yes."

Ricco would impugn Kherchtou's character, emphasizing how he had pled guilty to the conspiracy to kill Americans, while his client, Odeh, maintained that he had never participated in such a conspiracy. Furthermore, despite his willing participation—as confirmed by his guilty plea—Kherchtou testified that he had not been informed in advance that the U.S. Embassy was a target. Therefore, Ricco was saying, how could Odeh, who denied being party to the conspiracy, possibly have known?

At least in retrospect, Schmidt has a sympathetic opinion of Kherchtou: "I have great respect for him. He lived with Wadih and his family for a couple of months in hotel rooms and, then, in their home. He doesn't have a bad word to say against Wadih, he's appalled by how it all turned out. If you dissect what Kherchtou said, the crime he admitted participating in was shopping for guys who were going to Somalia. That's really all he said. He wasn't even interested in Somalia, he was just told to help some guys, to buy some stuff. And that was because he had to plead guilty. You can't be a government cooperator in these kinds of cases unless you plead guilty to something that looks really serious and you face a lot of jail time. I think Kherchtou was a decent person, and we wish him well."[15]

Josh Dratel allows, "I have nothing positive to say about al Qaeda, but many people joined to fight for a Muslim cause in what they saw as a fair fight on a battlefield, not to be terrorists. Kherchtou is one of those. I don't think Kherchtou ever viewed himself as a terrorist. He denied, at trial, that he shared the same goals as al-Fadl, that he would get involved in killing innocents. When he was in al Qaeda, he was as al Qaeda as anybody. He just had a different concept of what al Qaeda meant."[16]

ALI MOHAMED

Publicly, the prosecution described Ali Mohamed as "one of Mr. bin Laden's oldest and most trusted lieutenants" and his acceptance of a plea bargain that saw him agree to cooperate was characterized as "a tremendous victory for the government."[17] Indeed, he was the first suspect to affirm bin Laden's direct involvement in planning al Qaeda's terrorist attacks.[18]

Privately, Pat Fitzgerald, who brokered the plea called Ali "one of the most dangerous men we've ever interviewed." FBI agent Pat D'Amuro adds, on his own account, "This is a bad, bad guy, one of the worst."[19] Ali Soufan concurred: "He is dangerous, and fully committed to Egyptian Islamic Jihad and to bin Laden. He is very smart. He will only tell you what he believes you already know. I still don't think we have the full story about him. He was certainly not 100 percent cooperative."[20] Consequently, Fitzgerald was determined, one way or the other, to secure a long jail sentence for him.

Ali's was a checkered career of shifting and contradictory alliances. Or, perhaps, a career of no alliances whatsoever. There are those who enter the netherworld of terrorists and counterterrorism agents because it is the most exciting place on earth. They are, with childlike indifference, consumed by the adventure and the intrigue, paying no heed to the consequences of their actions. Their ego swells with the conceit that they are manipulating events unbeknownst to anyone with whom they deal and double-deal. Ali Mohamed was that kind of an operator. And, while Soufan assessed him as fully committed to the jihadi cause, his final act before being incarcerated was to betray it.

"Ali was so adaptable, so keen to please whoever was in his orbit at the moment," said Cloonan, who spent considerable time with him. "He was innately intelligent, tactically oriented. He was a great storyteller and a worthy trader. He worked for Egypt, he worked for [Egyptian Islamic Jihad's leader Ayman] al-Zawahiri, he worked for the Bureau; he tried to get recruited by the Agency. I think he was the victim of his own treachery."[21]

An early member of EIJ, he was allegedly tasked by al-Zawahiri to penetrate U.S. intelligence. In 1984, while an active-duty major in the Egyptian Army, Mohamed walked into the CIA station in Cairo and offered his services. Suspecting he was an Egyptian government provocation, they were reluctant to take him. Still, not ready to dismiss outright a potential source within the military, Langley was cabled to see if any other station might be interested. Frankfurt, which was responsible for operations against Iran, responded affirmatively. Mohamed was tasked to penetrate a Hezbollah-linked mosque in Hamburg, the city where Mohammed Atta, leader of the 9/11 hijackers, once lived and studied.

Ali immediately revealed to the Iranian cleric that he was an American spy. However, the CIA had already penetrated the mosque and quickly learned of his betrayal. They cut ties immediately, labeled him untrustworthy, and put him on a watch list that was supposed to prevent him from ever entering the United States.[22]

Nonetheless, the very next year he was on a flight to America, during which he met the American woman he would marry in order to secure citizenship. Even more inexplicably, he succeeded in enlisting in the U.S. Army. He so impressed his superiors with his knowledge of Middle Eastern politics and culture that he was soon giving lectures at the Special Warfare Center, Fort Bragg, home base of America's elite and secretive Special Forces. His supervisor, Norvell De Atkine said, "He told me pretty near the same things that I had heard from my time in the Middle East—almost eight years—that I heard every day, which was that American policy is dead wrong."[23] Hearing that in the Middle East, sure, but from a serving member of the military recently arrived from Egypt, some misgivings should have been triggered.

Neither his fundamentalist Islamic beliefs nor his controversial political opinions raised any concerns. For example, he revealed to his commanding officer, Lieutenant Colonel Robert Anderson, that he'd served in the same Egyptian Army unit as President Sadat's assassin. Anderson referred to Sadat as a patriot. "No, he had to go, he was a traitor," Ali replied.[24]

All the while, Ali was exploiting his access to American training material to write al Qaeda instruction manuals.[25] A search of El Sayyid Nosair's apartment following his arrest for the murder of Rabbi Meir Kahane revealed documents acquired from the Special Warfare Center. As well, Ali would periodically travel to Brooklyn and Jersey City to provide military training to jihadi hopefuls.

In 1988 he made no secret that he was going to spend his leave time in Afghanistan fighting with the mujahideen against the Soviets. His superiors took no steps to forbid this adventure.[26]

The following year, he was honorably discharged from the regular army with the rank of sergeant and continued to serve with the reserves. He never gave up on his long-standing objective of gaining entrée into U.S. intelligence. After relocating to California in 1990, Ali offered himself as an informant to the FBI's San Francisco Field Office, claiming to have information about a local Hamas document forging operation. All the while, he withheld knowledge about a West Coast fundraising tour by al-Zawahiri, to whom he played host and bodyguard. Nor did he let the Bureau know of his 1991 trip from Afghanistan to Sudan when he helped bin Laden set up shop.[27]

He later admitted to helping bin Laden establish the Nairobi cell. It was not determined from the outset that the cell would strike the U.S. Embassy. Ali revealed that bin Laden had tasked him to conduct surveillance of several targets around Nairobi in 1993, among which was the embassy. On at least one occasion, during 1994, he actually entered the premises for a firsthand look. He was assisted in his mission by Abu Anas al-Liby. They, along with Hamza al-Liby, stayed for a time in the apartment shared by el Hage and Kherchtou, where they set up a makeshift darkroom to develop their surveillance photos.

"I took pictures, drew diagrams and wrote a report," he said. He brought the material to Khartoum, where it was reviewed by Osama. "Bin Laden looked at the picture of the American Embassy and pointed to where a truck could go as a suicide bomber," he said.[28]

Schmidt sought to establish that el Hage was unaware of any of this activity. "This was a very secretive operation, is that right?" he asked Kherchtou.

"Yes," he agreed.

Ali Mohamed also traveled to Djibouti in 1994 to do surveillance of the French and American embassies and French military facilities. There were plans for Kherchtou to accompany him to Senegal "to make surveillance for French targets there." Kherchtou explained, "Because France was against the Muslims in Algeria and Osama bin Laden said once in one of the meetings that he was helping Algerians." Bin Laden was angry over France's support for Algeria's military regime, which overturned an election that would have seen the radical Islamists of the Front Islamique du salut (FIS) take power in 1991. This sparked a protracted and especially bloody civil war.

However, the trip was cancelled when Ali learned the FBI wanted to interview him in connection with the trial of the Blind Sheikh. Mohammed Atef, by then leader of al Qaeda's military council, instructed him not to come back to Kenya for fear he might tip American authorities to the existence of the cell.[29]

In 1994, following an assassination attempt against bin Laden, he returned to Khartoum to train his bodyguards and to coordinate with the Sudanese intelligence agents responsible for security around his compound.[30]

Al Qaeda's management style—evident in both the African embassy and 9/11 attacks—has been referred to as "centralization of decision and decentralization of execution": "Bin Laden decided on the targets, selected the leaders, and provided at least some of the funding. After that, the planning of the operation and the method of the attack were left to the men who would have the responsibility of carrying it out."[31] Local participants, therefore, had considerable autonomy.

Evidence of its approach was found in a memo that Harun wrote when the cell went operational: "We, the East Africa crew, do not want to know how work plans are operated because we are not fit for plans. We are just implementers. We, thanks to God, trust our command and appreciate their work. . . . But the advice here is for work purposes only, because this work we are doing, the return of an Islamic state, is a team effort and not an individual one; we are all participating in it."[32]

Kherchtou explained to the court how an operation worked: "During the training, [Ali] Mohamed explained us that this job is the first part of military part. I mean, you collect the information about this certain targets, and whenever you finish your work, our group, we just leave, we send our reports to our bosses and we leave. So this number two—our bosses are number two. Those people, they go through this report and they read all the information, and everything. Then they decide, they make some decisions how to attack that target, and the first—then they send another group who supply everything so as to attack that target. Whenever that group, third group finish his job, he has to leave. No one at the end, the fourth group, who can do the job come so as to finish the job."

Under interrogation, Odeh described it in similar terms, though he spoke of two teams, one that handled logistics and surveillance and one to carry out the operation. Al-'Owhali described four components of the cell: intelligence, administration, planning and preparation, and execution.

Defense attorney Fredrick Cohn, referring to the clear division between planning and execution, said al-'Owhali was obviously part of the execution team and, therefore, had not participated in the conspiracy. "In a real way, Mohamed was the most minor participant in this event in terms of what he knew," he argued.

During a search of Ali Mohamed's California residence following the bombings, a number of incriminating documents were discovered. He had manuals detailing surveillance techniques, specifically relating to military, diplomatic, and government targets. He had plans for how to structure terrorist cells and military training methods. He had instructions for deploying a variety of explosives, assassination techniques, and manuals for weapons, including rocket propelled grenades. He had codebooks and coded correspondence. He also had a report on the drowning death of Abu Ubaydah, copies of a document that had been forwarded to bin Laden, and a coded letter from a coconspirator about el Hage's 1997 trip to visit bin Laden and his subsequent interview by American authorities.[33]

On May 19, 1999, Ali Mohamed was indicted for conspiracy and for lying to the grand jury investigating the bombings. Negotiations had apparently been under way to get him to cooperate, but the indictment suggested they had broken down.[34] Ali appeared in Judge Sand's court on October 20, 2000. He pled guilty to conspiracy to kill American nationals; conspiracy to murder, kidnap, and maim at places outside the United States; conspiracy to murder; conspiracy to destroy buildings and property belonging to the United States; and conspiracy to destroy American national defense facilities.

He confessed, before the court, to providing al Qaeda operatives, including Harun, with military, intelligence, and explosives training. He taught them how to establish operational cells. He admitted to participating in the establishment of al Qaeda's presence in Nairobi in the early 1990s, in which effort he implicated Wadih el Hage, revealing that his code name was "Norman." This was significant, for among the evidence of el Hage's perjury was his denial that he knew anyone by that name.

After the bombing of the embassies, Ali intended to leave the United States for Egypt, and continue onward to Afghanistan to join bin Laden. But before he could leave, he was subpoenaed to testify before the grand jury. "I testified, told some lies, and was then arrested," he said.[35]

Under the conditions of the plea, Sand said that he would face no less than twenty-five years in prison. To this day, he remains incarcerated. And still to this day, Cloonan contends, Ali believes he'll end up with a deal.[36] However, the government is not likely to offer many concessions beyond the possibility of parole after twenty-five years.

"You never like to strike a plea agreement with an individual who is that bad." D'Amuro shrugs at the compromises the criminal justice system engenders. "Still, Ali Mohamed pled guilty, cooperated, and was willing to testify against al Qaeda. There needed to be a decision whether this was the most strategic way to get a very bad guy off the streets. I'm very comfortable with the call that was made to do that."[37]

Cloonan speaks sympathetically about Ali, for the level of cooperation that he ultimately gave. He knew he had no way out when he was caught and he made the best deal he could, which was, in effect, no deal at all. Seeing no possible alternative, he threw his lot in with the Americans.

"He was, I'm convinced, looking for a way to get it off his chest without being embarrassed," Cloonan said. "He was extremely ashamed by what he's done. I think he liked the idea of training and planning, but when the operation actually happens and you're a part of it, you have a price to pay."[38]

In December 2000, the U.S. Attorney indicted an additional four coconspirators in the bombings. The timing suggests a likelihood that these indictments were predicated on information Ali Mohamed provided. Those named were: Abdullah Ahmed Abdullah, said to be a senior advisor to bin Laden and to have participated in surveillance of the Nairobi embassy just four days before the bombing; Saif al-Adel, alleged to be a senior advisor to bin Laden; Muhsin Musa Matwalli Atwah (aka Abu Abdul Rahman al-Muhajir), the bomb maker who would ultimately go on to become al Qaeda's chief bomb maker before being killed in a Pakistani helicopter assault in Waziristan in April 2006,[39] and Ahmed Mohamed Hamed Ali, who served as a trainer in Somalia.[40]

[10] WADIH EL HAGE

Wadih el Hage presented the biggest challenge for prosecutors because, no one contested, he'd left Kenya a year before the bombings and, therefore, did not stand accused of any murders. He was charged only for his participation in the conspiracy to kill Americans, as well as with twenty-two counts of perjury for giving false statements to a federal grand jury.

"He was never alleged to have participated in any violent activity or planned any violent activity. The government, itself, described him as a facilitator. He got caught up after the fact," said Sam Schmidt, his attorney. "Probably in any other legal system, the role he played would not have held him up for criminal charges. But the conspiracy laws in the United States, under certain circumstances, are very expansive. If someone you know is planning an attack and you help them in the sense that you work with them so that they make money, and they use that money to buy arms, you're held responsible for their conduct. Even if you don't buy the arms for them."[1]

Judge Leonard Sand's explanation of the law of conspiracy sounded eminently more balanced: "The standard law of conspiracy calls for the jury to find a meeting of the minds to commit an illegal act and that the defendant joined in the conspiracy."[2] If the jury found that el Hage was active in al Qaeda, it could find that he was a party to its conspiracy.

"Wadih really didn't believe he was doing anything against the United States. He didn't flee to Sudan or Afghanistan. He returned to the United States," said Josh Dratel, another of his lawyers. "It takes a pretty sophisticated legal understanding to appreciate how his activities could be construed as a crime against America."[3]

El Hage was called before the grand jury twice—on September 24, 1997, and September 16, 1998. Both appearances followed grueling travel.

In the first instance, he'd been en route from Nairobi, with a lengthy delay in Jeddah, for nearly two days with his wife and their six children, all of whom were under the age of ten. He was met by federal authorities at JFK Airport in New York and immediately served with a subpoena. While his wife and children were brought to a hotel, el Hage was taken to the U.S. Attorney's office in Manhattan and questioned for several hours. He was brought to the hotel later that evening. As Dratel recounts, "he did not get a lawyer. He's subpoenaed for the grand jury the next day. He found it all very disorienting and it affected his ability to answer questions."[4]

On the second occasion, he had driven from his sister's home in California, stopping at his mother-in-law's in Tucson, when he was served with a subpoena upon arriving at his home in Arlington. He was flown to New York that afternoon. He appeared before the grand jury the very next morning.

FBI Agent Jack Cloonan expressed disbelief at el Hage's intractability: "He just could not fathom cooperating with the United States government. It's hard to comprehend, with as much time as he'd spent in the U.S., educated here, and raising all those kids."[5]

On August 20, less than three weeks after the embassies were bombed, Special Agent Robert Miranda of the Bureau's Dallas Field Office and Dan Coleman, the agent who had interviewed el Hage in Nairobi, went to his residence to interview his wife, April Ray. They arrived at 2:15 pm. Around forty-five minutes later, Wadih came home. April Ray left to pick up their kids at school; el Hage remained with the agents. After about an hour, he said he had to return to work, but agreed to continue the conversation later that evening. He voluntarily went to the FBI's office at 8:00 pm and spoke to the agents for approximately two hours.

He acknowledged having worked for bin Laden in Khartoum from 1992 to 1994, but said they hadn't spoken since Osama left Sudan. Asked whether he was able to contact his former boss, he said the only way he could think to do so would be through the unlikely and convoluted process of flying to Pakistan and seeking the intercession of the Taliban Embassy to let bin Laden know that he was looking for him.

Wadih conceded that Osama valued his American passport, which made it easy for him to travel on behalf of his business interests. The defector source Jamal al-Fadl had told the Bureau of his difficulties traveling on a Sudanese passport, which invariably attracted enhanced scrutiny at points of entry, especially in Europe, and agreed that el Hage traveled frequently in support of exporting the produce of bin Laden's farms, as well as to purchase goods like tractors, asphalt and cement.

El Hage denied knowing any al Qaeda operatives in Kenya. Asked directly about Harun, he said that Harun worked for him at Help Africa People, but insisted he was unaware whether he was acquainted with bin Laden. They discussed his trip to Tanzania to look for a Mr. Habib, who had been on a ferry that sank in Lake Victoria. Wadih admitted to having met Mr. Habib in Nairobi in 1994, but said this was not the same person as Abu Ubaydah al Banshiri, who was then al Qaeda's military chief.

El Hage denied knowing Mohamed Odeh personally, but volunteered that he heard he'd been arrested with a Yemeni passport that bore someone else's photograph. He failed to identify a picture of Odeh.

According to Miranda's testimony, el Hage offered that "he did not believe Usama bin Laden was responsible [for the embassy bombings] because Usama bin Laden was a humanitarian."

"Did you ask Mr. El Hage why it was that bin Laden hated Americans?" Fitzgerald asked the FBI agent.

"His answer was that it was the duty of any true believing Muslim to drive out the U.S. from the Saudi peninsula because the Koran had reserved the Saudi peninsula only for Muslims. He also said that the U.S. government unfairly supported Israel . . . by saying that the U.S. was quick to come to the aid of Israel if something happened to it, but that if Israel did something illegal that the U.S. was slow to act. He also said that Israel was expanding to take control of the entire Middle East. And, finally, in response to that question, he said that many people wanted to make the world live according to the Koran, but they don't have the resources. But bin Laden has the resources to make the world live according to the Koran." Added Miranda, "During that answer, he often switched between using 'he' for bin Laden and 'we' when describing the hatred to the U.S. and the West."

Fitzgerald emphasized all those points where el Hage had been untruthful during the interview. He pointed out how el Hage said he didn't know anything about Abu Ubaydah dying on the ferry, claimed not to have had any contact with bin Laden since 1994, that he didn't know whether Harun was acquainted with bin Laden, that he denied having a phone number to contact bin Laden, that he said he was unaware of anyone in Kenya or Tanzania who knew bin Laden, and that he didn't communicate policy enunciated by bin Laden in 1997 to his people in Kenya.

Schmidt sought to call into doubt the entire contents of Agent Miranda's testimony by challenging him for his failure even to take written notes during the interview. "You're telling us now when you reached the point where you're now describing your conversation with Mr. el Hage that, without any notes at all, you were able to quote things that he said earlier to you absolutely verbatim, is that what you're telling us?"

"Sir, I said that in instances where his answers were significant or he used words that struck me as significant, yes."

Schmidt elicited that Miranda, not el Hage, injected the word "hatred" to characterize bin Laden's feelings toward America. "When you said 'when describing the hatred of the United States and the West,' that was basically referring to the first question that you asked him even to bring up the topic, isn't that correct?"

"That's probably correct, sir."

With each FBI agent who testified about having taken a statement from a defendant, the appropriate defense attorney criticized them for not taping interviews. The court was told that it was Bureau policy not to use tape recorders, but to rely on reports written from agents' notes.

In his closing, Ruhnke remarked, "I suggest, respectfully, it is a decision that is made that the government would rather have you hear it from the FBI than hear it as it happened. So you don't have it [the statements] as it happened, you have it as the FBI said it happened."

During his cross-examination of L'Houssaine Kherchtou, the al Qaeda defector who had once lived with el Hage and his family, Schmidt painstakingly elaborated on the legitimate side of bin Laden's business interests, which were extensive. For instance, Schmidt emphasized how hundreds of laborers worked on the road bin Laden built between Khartoum and Port Sudan, none of whom had any connection to terrorism. There was no proof that el Hage had pledged bayat to al Qaeda. That he left Nairobi before the bombing, his defense would posit, demonstrated that he was just a hardworking businessman, not part of any conspiracy to kill Americans.

"Do you remember saying to the government that the Nairobi station was only established for the legitimate purpose to help the guys traveling to and from Somalia?" Schmidt asked.

"Yes," said Kherchtou.

He would have Kherchtou testify that el Hage had many books about gems in his home, to support his assertion that gem trading was one of his enterprises.

Because the prosecution introduced every document or phone record with which it could possibly incriminate el Hage, Schmidt went back over those same documents and records to elicit every one of his legitimate contacts and transactions. The idea was to dispel the perception that the preponderance of his activity could be tied to al Qaeda, or that he could even be expected to distinguish who, among those with whom he had business dealings, was al Qaeda. Schmidt ran past Kherchtou a confusing array of names drawn from el Hage's address and date books and phone records, asking whether each individual was or was not a member of al Qaeda.

Sand was moved to chide, "I do suggest that if you're really trying to communicate something to the jury, an hour of asking a list of names is not a very effective way of doing it."

Schmidt complained that the prosecution took isolated instances out of context, making them appear to be nefarious and presenting them as representative of el Hage's overall conduct, explaining, "Mr. el Hage's conduct concerning large numbers of activities were not only open, but his home, which is supposedly the al Qaeda office, his telephones, which are supposedly being used for al Qaeda, the people he is in contact with, show all the activity, that for him to be a secret member of a secret organization capable of committing horrendous acts, it is inconsistent with the manner in which he carried himself, spoke to people, involved himself in public activities. It would be completely inconsistent with the government's theory of Mr. el Hage's involvement with the . . . conspiracy [and] that is why a little bit wouldn't make a difference, but more than that, a not overwhelming number will make a difference."

Schmidt argued that, in order to give context to what the government presented, the jury needed to appreciate the full scope of el Hage's activities, as captured in the very wiretaps and documents upon which the prosecution depended. Only by appreciating all that he did that was legitimate would they see how the prosecution cherry-picked incidents to paint an inaccurate picture of who and what el Hage was.

Of course he was connected with bin Laden. He had never denied that. What he denied was an association with al Qaeda. While the government blurred that distinction, Schmidt endeavored to show, by exhaustively detailing every aspect of el Hage's life, that guilt by association was not proof beyond a reasonable doubt that he had participated, in any way, in a conspiracy to kill Americans.

Eventually, as he seemingly tried to enter every legitimate conversation, appointment, and undertaking into evidence, Sand lost his patience: "Mr. Schmidt, you will have to pick it up. We want to move forward because, you see, it is very slow and tedious."

"He was engaged in bona fide commercial transactions with people that the government claims are al Qaeda," Schmidt told the court, "whose goal is to kill Americans, and I am trying to show that they have put a very distorted picture on ambiguous conversations and that his conduct and contact with these people is legitimate."

Schmidt introduced conversations captured on the wiretap on Wadih's Nairobi home that he had with U.S. agents in August and September 1997. He is heard complaining to the Americans that his house was searched by Kenyan police, and asking for their assistance in retrieving items that were seized.

On the significance of this evidence, Schmidt told the court, "His perception of the Americans and of him being an American and the Americans on his side is consistent with innocent conduct, consciousness of innocence. . . . Mr. el Hage is charged with being a member in a nine-year worldwide conspiracy against the United States. . . . His first regular contact with officials of the United States is in August of 1997. After his contact with the Americans, he maintains close, personal and informational ties with them. I think that's relevant."

As Sand considered his argument, Schmidt pled, "I believe a very important part of our case is Mr. el Hage's conduct from the time he was approached by the government in August of 1997 until his arrest in 1998, including testifying two times in the Grand Jury, not asking for an attorney. I think this is consistent with his consciousness of innocence, and to eliminate these conversations, your Honor, I obviously very strenuously object."

For all its tediousness, the Judge allowed him to go on.

To speak to the point of how the lines between business and terror were not clearly delineated, the government called Essam al Ridi. An Egyptian, al Ridi had become acquainted with Abdullah Azzam, al Qaeda's cofounder, while studying in Pakistan. In 1979, he went to the United States, where he earned his pilot's license, after which he returned to Pakistan to join Azzam in the anti-Soviet jihad in 1983. Two years later, he settled in Arlington, Texas, but agreed to continue helping Azzam however he could. This included sending a shipment of twenty-five Barret .50 caliber rifles to Afghanistan in 1989. According to FBI Agent Ali Soufan, al-Ridi "resented people like bin Laden—rich outsiders who controlled decision making,"[6] a sentiment that obviously did not deter him from trying to earn a buck.

In 1993, el Hage contacted al-Ridi from Khartoum regarding Osama's interest in buying an airplane with a range of at least 2,000 miles, so as to be capable of flying non-stop from Peshawar to Khartoum. Asked by the prosecution what it was they needed to transport between the two cities, al-Ridi responded, "Stinger missiles."

Al-Ridi found a plane in storage in Tucson, arranged the purchase, and agreed to fly it to Khartoum, a hop-scotch that took him a week because of the aircraft's limited range, as well as mechanical problems encountered en route. While he rejected a job offer from bin Laden, al-Ridi again agreed to freelance when called upon.

Around 1995, el Hage asked him to come to Africa to fix up the plane, which hadn't been used since its delivery. Al-Ridi met him in Nairobi. Asked what he was doing there, el Hage said he worked for the charity Help Africa People, adding flatly, "It's really a cover for our efforts in Somalia and here."[7]

Al-Ridi flew on to Khartoum, where he repaired the airplane. However, while landing from a test flight, he lost braking power and crashed into a sand dune at the end of the runway. Rather than risk having to explain what he was doing with bin Laden to local authorities, he fled the airport and terminated his employment with Osama then and there.

On cross, Dratel asked, "When you were asked by Mr. el Hage to purchase the plane, you went forward with that as a commercial, purely commercial business transaction, correct?"

"Absolutely," al-Ridi replied.

El Hage lacked the simple villainy of the killer. With his withered arm, he'd never picked up a gun. He was toiling away in a Texas tire shop when the bodies were mangled in Africa. Isolating his actions in furtherance of the conspiracy was difficult. That he perjured himself before the grand jury helped the prosecution make its case and convince the jury that there was more to his work than business as usual.

"Ladies and gentlemen, I submit to you that the evidence shows that Wadih el Hage was a facilitator, somebody who performed key logistical acts on behalf of the al Qaeda conspiracy and somebody who obstructed the investigation into al Qaeda within a year of the bombing and within weeks after the bombing," prosecutor Karas argued. "Wadih el Hage is given a choice: assist the United States in its investigation of al Qaeda and its leader who has declared war on the United States, or continue to side with bin Laden and al Qaeda. And you will see, ladies and gentlemen, that the evidence overwhelmingly established that el Hage made his choice. He violated his oath. He didn't tell the truth. He lied about al Qaeda. He lied about bin Laden. He chose, Wadih el Hage, the American citizen, chose al Qaeda and bin Laden over America.

"It is tragic, ladies and gentlemen, because it robbed the United States of an opportunity to investigate and crack the bin Laden cell nearly eleven months before the embassies are bombed by the East Africa cell that he ran."

The prosecution never contested that el Hage raised a family and engaged in a variety of business activities. "But like other people in al Qaeda, the evidence shows that Wadih el Hage led a double life, a secret criminal life on behalf of al Qaeda."

Explaining the business enterprises, prosecutor Kenneth Karas said, "The business is bigger than jihad, ladies and gentlemen. It provides resources that finance the operations. It provides a way that employs the people that you want to keep employed. It provides terrific cover if you want to bring in munitions or have people travel. Al-Fadl told you about the plane that went up with sugar to Afghanistan and returned with guns and rockets. It's a great cover."

The following day, Schmidt retorted, "Not a single piece of evidence points to Mr. el Hage ever agreeing to join in a conspiracy to kill Americans, to destroy American property, or to maim or injure those same people." Yes, Wadih was associated with people indicted in the bombing. Yes, he worked for bin Laden. Yes, he believed in jihad for the betterment of Muslims. No, he never killed anyone or assisted anybody else in killing. Citing all of el Hage's legitimate activity, Schmidt said, rather unconvincingly, "He doesn't have time [to conspire]. He has his work."

El Hage certainly had a different story than his codefendants, as reflected in the charges he faced. "El Hage played a different role than the active participants who were tried," said the U.S. attorney for the Southern District, Mary Jo White. "His was actually more significant in the broader conspiracy."[8]

[11] THE DAY IN COURT

The trial of al-'Owhali, Odeh, K. K. Mohamed, and el Hage opened on a blustery February 5, 2001, in the Southern District of New York, courtroom 318 of the Old Federal Courthouse, Foley Square, Manhattan. The building's architecture conveys the grandeur and stolidity of the law.

It had taken nearly a month to select a dozen jurors from a pool of fifteen hundred, the largest ever assembled for a federal criminal trial.

With al-'Owhali and K. K. facing the death penalty, it was the first capital case to go before a Manhattan federal jury in nearly a half century. All four defendants pled not guilty.

There was no real consideration given to a pretrial plea bargain. The government believed it had already extracted all intelligence of value from al-'Owhali, Odeh, and Mohamed, leaving them nothing to deal. El Hage had resisted cooperation to the point of perjury.

"Our office was always amenable to a plea, but it would not have meant agreeing to anything better than life without parole," shrugged Mary Jo White.[1]

With the government offering virtually no incentive beyond, perhaps, taking death off the table, the defense had little incentive to plead guilty.

And the prosecution was content to go to trial.

For all the formality meant to expunge passion from the proceedings, for all the isolation of fact from opinion, there is no denying the anguish at the heart of a criminal trial.

Odeh's attorney, Anthony Ricco, expressed what some of the jurors were undoubtedly thinking as they contemplated the enormity of the crimes before them: "I'm ready to jump over this bar right now and end this. Trial for who? For them?" He acknowledged the extreme suffering that the case would address and the pain inflicted on the victims and their loved ones. And he recognized that these things couldn't help but affect the jury. Nonetheless, he appealed to them "to overcome that anger and overcome that bitterness, to keep your minds open to . . . the concept of fairness."

And so al-'Owhali, el Hage, Mohamed, and Odeh entered the courtroom, presumed innocent of the monstrous crimes of which they were accused, to plead their case. The daunting task facing defense counsel was to humanize the defendants. A task exacerbated by their own difficulty winning the trust of their clients.

Judge Sand recalls, "What was quite unique, for me, about the case was the relationship between the defendants and their attorneys, who were all extremely able and vigorously defended their clients. But, it was common knowledge to everyone in court that the defendants hated them."[2] He noted how Fredrick Cohn seemed to have particular difficulty with al-'Owhali, pointing out that he was not permitted by his client to make an opening statement. (Interestingly, most of the defenders, in retrospect, at any rate, speak quite positively of their relationship with their clients.)

"We had a strange relationship," Cohn affirmed. "He didn't trust anyone from the West. From his point of view, we're part of a system, paid for by the government. And I'm Jewish, though certainly an apostate Jew and, in all candor, anti-Zionist. In any event, I try to stay away from philosophical discussions with my clients. It causes profound trouble, particularly if you disagree. He got along with my associate, Laura Gasiorowski, very well—spent an inordinate amount of time trying to convert her to Islam—and, quite frankly, it was her relationship with him that got us over hurdles when we had difficulties."[3]

Gasiorowski still seems rather perplexed at how she succeeded in earning al-'Owhali's trust, "I went to the jail every single day. We spoke for hours at a time. It was emotionally draining to spend every day trying to convince him that he could trust us. You'd just go in circles and circles. I read everything I could find to understand who these people were, what it's like to grow up in Wahhabi Saudi Arabia, what al Qaeda was. To grasp what was going on in his head, sitting in a room, maybe for the first time, opposite a woman who was not his mother or his sister. I had to let him educate me, to just listen to him. I think every human being wants to connect with other human beings in whatever circumstances they're in, and I think that's what he wanted."[4]

Certainly at the outset, al-'Owhali's conception was that representation paid for by the government was beholden to the government. "We eventually succeeded in establishing a relationship where he trusted us as his attorneys," Gasiorowski concluded.

Six months prior to the trial, al-'Owhali had dismissed what Cohn characterized as a "terrific defense team." Judge Sand cast about for replacements he thought might prove suitable. Cohn was the seventh call he placed.

"I said yes because it was a death penalty case and I didn't think, given that this kid was not Osama bin Laden, seeking death was right," Cohn related. "Then I went home and told my wife, who said, 'You didn't ask me.' I said, 'We've been married thirty-six years, when have I ever asked you if I could take a case?' 'This is different,' she said."[5]

Further complicating matters was the need to communicate through translators. That factor alone dampened any possibility of spontaneity, and the intercession of another person stifled the development of true intimacy.

Some of the problems were cultural. One of the defendants was explaining to his lawyer how seventy-two virgins awaited the martyr in heaven. The councilor quipped, "Can you imagine having all those fathers-in-law?" Abiding no humor at his religion's expense, he immediately demanded new representation, which Sand granted.

The defense teams for al-'Owhali, el Hage, and Mohamed all included Jewish attorneys, who insist that their religion gave their clients no pause.

Of K. K., Stern said, "He viewed us skeptically at first. He knew we were free, so that raised some doubts. But eventually we earned his trust. I made a point of seeing him every week. If I made a promise to do something, I kept it."[6]

Odeh's attorneys, Ricco and Wilford, are both African-American, which may have helped to win his confidence that they could serve on his side—but only to a point.

"I don't really know whether Mr. Odeh ever had confidence in anybody. I will say that he was able to, at least, move to the point where we could present his defense. He was forthcoming with information," offered Wilford. "But, as far as trust, his position was, 'You're either down with my cause, or you aren't.' And I'm not, so there was a fundamental difference, but that's not a barrier to our doing our job. I think he accepted, theoretically, that we worked for him, but whether he accepted in reality is a different matter. I believe we had the necessary attorney-client relationship."

He mused further, "I can say Mr. Odeh is a very interesting fellow, very different from most clients. He speaks seven languages, he was a soldier, he'd been in a whole plethora of places in the world, and he's dedicated to his cause. He's very bright, devoutly religious, very sincere. Mr. Odeh is a very insightful person."[7]

Two themes emerged from the opening arguments by the defense: that the accused are not monsters; and that they are the products of a very different culture and environment than anything the jury was likely to have personally experienced.

"Somehow, you have to make what your client did human. You have to make him fallible, but not evil," Cohn asserted. "If you let someone sit there with a monster mask on his face, they'll sentence him to death because it's not another human being. You've got to establish some kind of context where it seems rational and a juror says, 'If I were in that person's shoes, I might have done that.'"[8]

This was a jury of peers only in the very loosest sense. Stern acknowledged, "Few people here have encountered anyone from Zanzibar. K. K. was truly alien, and that presented a high hurdle for us."[9]

As Odeh's advocate Ricco explained to the jury, "The difficulty that you have in this case is that you as jurors have to try to understand actions and the associations of a person who is not a part of our culture. The nuances of his culture that are important to him, that help guide him in his decisions are something that's a little foreign to us."

Ricco didn't dispute that Odeh was involved with al Qaeda. He tried, however, to explain: "You're going to find that his participation as a soldier is based on one thing, his love of Islam, his complete faith in the Koran, the sharia." He emphasized that Odeh agreed to follow bin Laden "only to the extent that bin Laden would engage in acts that were Islamically correct. Odeh was proud to go to Afghanistan to fight Russia." But, he cautioned, being a part of al Qaeda did not prove involvement in a plot to kill Americans, generally, or, specifically, in the attack against the embassy in Kenya.

As far as explaining who Odeh was, there were practical limitations. Wilford said, "We were defending charges where his life story didn't really make a difference. Why he did what he did was not much of a defense. There was no way we were going to get a jury nullification when you had two hundred-some people dead."[10]

Al-'Owhali, Odeh, and K. K. Mohamed all sought to have the statements they made while being questioned overseas suppressed by the court. The defense argued that standards observed during these interrogations failed to conform to American norms. They called into question whether statements were given freely and following a full explanation of the right to counsel, the right not to answer questions, and the consequences of assenting to do so, as is required in the United States, where a suspect must be provided an advice of rights (commonly known as the Miranda warning), and must clearly indicate an understanding of these rights. Not only are suspects not to be coerced, but there can be no intent to trick suspects into cooperating with investigators by capitalizing on their ignorance of their rights under the law. In the absence of explicit warning as to their rights, nothing suspects say may be admitted into evidence at trial.

On cross-examination, Anthony Ricco reminded Special Agent Anticev that Odeh had suggested he would like to speak to American officials alone, to the exclusion of the Kenyans, "and the Americans got up, left the room to discuss it, right?"

"Yes."

"And when you left the room, you left Mr. Odeh in the room with the people who he did not want to talk to alone, correct?"

"Yes."

"Then, all of a sudden, you are called back into the room and Mr. Odeh says, 'I'll speak to both groups, right?"

"Yes."

He left it for the jury to imagine what might have happened during that brief interlude in that closed room with no Americans present.

Later in his examination, Ricco returned to the theme, "During the evening hours when the interviews ceased, Mr. Odeh was taken back into Kenyan custody, isn't that correct?"

"Yes."

"You didn't spend those evening hours with Mr. Odeh, isn't that right?"

"That's right."

"There were times when Mr. Odeh was in the presence and custody of the Kenyans without the American officials being there, isn't that right?"

"Yes."

"Often, isn't that correct?"

"Yes."

"You, I take it, took steps to ensure that the interviews took place in an area that was free of intimidation and fear?"

"Yes, I think we did that."

On redirect, Pat Fitzgerald countered Ricco's insinuations. "Did he [Odeh] ever indicate to you during that time that he was physically mistreated by the Kenyans?"

"No."

"Did he ever look like he was physically mistreated?"

"No."

"Isn't it fair to say that Mr. Odeh did say that he was upset that the bomb had deflected and affected many buildings around the embassy and killed many people?"

"Yes."

"Did he ever indicate that he was concerned or upset that Americans in the embassy had been killed?"

"No."

When examining Kherchtou, Edward Wilford questioned him about an incident where he'd paid a $3,000 bribe to get an al Qaeda member released from jail, as well as how the police had stolen cash when they searched his home. This, to establish the corrupt nature of the Kenyan police.

Judge Sand ruled that all statements were admissible, saying the Miranda warnings, as strictly mandated within the United States, may not always be practicable abroad. For example, he pointed out, Kenyan law does not provide for access to a lawyer prior to any questioning. He was reluctant to establish a precedent whereby all interrogations of terror suspects overseas would automatically be bound by Miranda. Despite such practical allowances for local conditions, Sand did assert, "The Constitution applies when questioning is conducted by the U.S. Attorney's Office for law enforcement purposes."[11]

This was the first time that an American district court had been called upon to rule on whether U.S. agents, operating in a foreign country under foreign laws, interviewing a foreign national for the purpose of a prosecution in the United States, were obliged to uphold constitutional rights.

"Until al-'Owhali confessed, they had suspicions [of his involvement], but, in my view, the government really didn't have much," said Cohn. "If they had suppressed the confession, the government would have had an awfully hard time."[12]

Stern contended, "Once K. K.'s statement was admitted, it was basically the end of the case in terms of winning a not-guilty verdict. From that point forward, we were playing to the penalty phase to save his life."[13]

Gasiorowski acknowledges a similar approach for al-'Owhali: "Our focus was primarily on mitigation. You'd always prefer to defend on the basis of innocence, but in the back of your mind, you have to consider the ultimate possibility of a death sentence, so, from day one, no matter what, you're thinking about how to put together a mitigation case."[14]

Strategically, this presented a problem for the non-death-eligible defendants, Odeh and el Hage, because they were arguing to establish reasonable doubt, which gave rise to periodic requests to sever their trial from al-'Owhali and Mohamed. There was a fundamental tension between defendants intent on instilling reasonable doubt as to their guilt and those whose best hope was to introduce mitigating factors to save their lives. Their arguments could be at cross-purposes and, according to the non-death-eligible defendants, prejudicial to their interests.

"Some of the things the other lawyers were trying to do for their clients who had no defense, but just wanted to make sure they weren't executed, were inappropriate for our efforts to present a defense," insisted Schmidt.[15]

The divergence between the two approaches emerged at several junctures in the trial. For instance, when cross-examining Jamal al-Fadl, Stern sought to discredit him as a participant in al Qaeda's conspiracy to kill Americans. "You knew that money you were making [through bin Laden's legitimate business activities] would go to buy weapons, didn't you?"

"Yes."

"And you knew that those [al Qaeda] soldiers would use those weapons to kill people in other countries, right?"

"Yes."

"And you were proud to be helping al Qaeda the way you best could be, being a businessperson?"

"Yes," al-Fadl conceded.

Josh Dratel objected on behalf of el Hage because this line undercut his contention that one could be conducting business for bin Laden without any knowledge of al Qaeda's terrorist activities. Upholding the distinction between business and terrorism was critical to el Hage's defense. Sand denied him.

El Hage had another argument for severance: that he was the only defendant not facing a single charge of murder for having been an active participant in the attack.

"About a third of the trial dealt with the bombing itself, and the aftermath. The descriptions were horrendous. But Wadih was not charged with any act of violence," pointed out Schmidt. "From the beginning, he opposed terrorism against civilians. He thought what happened in Kenya and Tanzania was wrong. He truly thought 9/11 was an abomination."[16]

Odeh's defense tried to create reasonable doubt by calling into question the manner in which the local police might have handled physical evidence. Attorney Carl Herman called Dr. John Brian Ford Lloyd, an explosives expert who had spent twenty-five years with the Home Office in the United Kingdom. He reviewed FBI forensic reports and noted that they said only that trace explosives were detected on Odeh's clothing when he was arrested, failing to specify the amount.

Asked why it would be important to know how much explosive was present, Dr. Lloyd replied, "First of all, very simply, the more explosive there is, the more significant the evidence is likely to be. If there's a large amount of explosive on a person's clothing, that is clearly of greater significance or likely to be of greater significance than if a very tiny trace of explosive is present. If a person has been in recent contact with explosives, with intact explosive or perhaps has been trying to make a bomb or something of that sort, then one would expect to see a large amount of explosive on his clothing. One would not expect to see merely a trace of explosive."

Noting that the TNT was ground up, Herman asked, "Would the act of grinding up the TNT . . . create finer particles of TNT and therefore make it subject to greater dispersion?"

"Yes. Anything, anybody in the vicinity of this sort of operation would be contaminated with it. I think that cannot be reasonably doubted." The defense's point being that, without knowing the concentration of explosive found on Odeh's clothing there was no way to know whether he was in close contact during the making of a bomb or, perhaps, just innocently brushed against some surface that had been contaminated.

During his summation, Wilford would return to the issue of trace explosives, insisting, "The evidence that connects Mohamed Odeh to these crimes that the government is relying on is not overwhelming, it's underwhelming, and if you pay close attention to it and analyze it, which you must, it makes a difference." He claimed that microscopic traces of TNT do not eliminate reasonable doubt and suggested that Odeh's clothing could have become contaminated while it was in the possession of Kenyan police, who do not employ the rigorous forensic standards and evidence handling procedures of the FBI.

"Keep fast to the truth. Keep fast to the evidence. And keep fast to the instructions that his Honor is going to give you. And it points one way: Odeh is not guilty."

In a trial as long as this one, and as much as the dignity and seriousness of the proceedings were maintained, there were odd moments of levity. The judge and lawyers have, in many cases, known one another for years. They have appeared together in other cases. They work exceedingly long hours for months on end. Cohn and Sand, for example, had a relationship that allowed for banter not seen with other attorneys.

Cohn refers to Judge Sand as "the Saint of Foley Square."[17]

"Your Honor, if I stand up, you yell at me, if I don't stand up, I don't get heard," Cohn complained upon entering an objection.

"If I don't have the opportunity at least once a day to yell at you, you know," Sand retorted.

"I know."

"There has to be some compensation."

"Given the limited salaries of federal judges, I try to give you what compensation you can get."

"I appreciate it." Sand then pointed out, for the record, that the exchange was in a light-hearted tone, so that future transcript readers would not come away with the wrong impression.

Closing arguments began on May 1 with the prosecution playing a video shot in the immediate aftermath of the attack to serve, Kenneth Karas said, "as a painful reminder of why it is that we have spent the last two and a half months together to review evidence that was collected from all over the world."

He concluded, "One of the defense counsel said in the opening statement, this case is a rare opportunity to demonstrate to the world that we can abide by our principles of justice in a case of this magnitude. I submit to you that that is absolutely right and we have done just that. While the defendants hated, targeted and killed people, and killed people merely because of their nationality or their religion, the government has responded by presenting you with evidence of what these individual defendants did that make them guilty."

In his closing, Cohn made the point: "This is something not about morality, not about justice, but following the law. Justice is something else that we may or may not get to here, but you have to follow the law." He raised an important principle about the legal system. The law has primacy, he was arguing. And if justice need be sacrificed in applying the law, so be it. But you do not overrule law in the belief of achieving justice.

Ricco, as was his style, gave a rambling, discursive summation, admitting, "There is always so much that we want to say, but there is only really but so much of it that is really important, and lawyers have a bad way of not just, like, this is what we're trying to say and be done with it."

This remark holds relevance to the entire trial process. Because of its interrogative structure, lawyers can only state the points they are trying to make at opening and closing. Otherwise, they are limited to eliciting facts, often leaving jurors unsure about the significance of specific testimony or of how a particular piece of evidence relates to the whole. Certainly, after a lengthy process, jurors can be forgiven if some subtle allusions escape them by the time they are sent off to deliberate.

Bearing the burden of proof, the prosecution is afforded the opportunity to make a rebuttal argument to the summations of the defense. Pat Fitzgerald concluded his by invoking the name of Roselyn Wanjiku Mwangi, who was attending secretarial school on August 7, 1998. Rosie lay trapped in the rubble of the Ufundi House in Nairobi for two days while rescuers frantically dug to find her. Rosie succumbed to her injuries and lack of water just before they reached down to where she was buried. She died within arm's length of salvation.

"'This trial is about her murder. The pathetic part is, so many people got killed, so much human carnage. Roselyn Wanjiku Mwangi. She is count number 123 in the indictment. You have to get to page 45 of the indictment to see her name. But she is not just a name. She is not just a count. It is not a name on a list. It's a person."

Jury deliberation began at 3:45 pm on May 10. The jurors obviously did not take their duty lightly. Based on the clarifications they sought from the court and the exhibits they asked to review, it was apparent they were engaged in a substantive and careful debate on the evidence. They were not overwhelmed by passion or moved to exact revenge. They were thoughtful and contemplative, respectful of the law. On May 29 at 12:30 pm they returned with their verdicts.

All defendants were found guilty of all charges.

With the pronouncement of the word "guilty" after the reading of each count, the defendants were struck with the enormity of what they had done, or at least with the hopelessness of imprisonment. With the loneliness of being far from home. Without the camaraderie that made sense of the slaughter and destruction.

For al-'Owhali there must be dreams of the paradise that his decision to flee, his moment of doubt, denied him. His God rewards obedience extravagantly and punishes betrayal harshly. Perhaps experiencing the torment of isolation reinforces his faith, a constant reminder that his God holds him in contempt for his failure to martyr himself, for his weakness. Or does he feel utterly forsaken?

In practice, capital punishment is reserved for "the worst of the worst," that is, those crimes which most outrage the conscience of the community. Paradoxically, this makes for the capital system's undoing, because it is these extreme and repellent crimes that provoke the highest emotions—anger, especially, even outrage—that in turn make rational deliberation problematic for investigators, prosecutors, judges, and juries.
—Scott Turow, *Ultimate Punishment*

[12] LIFE AND DEATH

One day after the verdicts were delivered, the parties returned to court to consider the fate of the death-eligible defendants, al-'Owhali and Mohamed. There is no exact formula for balancing the aggravating and mitigating factors contributing to a crime, nor is there a mechanism to define who deserves to die. Yet, when sworn in, the jurors pledged that they could, in good conscience, vote for death. Without unanimous agreement in favor of capital punishment, the defendants would automatically be sentenced to life without the possibility of parole.

"Jurors are called upon to make a unique individualized judgment about the appropriateness of sentencing another human being to death," Judge Sand said solemnly. "This is not a mechanical process. Neither is the decision determined by raw numbers. . . . In short, what is called for in weighing the varying factors is not arithmetic, but an individual's careful, considered, and mature judgment."

Being the ultimate punishment, death must be meted out with the ultimate care. Its appropriateness as a sanction begs the philosophical question as to the propriety of the state engaging in willful killing. "It's chilling when a representative of the state rises and argues that a human being ought to be killed," offered David Stern. "The government should be dispassionate, not angry. I find it unseemly."[1]

"Justice is not done yet," Pat Fitzgerald told the jury; "the only just punishment, the only punishment that does justice for the victims, the only punishment that fits the crime is the death penalty."

It is an awesome responsibility of individual conscience put upon jurors, the decision of whether someone will die. Indeed, the seemingly arbitrary way in which it has been applied is one argument against the death penalty. And in this case, with so many coconspirators, seeking death for some, while others evaded punishment altogether, raised a potential problem for the prosecution.

Nothing made this more obvious than how the government agreed that suspects who had been taken into custody abroad—Mamdouh Mahmud Salim, the al Qaeda leader who headed the fatwa council, in Germany; Khalid al-Fawwaz, Ibrahim Eidarous, and Adel Abdel Bary, who were senior propagandists and facilitators, in the U.K.—would not be subject to the death penalty because both countries refused to extradite suspects to face possible execution. Thus, in order to get custody, the U.S. attorney had to pledge to seek only life imprisonment.

Why, the defense put forth, should their clients be executed and others not, merely due to the circumstances of their capture, having absolutely nothing to do with their culpability? In K. K.'s case, his extradition from South Africa had been in violation of that country's own laws, his attorneys argued as one of a dozen mitigating factors cited.

"One of the ways you defend a death penalty case is to show remorse to the jury, but al-'Owhali was never going to let us admit guilt," explained Cohn. "What I did was focus on how there were an awful lot of people similarly situated who were not getting death, which ended up being the biggest mitigating factor accepted by the jury. In my view, the jury found it important that Salim escaped death, even though he was no longer part of this trial, just because he had the good fortune to be apprehended in Germany. But, the fact they would find him guilty was written in stone. A lot of our effort was to limit the damage that would spill over from the guilt phase to the penalty phase."[2]

It was, the defense contended, pure happenstance—and thus inherently unfair—that al-'Owhali and K. K. faced death while others did not.

The prosecution would not get caught arguing the death penalty on comparative merit. Prosecutor Michael Garcia said simply, "Al-'Owhali is the rare exception, the criminal, the murderer, who deserves the ultimate penalty that is authorized by our law."

In order to pass a death sentence, the jury must find unanimously that at least one statutory factor has been met. These include that the killings were intentional, that the actions of the defendant were undertaken with the intent of causing death, or that the defendant participated in an act of violence knowing that it constituted reckless disregard for human life. Only upon crossing this threshold is the jury to consider statutory aggravating factors of the crimes for which the defendants have been convicted. These include that the deaths occurred during the commission of other crimes, that the defendant wantonly endangered people other than the actual victims, that there was premeditation or that the deaths were the result of an act of terrorism, or that there was an intent to take multiple lives by a single act.

In addition, the government offered three nonstatutory aggravators for consideration. That the defendants continued to pose a serious threat to those with whom they will come into contact. That the survivors of the bombing and the families of the victims suffered grievous economic hardship and emotional injury in the aftermath of the attack. And that the offense was motivated by an express desire to kill high-ranking public officials of the United States serving overseas.

The first defendant to be considered was al-'Owhali, facing 258 capital charges, including 213 for murder, 41 for murdering officers and employees of the United States on account of their duties, 2 for murdering internationally protected persons, and 1 each for destruction of U.S. government property resulting in death and using a weapon of mass destruction against U.S. nationals resulting in death.

"Death held no great fear for him," Cohn said, "and still doesn't. He believes he's going to paradise and the seventy-two virgins. Whatever you think of his beliefs, he is legitimately that religious. That's who he is."[3]

Fitzgerald opened the penalty phase as he'd concluded the guilt portion, by invoking Roselyn Wanjiku Mwangi, Rosie. He recalled the slow horror of her days suffering beneath the rubble, waiting in vain to be rescued. Though death brings an end to life, it marks not the limits of suffering. Not for families and loved ones left alive behind.

Rosie's husband, Lawrence Ndugire, was among those who journeyed from Africa to present the court with a victim impact statement. He and Rosie had been married for eighteen years and had two sons, aged sixteen and fourteen, and a daughter, eleven. He was among the rescuers working desperately to save her.

"I collapse when I hear that she had died," he said.

Victim impact ought to be the most important factor to consider, Fitzgerald advised the jury. "You need to understand the pain, the horror and the agony that that bombing put so many people, so many families, through. You need to weigh that in the balancing, in making your reasoned, moral judgment as to the appropriate penalty."

Gone was the dispassion, the resolve not to inflame that governs a trial. Here, less the criminal act than the consequences of the crime are laid bare before the jury. The dead, reduced to charges in the first phase of the proceedings, are returned their humanity. The human toll lives in the testimony of those they left behind. The loss so sudden and irrevocable, numbing and confusing, is made palpable.

Fitzgerald spoke movingly about several of the victims, including Teresia Karanja, who walked into the Cooperative Bank Building that day, nearly three years past, and was carried out a paraplegic. She would testify from her wheelchair how she waited to be rescued, under piles of debris, for four and a half hours. She would spend four months in a Nairobi hospital, followed by another four in South Africa, where she received additional treatment and rehabilitation.

The hardships caused by her condition were profound, she recounted: "I had to start from zero. . . . Up to today we are struggling to live day and day life. I have to reduce my hours of working because of health. My husband has to reduce working hours because he has to take care of me. It has affected our life up to today. But, thank Lord, I am alive."

Many of the survivors were left blind. Fitzgerald said, "We have to understand that you're going to hear a lot about flying glass in the course of the next few days, and what happens in a downtown, bustling area with buildings with windows, surrounded by more buildings with windows, and cars and buses with glass is that when a bomb goes off, all those windows turn into thousands and tens of thousands of little swords, fly through the air and cut and rip, and tear and maim and blind and kill."

Ellen Bomer, a commercial officer at the Nairobi embassy, was among those blinded. "Everything that gave me identity was ripped away, and I felt like I had no identity, no worth. I wasn't going to be able to go out to the ranch and walk around, because there are snakes, I can't walk out there. . . . You know, just little, simple things that if you could see you just take for granted. . . . I wasn't ready to give up my career. But, you know, here I am, I'm blind, what am I going to do?"

She added wistfully, "I keep thinking I'm going to see, I'm going to see, I'm not going to give up. My Lord is not going to take both eyes. He might take one, but he isn't going to take both, because I didn't do any of this. I was innocent. I was doing my job."

"You must weigh the pain of that horror that the defendant al-'Owhali caused by his bomb in making your decision," Fitzgerald told the jurors, "and remember when you see a cross-section, a glimpse of the pain and suffering, that it is the defendant who brought that horror into this world. It's the defendant, al-'Owhali, who is responsible for that snapshot of horror and pain that you will see."

Prosecutor Michael Garcia spoke contemptuously of al-'Owhali: "He threw his grenades and he ran. He ran fast and he ran hard across that parking lot and he saved himself. . . . And after he had killed those 213 people and blinded Ellen Bomer and blinded Sandi Patel, he went to the hospital and he got treated for his injuries. The largest injury he had was to his back, because his back was facing the embassy as he ran from it. Yes, he ran away."

While the penalty phase amounts to a continuation for the prosecution, defense counsel is required to pull an awkward about-face. With their client's guilt affirmed, the best they could do was to, somehow, present mitigating factors, which, as David Baugh, a death penalty trial expert brought in from Richmond, Virginia, to help with al-'Owhali's case, explained to the jury, "is not to offer you a justification for what the defendant has done, because there can be no justification. However, there can be, for whatever purposes it should be used, an explanation." What he could do was explain the totality of the circumstances that culminated in the bombing on August 7; how it came to be that young men were willing to kill and die for the cause bin Laden espoused.

Baugh impressed upon the jury the harsh power they wielded: "If all twelve of you vote that he will die, he will die, and no one can stop it."

As a kind of tribute, and a means of demonstrating that he wasn't shying away from the ugly truth, Baugh took it upon himself to read the names of each of the dead. He admitted that he could do nothing about the loss and the suffering. It was there. It would remain.

But, he said, "I hope you will find at the conclusion of this penalty phase, too many people have died, too many mothers, not just American mothers, not just Tanzanian mothers, not just Iraqi mothers"—a reference tossed in to support the claim that the death of Iraqi children as a result of American sanctions was among the factors that motivated al-'Owhali—"too many people have suffered and are suffering. And I will tell you this, if in the discharge of your duties, you find beyond a reasonable doubt that killing him will stop [the suffering], then that's the appropriate sentence and I will concede the point."

The victim impact statements were wrenching in their simple, subdued eloquence. Spoken from the heart, by parents, husbands, wives, and children, without hellfire demands for retribution, they led the jury inexorably down into the dark, desperate pit where consequences squirm and devour their innocent prey. It was all so private, the hurt they exposed, so intense as to make you wonder how these people maintain the façade that anything else in their lives matters.

Susan Bartley, who lost her husband, Julian, the Consul General, and son, Jay, a summer intern, spoke of her twenty-eight years of marriage, and the twenty years of Jay's short life. "This pain is with me every day. Oftentimes it is unthinkable. . . . When you know someone, when you have known someone as long as

I knew my husband and they are no longer there, what is left is raw emptiness. A part of me is missing."

Mary Khahenzi spoke of how her husband, Thomas, decided to wear his favorite T-shirt that morning, even though it was still damp from the previous night's washing. It was emblazoned with "I am a Catholic and Jesus loves me."

Four agonizing days passed before Thomas's body was recovered from the ruins of the Cooperative Building. Mary was asked to come to the morgue to identify him. "I found him laying on the mortuary floor. The T-shirt he had insisted on wearing was my means of identifying him. Yes, he was wearing, 'I am a Catholic and Jesus loves me.' He was very broken, but we identified him by the T-shirt he was wearing."

At the Nairobi Hospital, there weren't enough doctors and nurses to tend to all the wounded. Cleaners pitched in. Victims with lesser injuries helped the more critical. Hearing of the catastrophe, a maid who lived nearby and owned two sheets brought one to the hospital, rightly certain that somebody would need it. Channa Commanday, a nurse-practitioner in the hospital's emergency department, read from a note she wrote to herself after treating victims nonstop for three days: "One man lay with eyes swollen shut from corneal lacerations, amputated fingers, and clothes torn off in the blast. As I felt his rapid pulse and spoke to him, he said, 'I'm okay. You go help the others.' Most of the others said the same thing."

Fifteen victims' statements were heard on the first day.

The defense declined to cross-examine. In a sidebar at the end of the day, Cohn said, with an exasperation brought on by the emotional ravages of the testimony: "What we have gotten is witness after witness who tells us the same thing that we all know, which is that whenever you have someone who dies there is familial loss, which is terrible, and that there were consequences that are financial, as well. There is a limited amount of that record that the government is entitled to present to turn that into a personal experience that the jurors can understand without reaching the point that it is so duplicative that it becomes more prejudicial than it is supposed to be. I understand that it is supposed to be somewhat prejudicial, but we have to draw a line somewhere."

"What is a fair balance? Two hundred killed and 5,000 injured and what is the calculus of that?" Sand mused.

"I say, as someone who bleeds for somebody that I want to weep and stop myself because I can't do it in front of the jury, in front of the victims, where it is no longer factual, it is a roller coaster and it is enough," Cohn pled, with a humanity that superseded his professional responsibilities. "I don't care if it is another day or another hour. Ms. Bomer is enough to make anybody, make a stone, weep. It's enough."

"I think you have made your point, Mr. Fitzgerald," Sand agreed. However, he overruled Cohn's objection: "I don't believe there have been histrionics for the sake of histrionics."

Fifteen more victims took the stand on the second day.

Mordecai Thomas Onuno spoke about seeing his wife, Grace, in the morgue. It was August 9, their wedding anniversary. "I wanted to look at her face. I tried to hold her head to look at her face. There was no face. The skull had been crushed. There was no face. Only some hanging skin. I felt angry because this sort of very peaceful person should not have died violently."

From then on, Onuno's life hinged on this day. The day his marriage began; the day he discovered it was over. His life trapped in the precarious tilt of a spinning top, not quite toppling, not quite upright.

Geoffrey Manguriu lost his twenty-year-old daughter, Joyce, in the wreckage of the Ufundi House.

"How are you coping with the loss of Joyce?" Fitzgerald asked.

"Just keep on praying that she will be okay wherever she is."

Adams Titus Wamai was a commercial specialist at the embassy. His wife, Winfred, testified about identifying his body: "I just got him from his clothes. He didn't have a face. He didn't even have a heart. Part of his chest was gone."

The prosecution rested on May 31, leaving the defense to rise in air heavy and dank, thickened by the evocation of the blood and flames and smoke and tears of a still-reverberating explosion.

Baugh needed to win some sympathy by conjuring his own victims to stack up against those of his client. He argued vigorously—out of the jury's presence—that he be permitted to introduce evidence that American-imposed sanctions against Iraq had caused the death of as many as 1.5 million children. He wanted to enter into evidence pictures of babies born with a variety of deformities, allegedly as a result of depleted uranium from American ordnance used during the Gulf War.

"These are ghastly pictures of deformed babies," Sand suggested, "being offered for the point of showing that deformed babies are ghastly looking."

Though he did not claim that al-'Owhali had ever seen the images, Baugh proposed that American indifference to the welfare of Muslims and contempt for their suffering was what inspired him to join the jihad. Furthermore, it gave him an argument for why al-'Owhali showed no remorse.

He reached even farther afield, to include the American invasion of Panama as a mitigator. "One of the aggravators alleged by the United States is that my client showed a certain disregard for the safety of others who were not his target. There is a documentary called *Panama Deception* . . . showing when the United States went to arrest [President] Manuel Noriega, we killed two to three thousand Panamanians. If the United States sees nothing wrong with killing Panamanians to pull off a political objective . . ."

Sand was dumbstruck: "If you succeed, sir, in convincing the jury that actions taken by the United States military in an authorized military action . . ."

"Authorized by who? There is no declaration of war on Panama."

" . . . are comparable to the conduct in which the jury has found that the defendant has engaged, you will have engaged in a Herculean task."

The judge was adamant that the process would not degenerate into presenting gore for gore's sake. He would limit the degree to which the defense could introduce broader issues of international policy. Nonetheless, he permitted the playing of an interview with Secretary of State Madeleine Albright from the May 12, 1996, broadcast of *60 Minutes,* in which she acknowledged the impact of sanctions against innocent Iraqi civilians, including the killing of as many as five hundred thousand children, while insisting that U.S. policy objectives were worth it.

Baugh read into the record from a declassified Defense Intelligence Agency memo dated January 1991 about the vulnerability of Iraq's water treatment facilities. To purify its water supply, Iraq depended on imported chemicals, which were restricted under the sanctions. The memo said, "Failing to secure supplies will result in a shortage of pure drinking water for much of the population. This could lead to increased incidence, if not epidemics, of disease." With this, he purported to show that the United States was well aware of the impact its embargo was having on innocent civilians. Baugh quoted article 54 of the 1977 protocols to the Geneva Convention, which prohibits actions targeting drinking water supplies or facilities.

The defense called former Attorney General Ramsey Clark, an advocate for civil rights in the Kennedy and Johnson administrations, who had since become a champion for international human rights. He had visited Iraq frequently since 1991 to verify the conditions of civilian populations. He spoke about the destruction of the water system, how agriculture had been devastated, as farmers had no water with which to irrigate their fields or sustain their livestock: "It was a catastrophe of enormous magnitude."

On the issue of depleted uranium, Clark said, "It vaporizes and gets in the air and it gets in the ground water and it gets in the food chain. . . . There has been a substantial increase in cancers, tumors, leukemia, malformed infants, miscarriages, deformed infants." He opined that the estimate of 250 children dying daily as a result of the sanctions was probably low.

Clark had taken up the cause of terrorism defendants before, assisting the defense of the Blind Sheikh and submitting an affidavit in the extradition proceeding against Fawwaz in the United Kingdom.

Fawwaz had left his post as head of bin Laden's Nairobi operation in 1994 to run al Qaeda's London public affairs office. He was joined by Adel Abdel Bary, who had been sent by Zawahiri in May 1996 to run Egyptian Islamic Jihad's local cell. Bary was demoted to deputy when Ibrahim Eidarous arrived to take charge in September 1997. The three were arrested by British police on an extradition warrant at the Americans' request following the bombings. Fawwaz was accused of being involved in transmitting bin Laden's fatwas and vouching for their authenticity. A British court ordered him held pending extradition to the United States.[4]

The investigation into the three, dubbed Operation Challenge, revealed a treasure trove of intelligence. An early draft of the 1996 declaration of war was found on Fawwaz's computer. Phone records showed he had received a call from bin Laden's satellite phone the day before the 1998 fatwa was released to the media. Other documents connected Bary and Eidarous directly to al Qaeda's leadership.[5] In July 1999, however, a judge ruled there was insufficient evidence to hold them any longer. The case was appealed all the way to the House of Lords, where the suspects' detention was ultimately upheld. Fawwaz and Bary were finally extradicted to United States in October 2012. Both pled not guilty to all charges and will be tried in the Southern District of New York in November 2014. Eidarous, who had been released from British prison on compassionate grounds, died of leukemia in 2008.

"One of the things you told the court in the United Kingdom was your belief that in picking a jury for the trial in New York for Sheikh Omar Abdul Rahman [the Blind Sheikh], and I'll quote, 'In selecting the jury . . . there is no inquiry of prospective jurors concerning religious preference, exposure to prejudicial influence, personal history of anti-Muslim or Arab feelings, no probing for prejudice,'" Fitzgerald said indignantly.

"Yes, that's what I think."

Reminded that jurors responded to an extensive questionnaire designed to elicit prejudice and a month of voir dire, giving attorneys for both sides the opportunity to interrogate them at length, Clark responded weakly, "There was no development of any information that had any utility in terms of their religious beliefs or their preferences or how they felt about Islam or anything that was important to Dr. Abdul Rahman's defense."

"And did you not tell the court in the United Kingdom," Fitzgerald went on, "and I'll quote, 'In my opinion, to a reasonable degree of professional certainty, any defendant who has had the slightest contact or association with bin Laden or any other defendant or any of the co-conspirators will have little or no chance of receiving a fair trial or of acquittal even if completely innocent.' Did you tell the court in the United Kingdom those words?"

"That was my conclusion based upon my experience in civil rights and based upon my recognition of the difficulty of getting fair trials in an environment of intense prejudice and demonization of peoples and religions."

Later on, in his rebuttal argument, Fitzgerald would dismiss all references to Iraq as a distraction. "America's actions are not on trial here. We are on trial because this man [al-'Owhali] committed a crime. This man made a cold-blooded, calculated decision to kill 213 people and felt no remorse about it."

"This is the first case I have ever been involved in where the purpose given [for the death penalty] is to stop killing," David Baugh marveled in his folksy delivery. "Killing to stop killing. It's just a living example that killing always makes more killing. It always does, and you can't get around it."

He went on, "However, I do want you to understand, and I want you to appreciate, that there is a lot of sorrow over there [the Middle East] and there are a lot of deaths, and how anyone can stand up here and look at the suffering of these people, . . . realizing the suffering they are going to go through from this day forward, and not appreciate the children we are killing is a hypocrite." Whether intentionally or not, this echoed bin Laden's lament in the 1996 declaration of war: "that Muslims' blood has become the cheapest blood."[6]

Baugh argued that al-'Owhali committed murders in the context of the greater murders going on in Iraq. And on the killing would go. "Each of you, individually, today, is going to be asked to kill. That's right, to kill." He personalized it: "When you put Juror Number 1 or Juror Number 2 on that form, it's going to be like firing the bullet," he told the jury gravely.

When it was his turn for rebuttal, Fitzgerald responded to Baugh's accusation. "Mr. al-'Owhali being sentenced to death, he'll be given a sentence no worse than a sentence he imposed on 213 people without any sense of due process, without any right, without any decency." He went on, "The person who is responsible for al-'Owhali's death is al-'Owhali. He knew what he was doing. He had a free choice, and he went ahead and did it, and don't let anyone put that weight on you."

Baugh distinguished his role from that of the prosecution. "I'm fortunate in this case . . . because we get to come in here and argue for life. We get to argue for peace. We get to argue for reconciliation. . . . Too many people have died. Now, can I guarantee or can anyone guarantee that it will have any impact on stopping this killing? Probably not. But can it hurt? Could it possibly change one mind that thinks that America is indifferent to the suffering of those people? Yes."

The very nature of the crimes was bound to cause the factor of whether the perpetrators posed a continuing danger to weigh heavily on the jury. The defense attempted to demonstrate the Bureau of Prison's (BOP) capacity to control dangerous offenders by reading into the record the Attorney General's directive that allows for prisoners to be held under special administrative measures (SAMs), which stipulate isolation inside a cell for twenty-three hours a day, with only one hour of solitary recreation in an outdoor pen. Whenever the prisoner is moved from one place to another, it is with hands and legs shackled and under escort by three guards.

Addressing al-'Owhali's future dangerousness, Baugh contended that nobody in the courtroom feared him.

Fitzgerald was livid. The fact was that al-'Owhali's hands had been chained throughout the proceedings as a result of a violent incident at the outset of the trial when he tried to lunge toward the bench, ostensibly to get at the judge, but was restrained by the marshals. This was carefully concealed. Throughout the trial, the defendants were seated at a long table with drapery placed specifically so that jurors would not see that they were shackled out of concern that the perception they were dangerous might be prejudicial.

Outside the presence of the jury, Fitzgerald addressed Sand: "Judge, we have a situation where someone asked us to refrain from offering the courtroom incident. We haven't put in, obviously, the shackles. Then he [Baugh] takes advantage of that to argue to the jury that Mr. al-'Owhali has behaved well in court, when he knows that to be wrong, and we withheld proof on that basis."

Sand didn't contain his annoyance with Baugh: "We spent hours and hours making clear what the consequences of any misconduct would be."

According to Gasiorowski, the shackling wasn't a particularly big deal: "It was something that came with the territory. These guys were accused of horrific crimes. Besides, there was evident security right behind the defense table, marshals every four feet. They wore suits, but still, it was obvious this was a high-security setting."[7]

Trying to explain the basis of his comment, Baugh said, "Your Honor, I have sat next to this man, and I have my associate sitting next to him, and there has never, ever been . . . a problem. That's what I'm talking about."

"Officer Pepe probably could make the same comment about Mr. Salim," Sand retorted sharply, in reference to a horrific incident that would be discussed at length during K. K.'s hearing.

Baugh was incensed that the Judge would draw any connection between his client and Salim: "The broad brush you paint this young man with because he's Arab, and the people who attacked Officer Pepe were, is improper."

"Do not accuse me of being a racist," Sand shot back, "because there is no justification for that, and for you to say that I reach any conclusion because a defendant is an Arab is unspeakable."

"Your Honor, to me, it is not unspeakable and I don't mind saying it."

Sand struck from the record Baugh's reference to al-'Owhali's good conduct as prisoner and defendant.

Late in the afternoon of June 5, the jury began deliberations. It took nearly four days before they returned with a verdict on June 12.

They concluded unanimously that the gateway factors were proven beyond a reasonable doubt on all counts. As well, they found for all statutory aggravators on all counts. They agreed, furthermore, on all nonstatutory aggravators, except for future dangerousness, on which they were split. On the mitigating factors, the jury was divided. Eight found it to be a mitigator that other participating conspirators would not face the death penalty. Ten found that al-'Owhali's sincere belief that he was acting in accordance with his religious faith and believed the embassy was a legitimate military target was mitigating. And five found it mitigating that he was indoctrinated to believe in martyrdom at a formative age.

As is their right, the jurors introduced five mitigators of their own. Ten found that executing him would make him a martyr to al Qaeda's cause. Nine found that executing him would not necessarily alleviate the victims' suffering. Four believed that lethal injection was humane and that the defendant would not suffer. Five believed that life imprisonment represented a harsher punishment than death. Four found it mitigating that he was raised in a completely different culture and belief system.

It is noteworthy that some members of the jury voted against the death penalty, not to spare al-'Owhali, but because they perceived that they were actually imposing a harsher fate by voting for life imprisonment. Thus, the jury did not unanimously find that death was the appropriate sentence. As a result, the only option available to the court was life without possibility of parole.

"The jury was very thoughtful and very insightful," Gasiorowski said. "It showed that they really thought about what the justice system is supposed to do and what punishment is meant to be."[8]

The penalty phase for K. K. commenced on Tuesday June 19. He faced fifteen capital counts. The government cited exactly the same gateway factors and statutory and nonstatutory aggravators as for al-'Owhali.

The defense offered a dozen mitigators. He was not, they argued, a leader or organizer of the conspiracy, but was, in fact, considered expendable. His role in the murders was relatively minor, and others, who were more culpable, were not facing the death penalty. Moreover, as a matter of South African law, K. K. should never have been released into U.S. custody without prior assurance that he would not face the death penalty. K. K. was truthful in his postarrest statement, accepted responsibility for his acts, and provided valuable information to investigators. If not sentenced to death, they tried to reassure, he would be incarcerated for the rest of his life. He had no prior criminal history. His execution would cause his family to suffer grief and loss. He was remorseful and would never participate in such crimes in the future. He acted out of sincere religious belief and was only twenty-five when he committed the crimes. If executed, he would be seen as a martyr and his death could be exploited to justify future attacks. Because K. K. exhibited responsible conduct in other areas of his life, had shown himself capable of kindness, friendship, and generosity, and because he worked to support his family following the death of his father, he deserved to be spared.

Garcia countered by speaking of K. K.'s arrest more than a year after the bombing and how, even after having so much time to reflect, he, in fact, did not express remorse, telling investigators he was happy when he saw the news reports of the bombing. Not only that, but he said that he would have participated in more attacks against America had he not been apprehended. If released, he added with bravado, he would go back on the offensive.

As with al-'Owhali, the government began with a presentation of victim impact statements. Eight came from Tanzania to speak, including Asha Kambenga, whose husband, Omari Nyumba, was an embassy guard. He worked twelve-hour shifts six days a week to support his family. "When I heard the news [of his death], I fell down and I lose consciousness," she testified. Asha was twenty-two and her daughter four in 1998. "I don't have even the tuition to send my daughter to go to school. I can't afford that. Life is so difficult, and sometimes we don't even eat."

Henry Kessey was the mission's audits examiner. After the blast, he spent three weeks in the hospital in Dar before being transferred to Nairobi to undergo a cornea transplant. By 2001, he still found it difficult to work because his eyesight wouldn't allow him to focus on paperwork for extended periods without rest. Nonetheless, he remained responsible for the support of his entire extended family, including his mother, five siblings, and their children.

"If I lost my eye completely, it means I will not be able to work again, now I am going to turn to be a burden to my family and I don't want that to happen," he said. "So I was thinking of committing suicide in order not to be a burden to my family. . . . I'm responsible to my family. My family depends on me. So I have to struggle, you know, in order to do that."

Grace Paul described to the court how her seven-year-old daughter stares at a photo of her father, Elisa, in his pressed security guard uniform and insists that he is just away at work, speaking of him with immense pride in her voice.

Mohamed Jelani Mohamed spoke of the impact of the death of his uncle Abdurahman, a teacher who had played a key role as head of his family, a respected person in their village, and a preacher at the local mosque. His death was a loss for his entire community and a constant source of grief for his immediate family.

The prospect of future dangerousness became frighteningly real on November 1, 2000, calling into doubt whether SAMs were adequate to ensure secure confinement of terrorist prisoners and to protect society. Fitzgerald emphasized that reliance on SAMs ignored the constant risk to prison staff. "If he is in jail, he is in a jail of the United States, a sworn enemy, the enemy he wants so badly to kill. To him, the guards in that jail will represent the enemy forever." They will represent an opportunity; his last and only opportunity to strike at America. It had already happened.

In the maximum-security wing of the Metropolitan Corrections Center (MCC), known as 10 South, cellmates were regularly rotated as a security measure to prevent prisoners from bonding too closely. K. K. had been housed with his fellow defendant, Salim, for only five days. On this particular day, Paul McAllister and Charles Adler, two of Salim's court-appointed attorneys, came to see him to prepare for this very trial. Officer Louis Pepe was the lone correctional officer on duty on 10 South.

Salim had proven to be an extremely difficult client. He was uncooperative and it wasn't unusual for him to flatly refuse to meet with his attorneys. Only the week before, his request for new representation had been rejected on the grounds that he was being well served and there was no justification for removing his counsel. (McAllister and Adler would be relieved on November 8 because of what they were about to witness.)

When Pepe went to escort him from his cell to the visiting room, Salim said he hadn't decided whether he wanted to see his lawyers. Pepe could have sent them off then and there. Instead, the officer passed some time exchanging small talk with the lawyers and agreed to return to the cells to offer Salim a second opportunity. This time when he went to the cell, Salim was in the midst of prayer and Pepe did not wish to disturb him. Finally, once he was done, Salim consented to come to the visiting room. He brought with him a file-folder and some CDs. When he arrived, McAllister noted, he was handcuffed. Pepe exited the room and closed the door. Salim backed up to the door, and Pepe removed the cuffs through the tray port, in accordance with procedure.

Salim loaded one of his CDs into the computer, reacting with exasperation when it failed to launch. He demanded to go back to his cell to retrieve other CDs. Pepe was summoned to escort him. Contrary to procedure, he did not apply handcuffs. The two men walked together around a corner, beyond the view of McAllister and Adler.

A few minutes later, the attorneys witnessed a frantic commotion as COs converged on 10 South. They'd been summoned by the sound of Pepe's body alarm, which could be triggered only one of two ways: manually if he was in distress, or automatically because he'd fallen. In either event, it signaled trouble and the response was immediate. However, when the other officers arrived, they discovered that no one had the proper key for the secure door to the wing. It took a long ten minutes before they managed to find a key and get to their stricken colleague.

Officer Roderick Jenkins was at the head of the response column. He saw Salim, his hands covered in blood, running toward his cell holding keys. As Jenkins approached, K. K. lunged at him, squirting a liquid in his face. An FBI chemist would testify that it was a hot sauce available through the prison commissary, and was intended to temporarily blind the officer.

Jenkins, along with other officers, struggled to subdue K. K. while Salim tried to strike at them from behind. Officer Lance Maiden testified that he first saw K. K. as the team approached his cell, and he was poised in a "fighting stance." K. K. struck him in the face during the melee.

Lieutenant Glenn Carrino went immediately to assist the fallen Pepe, and helped guide him to the MCC's hospital. "All he kept telling me was, 'Lieu, I gave them a fight. I gave them a fight. I fought back.'" Elise Santulli, a prison employee who stayed with Pepe while he received first aid, rode with him in the ambulance, and remained with him at the hospital, also said that he indicated putting up a fight with "them."

K. K.'s defense called into question whether Pepe ever said that he gave *them*—plural—a fight, or could have referred to *him*—Salim in the singular, thereby indicating that K. K. was not involved in the assault. A statement taken from Santulli by the FBI at the hospital suggested that Pepe had said nothing to her except in reference to his physical condition.

The next thing McAllister saw was Salim being dragged by several guards, leaving a slick trail of blood along the floor. He was so lifeless that McAllister actually thought he was dead. They stopped just in front of the window through which he was watching. A guard pulled a blunt key off his belt and jabbed Salim in the corner of the eye with it, causing a spurt of blood. Then, he watched as Pepe was assisted down the corridor by four officers. He was covered in blood and a long object was protruding from his left eye.

McAllister was shocked by the sight. In the tough and unforgiving world of prisons, Pepe was well known for his humanity.

"Exceptionally courteously," McAllister replied when Garcia asked how Pepe treated prisoners. "He was really very well regarded and he treated them well."

"And would he do certain things for the prisoners that other guards would not do?"

"One example was that he occasionally didn't cuff them with short visits, and I think he would, again, just typical of his behavior was his going back to the client on the day that we visited to bring a message back and forth about whether we would be visiting. That would not be unusual behavior [for Pepe]."

David Stern, who continued to believe that K. K. was innocent of the assault, concurs: "Pepe was a gentle and caring person who wanted to make things as humane as possible for the prisoners. He was specifically nice to K. K. Unfortunately, it's a fine line between being kind and careless. Salim was very clever and very ruthless. He didn't distinguish between kindness and weakness."[9]

For all his gentleness of spirit, Pepe was a formidable presence, standing only five foot seven but a stocky 270 pounds. He was also a member of the Disturbance Control Team, for which he was trained to respond to, and quell, any altercations, from an unruly individual to a full-scale riot.

Pepe's life was very much in jeopardy when he arrived at Bellevue Hospital. Salim had stabbed him so hard with a sharpened comb that it penetrated all the way through his eyeball, wedging into the bone at the back of the eye socket, and a further two and a half inches deep into his brain. He required immediate surgery to extract the comb and remove a blood clot that was pressing against his brain. The eye was completely destroyed and had to be cut out. Pepe's condition was further complicated when he suffered a stroke a couple of days after the attack. As a result, his ability to communicate was severely impaired, his capacity to understand language was diminished, and he suffered partial paralysis to his right arm and leg. Along with the total loss of his left eye, the right-hand field of vision in his right eye was seriously diminished.

Fitzgerald spoke to the jury about Salim's physical condition. He'd suffered a dramatic weight loss since he'd been in custody, shedding some thirty pounds. He suffered from asthma. He had a bad back. How, he asked, could this man possibly have single handedly overpowered the 270 pound Pepe? How could Salim have done it, except with K. K.'s help? And why was K. K. holding a jar of hot sauce when responding officers arrived on the scene?

Because, Fitzgerald answered, hot sauce was part of the plan. The hot sauce was to be sprayed in the guards' eyes. If he wasn't part of the plan, what was he doing with the hot sauce? "That's the key," he insisted.

David Ruhnke rose to refute the prosecution's version of what transpired, "Khalfan Mohamed had no knowledge that Officer Pepe was going to be attacked. He did not participate in a plan to attack Officer Pepe. He did nothing to attack or injure Officer Pepe."

Though it was a perilous line of argument, Ruhnke, nevertheless, suggested that Pepe was at fault, for failing to follow proper procedure in handling a maximum-security inmate like Salim. Pepe should never have opened the door to the visiting room without first applying his handcuffs. Prisoners are always supposed to be cuffed when in direct physical contact with a CO.

As well, Ruhnke said, the Bureau of Prisons was responsible for leaving Pepe the lone officer on a maximum-security wing, also a violation of procedure.

Staffing was so short that attorneys would sometimes have to yell out for ten or fifteen minutes, even holding up a pad of paper to block video cameras, in the hope of attracting an officer's attention when they were done with a client.

Being anything less than vigilant around Salim was especially reckless because he was known to be disgruntled. Ruhnke asked McAllister, "Did he [Salim] tell you he was falsely accused?"

"Yes."

"Did Mr. Salim complain to you about the violation of his legal rights?"

"Yes."

"Did Mr. Salim . . . complain about your representation to a judge?"

"Yes."

"As the time for trial approached, did you observe Mr. Salim start becoming increasingly angry and frustrated and upset about events?"

"Yes."

The defense called the other attorney present on the day of the attack. Charles Adler confirmed that Salim claimed to have been wrongly accused, complained frequently about the conditions of his confinement, and wanted new representation. He had sought severance from his codefendants, which motion was denied on the same grounds as other motions to sever: that separate trials would entail substantial repetition of the same evidence and, therefore, unnecessary duplication of expense.

Ruhnke conceded that K. K. fought with responding officers, but argued, "probably in an effort, he thought, to save his life." K. K. suffered fractures to his nose and eye socket.

"We do have evidence," he went on, "that there was at least some overreaction by some of the guards, physical force over and above what was necessary to subdue Mr. Mohamed and Mr. Salim." However, he acknowledged, "Pepe paid a price that makes this appear to be nothing. But he paid the price, and the injuries he received, were not at the hands of this man, they were at the hands of Mamdouh Mahmud Salim."

Garcia, in contrast, insisted that Salim "lured him [Pepe] back to that cell where this defendant was waiting. Officer Pepe opened the door, stepped in, and was viciously attacked."

Evidence that the assault was a premeditated part of a plot to take hostages and effect an escape was revealed in a note retrieved from the cell K. K. and Salim shared. It read, "We are the Muslims who were falsely accused of bombing the embassy in Africa. We have captured the tenth floor in MCC and we have several lawyers and officials. They are under our full control. We were forced to resort to this solution after we were deprived of our legal rights. We request the immediate release of BLANK and send them outside the U.S. If the government worries about the safety of its citizens, it has to comply with all our demands. Otherwise, it will be responsible for any consequences." It was not, the defense showed, in K. K.'s handwriting.

When he was examining al-Fadl, Stern deliberately established the point that al Qaeda had a well-defined rank structure with bin Laden at the very top and many, many workers far below. Those latter individuals, Stern emphasized, did not make decisions, but followed orders. Salim was among al Qaeda's decision makers. He was even enough of a scholar that his interpretations of the Koran were accepted within the group. Al-Fadl described Salim as bin Laden's "best friend."

Stern asked whether Salim taught new al Qaeda recruits that participation in the type of jihad being fought in Afghanistan was mandatory for a good Muslim? Al-Fadl answered affirmatively. During cross-examination by Ruhnke, Kherchtou had agreed that Salim was held in high esteem within al Qaeda. The purpose of all this was to establish Salim's superiority over as insignificant a pawn as K. K., someone far too lowly for Salim to ever trust as a partner in the assault against Officer Pepe.

To reinforce the themes of his low status within the group and his impressionability, the defense called Dr. Gerald Post, a psychologist and former CIA analyst who had done extensive research on the psychology of terrorists—both within the intelligence community and as an academic. He was given the opportunity to interview K. K. for several hours over the course of four meetings, as well as Odeh, once for about forty-five minutes.

K. K., Post said, had a predisposition to defer to authority and obey instructions. Post described as "poignant" a moment when Hussein, who had recruited him to partake in a jihad job, ordered K. K. to stop asking questions about the operation, just go fetch him a Fanta. "When he told me this story, he looked rather pained because it had, I think, become kind of clear to him just how down the totem pole he was, what a minor actor he was."

When Post asked what he thought about the bombing now, K. K. "was really horrified, especially with some of the pictures of the victims, and said to me, 'I guess I should have thought of this, those innocent victims.' And tears came to his eyes as he said that. . . . He said, 'My understanding of the Koran is that . . . there are no circumstances that justify taking innocent victims, and had I asked questions or thought, I now regret that I did not ask more questions about what they were doing.'"

When closing, Fitzgerald was contemptuously dismissive of Post, saying to the jury, "You know a lot more about al Qaeda than he did. What was he doing here? To give a dog and pony show, to stand up and say, 'I'm an expert, I spent a half-hour with Odeh.'

" . . . Dr. Post was a fraud. That was a fraud put on you to make you think that Khalfan Mohamed was remorseful."

In closing, Stern denied that the government had proven future dangerousness because it hadn't proven beyond a reasonable doubt that K. K. was a willing participant in the attack on Pepe. "It's all speculation, mine and his [the prosecutor]. Don't confuse that for proof beyond a reasonable doubt." As for the words attributed by witnesses to Pepe, Stern wondered, "He says I gave *him* a fight, I gave *them* a fight. You think he was really saying those precise words?"

According to the account Salim gave at his sentencing, he'd complained bitterly to K. K. when his motion for a new attorney was denied. K. K. agreed to assist in the assault "in part to atone of his 'sin' of testifying in a way that led to Salim's imprisonment." As Pepe led him back to their cell, Salim began to sing, a signal to K. K. that the attack was to begin. K. K. grabbed at Pepe's walkie-talkie while Salim knocked the legs out from under him and sprayed hot sauce in his eyes. When Pepe was on the ground, Salim reached for his keys and suddenly "became crazy" and stabbed him through the eye. He left no doubt that K. K. was a willing participant in the vicious incident.[10]

K. K.'s brother, brother-in-law, two sisters, and mother all came to testify on his behalf, speaking well of him and how deeply they would be hurt were he put to death. They were simple people, who had never before been outside of Tanzania. The experience of venturing to the United States and appearing in an American courtroom could only have been overwhelming.

Ruhnke suggested, "One of the things about the death penalty is that it disrespects and disregards the potential that people can change, the potential that people can say I have thought about where I have been and I have thought about where I am going, and where I have been is perhaps not the right place to have been."

He returned to the theme of equal application of the death sentence, invoking Ali Mohamed, the former U.S. Army soldier and al Qaeda trainer who had helped to plan the East Africa attacks, saying, "If justice can be served by striking a deal with Ali Mohamed . . . and allow him to walk free some day, then surely justice can be served by taking Khalfan Mohamed and putting him in a prison from which he will never walk free. And that's one of the points of comparing the involvement of people."

He echoed Baugh, drawing an analogy between the twelve-member jury and the traditional twelve-person firing squad. In the latter instance, one shooter was given a blank so that every squad member could ease their conscience by convincing themselves they were not responsible for the fatal bullet. Ruhnke said that jurors could take no such comfort, because imposing the death penalty demanded unanimity. None, then, could escape the weight of killing K. K.

When closing, Fitzgerald turned this remark on its head, saying that K. K. had fired eleven bullets, one for each of the dead in Dar es Salaam. His twelfth bullet, he added, was fired at Officer Pepe. "He was that firing squad, with no jury, with no trial, with no mitigating factors. He just killed."

Added Garcia, "Khalfan Mohamed has killed and he tried to kill again, and a life sentence for Khalfan Mohamed is a death sentence for the next guard in one of those prisons who makes a mistake. That's the choice. Stop Khalfan Mohamed's mission of murder, and the only penalty that will do that, the only penalty that addresses this crime and the threat this defendant poses every day is the death penalty."

Stern made no attempt to minimize the magnitude of the crimes K. K. committed. But he made a plea for the future and an appeal for optimism: "If you kill him, you say there is no hope, not just for him, but for us. You say there is no hope for the astounding human capacity for change. You destroy the chance that he will age and have the experience we all share. We say, 'If I had only known that before,' and then pass it on to others. You eradicate the hope that others will see the price Khalfan has to pay for what he did. That price, getting old and dying in jail, frightens the young more than death."

He concluded, "In the end, if you give him life, Khalfan will disappear. No one except those he loves will remember him. Someone has to say enough. Someone has to say, I will not hurt another family. Someone has to say, I will not become those I detest by doing what they do and killing in the name of justice. Let that be you."

When Fitzgerald rose to deliver his rebuttal, he sounded perplexed at the defense's effort to make it sound as though circumstances had happened *to* K. K. The truth, he made clear, was that K. K. made choices that *caused* the events that brought him to his current predicament. The bombing didn't happen *to* him, Fitzgerald emphasized, he *did* it. The attack on Officer Pepe didn't happen *to* K. K.; *he* assaulted Pepe. When he confessed to the FBI that he'd participated in the bombing, he didn't express remorse, he threatened to do it again! K. K. was not just someone who fetched Fanta. He was trained to use weapons, he was trained to build bombs, he was trained to kill. He had been to Afghanistan. He had been to Somalia. He was in Dar es Salaam.

"Hussein came to him and asked him to do a jihad job," Fitzgerald reminded the jury. "He gave him a choice. He had free will. He could decide to do the jihad job or not. He's not brainwashed. But he didn't equivocate. No moral struggle. He did it."

Stern disputed Fitzgerald's contention that K. K. felt himself to be a victim of circumstances and denied responsibility for what happened. "It's his fault. He put himself here, but there's a road he took to get here and if you don't understand that road, you can't possibly judge him fairly." He did not dispute that the gateway factors for the death penalty had been established. He also conceded that the verdict proved the presence of the statutory aggravators.

Fitzgerald rejected the notion that K. K. was expendable, as suggested by the fact that he was left behind when all the other conspirators fled Tanzania. No, he was left behind because he was the local guy who knew the language and knew his way around. They needed him to wrap up affairs in Dar. That isn't an indication of expendability; that was his job.

"Al-'Owhali was expendable," said Fitzgerald. "He was supposed to die, but did not. Azzam was expendable. He did die, the driver of the truck in Nairobi. Ahmed the German was expendable. He did die in the truck in Tanzania."

Fitzgerald went on, "Khamis does not have fire in his eyes. What he has is ice in his veins, and that's what makes him more dangerous, because he coldly, coolly, decides, 'I'll kill, I won't look back, I'll go be nice to people in South Africa and I'll come to America.' When the chance is given to attack Officer Pepe, he's in there."

Moreover, you might have a chance if you see fire in someone's eyes, but you can never, ever see ice in their veins. And that is what defines the cold-blooded killer.

Fitzgerald obviously recognized the power in this phrase. So much so that he repeated it a half-dozen times in his speech, causing David Stern to quip in his closing, "Mr. Fitzgerald crafted a very good line: 'He doesn't have fire in his eyes, he has ice in his veins.' Really excellent. You will remember it. Newspapers will write it. But is it really completely true?"

Concluded the prosecution, "I submit to you that the victim impact in this case, the magnitude of the crime, what he did to people is a sufficient reason to vote for the death penalty. When you take other people's lives away so coldly, so callously, after a moral choice to do so, you have lost your right."

Judge Sand charged the jury on July 3. Following the holiday weekend, they deliberated for two full days, returning a verdict on the morning of July 10. They found each gateway factor and all statutory aggravators had been proven beyond a reasonable doubt for all fifteen capital counts. On the nonstatutory aggravators, they did not find unanimously that the government had proven future dangerousness. They did find the defendant's acts posed a hardship to the victims and that he was motivated by the desire to kill high-ranking officials of the U.S. government serving abroad.

On the mitigators, ten found that K. K.'s role was minor in the context of the overall plot. Eleven agreed it was mitigating that others of equal or greater culpability would not be sentenced to death. Nine agreed that he was truthful in his postarrest statement to the authorities and that he accepted his responsibility. As well, nine found that his lack of criminal history was mitigating. They were unanimous that his family would suffer grief and loss were he to be executed. None found mitigation in his expression of remorse. Nine agreed that he had acted out of sincere belief. All took into account his age at the time of the offense. Seven were concerned that his death could be exploited for future attacks. In his capacity for kindness and friendship, that he exhibited responsibility in other aspects of his life, and that the loss of his father at an early age made a deep impact on him, ten found mitigation.

The jury came up with two mitigators of their own: nine took into account that his last psychological report, dated March 2001, concluded that his potential to harm others was low. Three adjudged that life imprisonment was a harsher punishment than being put to death. Ultimately, then, the jury failed to reach a unanimous verdict. As a result, K. K. was sentenced to life without possibility of parole.

Court was adjourned until sentencing, set for September 19, 2001. Of course, this was a mere formality, as the defendant's guilt, and the jury's rejection of the death penalty in the cases of al-'Owhali and Mohamed, required life without possibility of parole.

An urban legend circulated that September 11 was selected for the attack against the World Trade Center and Washington because sentences were to be handed down in the bombing trial on that day.[11] In fact, in early August, the date of sentencing was pushed back from September 19 to early October,[12] besides which, planning for 9/11 must have been far too advanced by the time the trial had progressed to its final phase for it to revolve around the vagaries of the court's timetable.[13]

In the wake of 9/11, the defense thought October was too soon to return. Smoke was still rising from the ashes of Ground Zero.

"It was tough walking into court because you felt as if anything you said was trumped," said Josh Dratel. "I remember sitting there, thinking, 'I can't believe I have to get up and make arguments.' I felt like there was a desire to get this out of the way, to get this chapter closed without further ado."[14]

[13] SALIM

Mamdouh Mahmud Salim was forty years old when he was arrested by German police, acting on a request from the FBI and CIA, on September 16, 1998, near Munich. Though he denied any association with bin Laden, Bavaria's Interior Ministry was prepared to extradite him.[1] On September 29, charges were filed against him in New York for conspiracy to attack U.S. military sites abroad, conspiracy to commit murder, and use of weapons of mass destruction.[2] He was alleged to have made false statements to German law enforcement officials and FBI agents over the course of several days' questioning. On December 20, he was returned to the United States.

Salim was to have been the fifth codefendant at trial. However, the need to recuse his attorneys for having witnessed the assault against Officer Pepe at the MCC would have resulted in an inordinately burdensome delay. It would have been extremely costly, have caused significant hardship for witnesses who had traveled a great distance to testify, and left the other defendants in an extended limbo. Consequently, the government chose to drop him from the bombing case in favor of charging him with conspiracy to murder and the attempted murder of the CO. Since he wasn't facing the death penalty in any event, the consequences, should he be found guilty, promised to be the same—life imprisonment.

His initial defense strategy was to claim temporary insanity. Prior to the attack, Salim had experienced progressive weight loss, dropping from 185 pounds when he was arrested in 1998 to 155 by November 2000. He reported feeling increasingly "hateful, angry and humiliated" during his incarceration. In particular, he was enraged by the strip searches to which he was regularly subjected. He felt "sad all day" and was no longer, he said, a "very cheerful person." He worried constantly about his family.

According to an evaluation prepared by a government psychiatrist who spent nearly thirteen hours examining him, Salim claimed to have "lost his ability to freely forgive others for transgressions and he felt extremely lonely and he thought about ending his life, but never made any effort toward doing so because Islam forbids such action." Nonetheless, "he had been battling for control of himself, with a part of himself which wants to violate his 'principles,' including to act violently." Asked to describe his mental/emotional state, Salim said he felt "hopeless, grieving, angry," "no control over myself," "doing things against my will," "anything I did that day, I was not the same person, maybe it was my body."

Asked specifically to explain his actions on November 1, Salim said, "I wanted to escape this ridiculous condition," and, "Since I did nothing, I have the right to be with my family." He was convinced that he had a chance to escape from the MCC.

On June 26, 2001, Barry Rosenfeld, a clinical psychologist, examined Salim. He concluded that "several factors limit the conclusiveness of the evaluation, including Mr. Salim's apparent lack of candor in both reporting his psychiatric symptoms (i.e., apparently exaggerating his psychological problems) and refusing to discuss many aspects of the instant offense."

Salim claimed that his decision to attack Pepe was a response to the voice of what he called "the creature," telling him, "Now, now is the day you take the key—it's a chance—if you miss it today, you'll regret it." Rosenfeld assessed that Salim's claim of auditory hallucinations was "possible," but "much more likely is the possibility that Mr. Salim fabricated this symptom in an effort to explain the instant offense as due to the stress of his confinement."

Salim ended up pleading guilty on April 3, 2002. The government sought life imprisonment under sentencing guidelines applicable to a crime deemed an act of terrorism, citing his plan to seize hostages and escape. However, Salim argued he was motivated simply by his frustration over the magistrate's decision not to assign him new council when he sought to replace McAllister and Addler. His plan was not to escape, he asserted, but to incapacitate Pepe and get hold of his keys so he could return to the visiting room and assault his attorneys, an act he was sure would cause them to withdraw and force the court to provide him with new representation.

Judge Deborah A. Batts ruled that the assault did not constitute an act of terrorism "because there is no evidence that defendant's attack on Officer Pepe involved conduct transcending national boundaries,"[3] and sentenced him to thirty-two years.

The government appealed the sentence, and the appellate court ruled that the application of the terrorism guidelines was not dependant on any "transnational conduct."[4] It found that the trial judge had erred in not applying the guidelines.

Thus, on August 31, 2010, Salim's sentence was extended to life without parole. Judge Batts was clearly not upset at being overturned, saying, "The cold immediacy of the precision with which he plunged the sharpened weapon deeply into the eye of the downed but struggling man is appalling."[5]

The repercussions from the attack on the other terrorism prisoners housed at the MCC were intense. COs came to perceive each of them as grave threats to their safety and were furious over the severe injuries inflicted on Pepe. The maximum-security wing was kept on lockdown for two weeks, during which time attorneys were prevented from seeing their clients.

"By the time we got in there, el Hage was in bad shape," recalls Dratel. He was, according to the attorney, roughed up, pushed into walls, picked up and thrown on his head. He was subject to frequent strip searches and orifice probes, which are extremely humiliating. The lights were kept on in the cells at all times. It was freezing cold. He was denied such amenities as a tooth brush, on the grounds that it could be sharpened into a deadly weapon in the same fashion as Salim had done with the comb.

"Our conclusion," Dratel went on, "was that it was a façade of security that allowed prison officials to be extremely harsh with him, and to exact retribution for his being, from their perspective, a terrorist."[6]

A motion was submitted on behalf of el Hage to delay the proceedings against him on the grounds that he was no longer competent to participate in his own defense. He became borderline catatonic for a time and claimed amnesia. However, a psychiatric evaluation ruled he was malingering. This does not mean faking, as in the vernacular, but merely that there was no clinical basis for diagnosing an illness. As a result, Sand denied the motion.

Following this incident, there was no way he could be called to testify on his own behalf.

"In the state of mind he was in at the time, it was impossible to get him to focus sufficiently for him to make a good witness," said Sam Schmidt. "It was a tough decision, because to get the full benefit of the presumption of innocence, you want the jury to see the defendant as a human being and to feel some resistance against finding him guilty, but it wasn't possible."[7]

Odeh, too, felt the wrath of the MCC. "The conditions at 10 South were terrible," said Edward Wilford. "It's tough to go in there just to have a conversation with somebody, imagine being in there twenty-four hours a day."[8]

How very gravely he had underestimated life. His own he had hated, and had wished away; but see how long it was taking to absent itself—and with what helpless grief was he watching it go, imperturbable in its beauty and its power. Even as his flesh fried and his blood boiled, there was life, kissing its fingertips, then it echoed out, and ended.
—Martin Amis, "The Last Days of Muhammad Atta," *New Yorker,* April 24, 2006

[14] SUPERMAX

After observing the accused on a daily basis over several months, Judge Sand offered, "I have no doubts about the sincerity of the defendants. I don't know of any motivation other than their beliefs." He paused thoughtfully before adding, "That makes them more dangerous."[1]

Those convicted for the African embassy bombings have been dropped into the void at the super-maximum-security facility in Florence, Colorado, under strict SAMs. They live in total isolation, except for perfunctory contact with prison staff. As a result of the assault against Officer Pepe, terrorist prisoners are handled with absolutely rigid adherence to procedure. For twenty-three hours of the day, they are alone in their cell. For the remaining hour they are brought to a pen where they can exercise alone. Their situation is harsh and hostile. It's difficult to imagine that any one of them has much to think about other than his sins, whether he perceives those to be of commission or omission.

Josh Dratel believes that the harsh application of SAMs is meant to compensate for their having escaped the death penalty, "As if ordinary prison is really too good for them. There has to be a way to ratchet up the punishment so they can suffer more."[2]

Of the supermax, Schmidt said, "It's about the worst in our country. I think it's inhumane and inappropriate. Being incarcerated there, el Hage is troubled."[3]

The medical literature shows that solitary confinement has a deep psychological impact on prisoners. There seems to be a consensus that incarceration in isolation for periods exceeding three months causes "serious psychiatric symptoms." The sensory deprivation of the stress concrete cell and the absence of human contact leaves inmates confined in solitary to suffer mental torpor, frustration, anger, anxiety, hypersensitivity, and agitation. Thoughts can become confused and obsessive.[4]

Without a past on which to reminisce fondly or a future on which to project hope, the mind tends to spin like a gyroscope unable to find its bearing. Life without possibility for parole is life without possibility.

Approaching a fork in the road between life and death at breakneck speed, human nature reflexively veers to life. Horrifyingly, the suicide terrorist breaks the grip of this primal instinct and turns toward death. Of course, of these defendants, only al-'Owhali ever agreed to die for the cause. But he too, given a split second, grabbed onto his last ditch opportunity to survive.

"People find solace in life," David Stern said reflectively when addressing how K. K. copes with his prospects in Florence. "He does his time uncomplainingly, living as best he can. He is treated professionally by the staff. He has grown a tremendous amount, and he's done it all on his own. He has thought deeply about what he did. It was a terrible thing. He killed people doing menial labor. And he's dealing with the consequences with dignity."[5]

Is this remorse? Only K. K. could say. Removed from the camaraderie of the jihadi brotherhood, and the reinforcement that comes from the support of people with shared beliefs, remorse may seep through the cracks in his hatred. Whether it is remorse for his own hardship or for his victims, we'll never know. In any event, hopelessness may be cause for remorse in itself.

Al Qaeda invests "significant care and feeding into its operatives. During the investigation into the 2006 aviation plot, the British discovered how often they had to pull people in from the field," said former FBI Agent Joe Billy, referring to an abortive conspiracy to blow up as many as ten Canadian and American flagged trans-Atlantic flights departing from London using liquid explosives disguised as beverages. "You're ready to be a martyr, but maybe not this year. Maybe next. They think a guy's all set to go, then he gets cold feet. So they bring in the spiritual people, put an arm around him. They need a degree of spiritual support to prop them up, keep them on track."[6]

For all that, the most impressive part of al Qaeda operations (and this applies equally to the embassy attacks as to 9/11) is the discipline of the conspirators. There weren't many defections during its formative years. You didn't see serious indiscretions. You rarely observed the kind of careless behavior that typically leads to cells being exposed. The ruthless dedication of the participants over the course of years and the steadfastness of those who've agreed to die is undeniably impressive.

"K. K. was very young when he got involved in all this," Stern went on. "I'm sure he experiences horrendous moments when he thinks ahead. He's losing his hair, and that causes him to contemplate the passing of time, that he'll never have children."

When Stern speaks of K. K. he sounds protective. "Al Qaeda doesn't care about liim. He's nobody to anyone. They abandoned him over in Africa, and they've abandoned him here."

He makes no attempt to excuse, only to humanize. "We [defense attorneys] have the good fortune to see the humanity in people who have done horrific things, to learn why they are so damaged. K. K. could have been something different, but something happened."[7]

"Aside from what drove him to this, he wouldn't hurt a fly, unless he received an order from a religious leader he worshipped, in which case he'd do almost anything," Fredrick Cohn said about al-'Owhali, adding, "Or at least he would have. I don't know what he would do today. He's a different person than he was then. He's been in a solitary cell for ten years now."

He's staged several hunger strikes, usually in a bid to improve the conditions of his confinement. On occasion, it has gotten to the point where he had to be force-fed. "I wouldn't say he's unbalanced. He's affected by his situation. There's no view that the government will ever do anything sensible like put him in general population. Essentially, this is a form of torture, in my opinion." Cohn goes on, "He's treated, I guess, as decently as you can treat anybody, but he lives in a cell. He never sees the sky, everything is made out of stress concrete. When we've seen him, it's through glass. He's handcuffed. Who knows how he's functioning?"[8]

Cohn seems ambivalent when reflecting on al-'Owhali, "We aren't friends, but I like him. He's a highly moral man. His morality is different than yours or mine, but he's highly moral. I don't believe he would hurt anyone, except for his moral purpose. He's not the same as your average thug. Salim, he's a thug. People like him gravitate to terrorism because it's a place where they can express their rage. Al-'Owhali is not like that."[9]

[15] HARUN

We know a great deal about Harun, one of the leaders of the East Africa cell and a key logistician for the embassy bombings, because of the diary he kept between 1998 and January 2009. Khalid Sheikh Mohammed, the mastermind of 9/11, was aware he was writing it and encouraged him to turn it into a book. Compiled in two volumes under the title *War against Islam: The Story of Fazul Harun*, it ultimately ran to more than eleven hundred pages and was published on a jihadi website. It was eventually removed, likely because some mujahideen objected to its content.[1] American authorities became aware of it when they found an early draft during the course of searching his home in Moroni in the aftermath of the attacks.

Harun posted his memoir to serve as a "corrective history," a reminder of what the "original" al Qaeda stood for, and, to his mind, the ideals from which the jihadi movement had strayed since 9/11, with the emergence of regional variations, including al Qaeda in the Islamic Maghreb (AQIM), al Shabab of Somalia, al Qaeda in Iraq, and al Qaeda in the Arabian Peninsula. He was very critical of the new generation of mujahideen who flew the al Qaeda banner yet had little contact with, and did not get direction from, the organization's central leadership. To Harun, publishing his book represented an opportunity for the old guard to distinguish themselves from upstarts who, he worried, were espousing a more intolerant Islam than his beloved "original" al Qaeda, and risked alienating the Muslim masses from whom the jihad needed to draw support.

Harun had begun studying the Koran at a Wahhabi madrassa in the Comoros in 1977, when he was only four, memorizing it by the time he was nine. Despite his tender age, he gave religious instruction on a local radio program. At fourteen, he went to Karachi on a scholarship for further Wahhabi studies. He was described as a "tightly wound, brilliant student of the Koran."[2] Devout, but not doctrinally zealous, he wasn't shy to denounce those who were driven by a rigid theology.

His ambition to serve the entire Muslim community as a fighter against all the injustices it suffered is what inspired him to move to Peshawar in 1991 to join the Afghan jihad. He was drawn to al Qaeda because it shared his notion of a cosmopolitan Islam and he appreciated how every Muslim was welcome at its guesthouses, irrespective of their country of origin. This would obviously appeal to an African, who probably felt excluded from groups with a more nationalist agenda, like Ayman al-Zawahiri's EIJ.

The "original al Qaeda," as Harun would later refer to the early leadership with whom he felt such strong kinship, embraced the global Muslim *umma* and rejected the sovereign nation-state, which served as the power base for those Muslim leaders it vilified as apostates. Al Qaeda's vision was to have "all work under the same roof, follow the same path under a single direction . . . we were all holding different nationalities, [yet united] in one group," he wrote.[3] In contrast, the regional groups reinforced the petty sovereignties that weakened their collective influence. "We blame our regimes for their lack of unity and yet we divided ourselves according to the borders that the colonizer drew for us," he lamented.[4]

Mohamed Odeh expressed similar sentiments according to the testimony of FBI Special Agent John Anticev: "He liked al Qaeda because it represented the whole Muslim world. Al Qaeda was Islamically pure and . . . the leadership in other groups might do things that were not Islamically correct."

Obviously, this was a highly idealized impression, given that the feeling of being treated as a second-class member was what had so disenchanted the Sudanese Jamal al-Fadl, culminating in his breaking from the organization.

FBI Agent Ali Soufan disputes Harun's version of al Qaeda's global vision. "Different issues from across the Muslim world drew people to the group. In fact, most recruiting was based on local issues. At one point the Saudis encouraged young men to join the anti-Soviet jihad to export their problems and relieve internal pressures, and also wanted to extend the influence of the Wahhabi school against Iran's export of its Shiite revolution. Egyptian members were upset over their government's accord with Israel."[5]

In May 1998 Harun rented the villa at 43 New Runda Estates, Nairobi, where the bomb that destroyed the embassy was assembled. Harun was to remain in Nairobi following the attack to oversee the cleaning of the villa.[6] A day before the bombing, he informed his landlord that he had to leave suddenly because his father-in-law had taken ill. They met the next day so she could check that all was in order with the villa and he returned the keys. Until investigators spoke with her later, she hadn't known what had gone on at her property and, in a tragic irony, the landlord's brother-in-law, an embassy employee, would die in the bombing.

By August 14, Harun returned to his native Moroni, capital of the tiny Indian Ocean island nation of Comoros. He knew this was not a safe refuge as authorities there kept records of every arrival and departure. It was almost foolhardy of him, but even the most disciplined operative can succumb to sentimentality, often associated with family, upon whom such great burdens are hung. In this case, Harun wanted to bid farewell to his wife, Halima.

A thorough analysis of phone records from the Nairobi premises associated with the bombers led Bureau investigators to the residence of Harun's mother, his wife, and her family in the Comoros. Following on this promising clue, Pat D'Amuro led a team of FBI investigators and a hostage rescue team over from Nairobi on September 2. They came armed with a federal warrant issued in the Southern District of New York charging him with twelve counts of murder (one for each U.S. official who was killed), conspiracy to murder, and the use of a weapon of mass destruction. Since the only plane they could requisition was too small to carry everyone, they had to fly over in two sorties.

In the company of local police, they raided two homes in Moroni. Concerned about the reception they'd receive, they came in hard. The Comoran police tipped Harun's father-in-law out of his bed, even though he was ill with a bleeding ulcer and had a catheter. Later that day, he collapsed and died.[7] His wife Halima, brother Omar, and sister-in-law were all taken in for questioning.

Halima's deposition before a magistrate in Moroni revealed that she was kept in the dark about her husband's life. Though cousins, the two had met on only a few occasions before their arranged marriage in 1994. Asked about what he was doing while they lived in Sudan from 1994 to 1996, she replied, "I don't know as I left the house rarely. I simply went to visit others in the Comoran community in Sudan. My husband never spoke about where he worked. We spent two years there. . . . I did nothing in Sudan. I simply brought up my child. I do not know the address of our house in Sudan in 1995. We returned to the Comoros in May '96 with Fazul [Harun] and my child. I stayed for two months and he left three weeks later. I returned to Kenya in June and Fazul told me that he was working in a nongovernmental organization."[8] She knew the organization was called Help Africa People, and she was acquainted with Wadih el Hage, whose cover was serving as its director, and his wife. Asked whether she shared her husband's political and religious views, she answered, "I didn't know."[9]

Computers, diskettes, a camera, CDs and tapes, letters, passports, birth certificates, two copies of the Koran, newspaper clippings, and men's clothing were all seized.[10] It was reported that Harun possessed Kenyan and French passports and stamps for forging others. One of the letters taken was addressed to his brother Omar after 1991 (it was undated), in which he wrote, "I've done two months in a military base (mujahedin) on heavy weapons (bazookas) for planes and with smaller arms for urban warfare Russian, Israeli arms and another two months on explosives (how to blow up buildings, houses, palaces & etc), then I studied pistols (you fire when you are in a car), learning how you kill a president in full view while he's with his bodyguards. All that stuff I learned. Don't worry. Then I studied topography. That is for the bazookas, if you want to fire on airplanes or boats. The things I learned in the army, the Comoran army and even the police force don't learn. I learned how to plan terrorist acts; I learned how to use a walky-talky etc. Don't tell anyone about all of this."[11]

Also recovered from the home were documents indicating a plot to kill local government officials. "The Comorans were shocked, they didn't know they had that type of activity going on their territory," D'Amuro says.[12] Comoros was generally described as "a country with a relatively liberal Muslim character."[13] However, opportunities for young men being limited, they often accepted invitations to study at religious schools abroad, where they were susceptible to recruitment by fundamentalists. Local officials blamed "poverty, Islam, racism, and French colonialism" for their radical transformation.[14]

With incredulity, D'Amuro recounts how FBI headquarters suggested the agents chase off into the mountains in case Harun was hiding out there. "We're told that cerebral malaria runs rampant up there. We're absolutely drenched in Deet to fight off mosquitoes. There's some incurable parasite in the water that attacks the liver, nobody wants to shower, in case. I managed to convince HQ that all indications were he was no longer on the island."[15]

Police later recovered the transit card he filled out at the airport showing he had, in fact, flown to Dubai on August 22. He told his wife that he was bound for Pakistan.[16] It would later be determined that he continued onward to bin Laden's lair in Afghanistan. Just a week after the raid, the United States posted a $2 million reward for information leading to his arrest.

Harun remained in Afghanistan until 2000, when he returned to East Africa. During this time he was promoted to confidential secretary, a position of great trust, making him a key figure within al Qaeda's leadership. He reported to the administrative branch of the military committee. This certainly implies he was privy to a great deal of operational intelligence. As a measure of his status, he boasted that K. S. M. confided his plans for 9/11 only to him, bin Laden, and Abu Hafs, al Qaeda's military commander, as early as 1999.[17]

He brought a variety of skill sets to his job, including his knowledge of computers, fluency in French, Swahili, and English, and expertise in explosives. He was a highly skilled document forger and would fabricate travel papers for operatives, as well as for bin Laden's wives and children—meaning that he likely knew their whereabouts, a closely guarded secret. He used to shave Osama's head, a very potent sign of the intimacy of their relationship.

Harun was actually arrested in Nairobi on July 12, 2002, along with Saleh Ali Nabhan, for using forged credit cards. A native Mombasan, Nabhan was also a wanted man, suspected of running al Qaeda's Mombasa base and of handling communications directly with bin Laden during preparations for the embassy attacks. They fooled the police by using aliases and soon escaped custody, with tragic consequences.

The two successfully disappeared into Mombasa's teeming Muslim community, where al Qaeda had long had a presence and where they could set about planning their next attack.[18]

With its beautiful Indian Ocean beaches, Mombasa is among tourist-dependent Kenya's most popular destinations. It was a favorite vacation spot for Israelis, who felt safer and more welcome than in Muslim-populated destinations closer to home.

On the morning of November 28, 2002, 261 passengers and crew departed Daniel arap Moi International Airport aboard a regularly scheduled Arkia Israel Air flight to Tel Aviv. Two SA-7 Strela surface-to-air missiles were fired from shoulder-held launchers deployed from the back of a sport utility vehicle. Both just narrowly missed the Boeing 757. At almost the same time, an explosives-packed truck was detonated by two suicide bombers at the entrance of the Paradise Hotel, an Israeli-owned beachfront resort, just as sixty arriving Israelis were being greeted by a troupe of local dancers. Nobody aboard the aircraft was injured. Fifteen people, twelve of them Kenyan, died at the hotel, while another eighty were wounded. Once again, Kenyan victims outnumbered the intended foreign targets. Years later, during a hearing at Guantánamo Bay, the Mombasa attacks were among thirty-one plots in which K. S. M. confessed his involvement.[19]

Harun planned the attack with Abu Talha al Sudani, whose role was to finance the operation. Al Sudani, who was also a suspect in the embassy bombings, had operated primarily out of Somalia for the previous decade and took over leadership of the East Africa cell after Harun fled to Afghanistan. He would later be suspended from al Qaeda and set up his own jihadi operation in Somalia.[20] He was killed in early January 2007 in an ambush carried out jointly by American, Kenyan, and Ethiopian forces.

Nabhan, called by U.S. intelligence sources the mastermind behind the scheme,[21] supervised the construction of the bomb and was the registered owner of the Mitsubishi Pajero in which it was carried. The two who performed the suicide attack, identified as Kenyans Fumo Muhammad Fumo and Harun Abdisheikh Bamusa, were also suspected of taking part in the embassy bombing.[22]

These were al Qaeda's first direct strikes against Israel, and would have been by far the worst terrorist attack in that country's long history of confronting terrorism had the SAMs destroyed their intended target. While there was nothing novel about a suicide truck bombing, the use of a missile against a passenger plane was a new, if not especially unexpected, tactic. So many of these weapons had been distributed to various groups of dubious reliability, and subsequently gone unaccounted for, over the years. With limited, if not nonexistent, perimeter security around most civil airports, commercial jets are fat, juicy ducks as they slowly climb or descend. Israel has declined to confirm whether its commercial carriers are equipped with antimissile countermeasures, whether the missiles fired at the Arkia malfunctioned, or if the shooter, Nabhan, himself, erred.

Australia, which had suffered the loss of more than eighty of its nationals in an al Qaeda bombing at a Bali resort in October, had issued a travel warning on November 12 strongly advising against travel to Kenya in general, and Mombasa in particular. However, the nature of the threat was never specified.[23] Israel was reportedly aware: "Prior to the attack, Israel has received general vague information that al-Qaeda was conducting reconnaissance missions in Kenya in order to carry out terrorist attacks, with no specific details regarding the identity of the target, location or timing. The general information was not indicative to define any concrete threat to Israeli targets. The general nature of the information, which was based on undefined questionable sources, was not enough to match the Israeli intelligence community criteria to issue an alert."[24] This is yet another example of imprecise intelligence, indistinguishable from other such warnings, actually coming to pass. Another instance of the broken clock being accurate twice a day.

Harun professed that he was opposed to killing Muslims, or even non-Muslims, just for the sake of eliminating unbelievers. Though civilians would inevitably be collateral damage, reducing the number of innocent victims ought to be factored in to the target selection process. While Salim was citing ibn Tamiyyah, the thirteenth-century Islamic warrior philosopher, to justify killing whoever happened to be in the vicinity of an al Qaeda attack, Harun quoted the story of how ibn Tamiyyah negotiated with the Tatars for the release of all prisoners, not just the Muslims, being held in his adversary's custody.[25]

Only very late did bin Laden come to realize that killing Muslims threatened to alienate potential sources of support. Documents taken from his final hiding place in Abbottabad showed that he was aware of al Qaeda's waning popularity since those heady post-9/11 days when he seemed ascendant. He wrote that the practice of indiscriminately killing Muslims "would lead us to winning several battles while losing the war in the end." Consequently, he called for future attacks to target U.S. interests in non-Muslim countries.[26]

Harun clearly defined what he considered appropriate targets: the military, first and foremost, followed by political and economic targets. He felt comfortable that 9/11 was a legitimate operation: the Pentagon and the U.S. Capital were obvious objectives, and the World Trade Center, he believed, was a valid economic symbol. Obviously, this is a narrow and self-serving interpretation of who constitutes an innocent civilian. To justify turning every person who happens to be inside the World Trade Center at any given moment into a legitimate target means, in effect, that there are no practical limitations on operations.

As an example of the just operational limits and principles he imputed to the "original" al Qaeda, Harun wrote that the Israeli Embassy in Nairobi was initially under consideration as a target, but was, he maintained, spared for the unlikely humanitarian reason that it was located near a school and that it would be Islamically incorrect to kill Kenyan children.[27] He insisted—perhaps because he needed to believe—that fewer Kenyans were killed in the bombing than was reported, and that there were more American casualties than has ever been admitted.[28]

Like all who have sought moral justification for inherently immoral positions, Harun ultimately lost his footing. When faced with a clear ethical choice, he simply evaded. For example, he rationalized the attacks on the Mombasa hotel and the Arkia jetliner by denying that any Israeli is a true civilian, therefore all are fair game as military targets. He doesn't explain the legitimacy of killing Kenyan dancers. In his memoir, he glosses over the 2002 bombing of a synagogue in Tunis—obviously directed against Tunisian Jews—which, by his own logic, he could not legitimize.

During his years on the run, Harun had enough narrow escapes to make a cat envious of his many lives. In addition to the post-embassy raid to capture him in the Comoros and his escape from Kenyan custody just before the Mombasa attacks, he evaded capture in August 2003, when the person with whom he was staying in Mombasa blew himself up with a hand grenade as police moved in to arrest them. In October 2003, he missed a meeting with a colleague turned informant, who was setting him up. In January 2007, he, al-Sudani, and Nabhan survived U.S. air strikes aimed at killing them at al Qaeda's Ras Kamboni training camp in Somalia.

Nabhan would be killed on September 14, 2009, during a U.S. Special Forces attack against a convoy near Barawe. He was thirty at the time. Media reports suggested that Harun succeeded Nabhan as leader of al Qaeda in the Horn of Africa, which, if such an organization existed, would have been a cell responding to bin Laden's direction, not a franchise operation.[29]

"He [Harun] was certainly one of the leading al Qaeda figures in East Africa," said Rashid Abdi, an analyst with the International Crisis Group.[30] An unnamed American adviser called him "a main conduit between the East Africa extremists and big Al Qaeda."[31]

By 2007, Harun found that his situation in Somalia had become tenuous. So much so that he sent his wife, Halima—who had only recently rejoined him from Waziristan—along with a number of other jihadis' wives and children across the border into Kenya, where they would be safer. In the event that she was ever taken into custody by local authorities, he instructed her to inform them of her identity. Explaining why in his autobiography, he wrote, "The moment the Europeans and Americans found out that the wife of Fadil Harun was in the custody of Kenyan authorities, they would want to interrogate her themselves. . . . I wanted her file to be transferred from the Africans to the Americans because the latter would treat her with respect."[32]

In August 2008, Kenyan police raided a house in the coastal town of Malindi, but again Harun eluded them. Police confirmed that he had been at that location because they found two passports issued in names that he was known to use. An ensuing manhunt failed to capture him.

Late on the night of June 7, 2011, Harun's luck finally ran out. Few ventured out after dark around the chaotic city of Mogadishu, a patchwork of hostile neighborhoods under the constantly shifting control of warring factions. When faced with persons unknown, jittery government soldiers, under the fiction of maintaining order, made it a practice to shoot first rather than ask questions. That's exactly what happened as a black Toyota 4×4 approached one of their checkpoints. The two occupants returned fire, but were both killed. The soldiers suspected their importance upon searching the vehicle and discovering $40,000 in cash, several laptops, cell phones, and a South African passport with a visa indicating the bearer had recently traveled to Tanzania.[33]

DNA samples taken from the corpses were sent to American officials in Kenya. The following week, the United States confirmed that one of the dead men was Harun, the most wanted terrorist in Africa. The other man was identified as Musa Hussein Abdi, aka Musa Dheere, a suspected senior al Shabab member.

A Somali security official said, "This was lucky. It wasn't like Fazul was killed during an operation to get him. He was essentially driving around Mogadishu and got lost."[34] He had reportedly been on his way from Merca, a Shabab-controlled town, to Deynila, a Shabab-controlled part of Mogadishu.

Nelly Lahoud, a scholar at West Point's Combatting Terrorism Center who studied Harun's diary is dubious about the official version of his death. Her impression is that, having spent many years in Somalia, he was too savvy to get lost in Mogadishu and end up at a government checkpoint. She believes that his criticisms of al Shabab and insistence that they lacked legitimate claim to the al Qaeda moniker had made him many enemies. Moreover, he had always asserted his personal loyalty to bin Laden and had likely alienated Ayman al-Zawahiri with his less-than-flattering attitude toward him and by questioning his rightful claim to being al Qaeda's second in command.

"It is possible that al-Shabab reasoned that eliminating Harun would be a welcome gift to al-Zawahiri, hoping that in return, al-Zawahiri would grant the group membership in al-Qa-ida," she wrote.[35] On February 9, 2012, he did, indeed, announce that al Shabab had been admitted as part of al Qaeda.

Secretary of State Hillary Clinton reacted, "Harun Fazul's death is a significant blow to Al Qaeda, its extremist allies, and its operations in East Africa. It is a just end for a terrorist who brought so much death and pain to so many innocents in Nairobi, Dar es Salaam, and elsewhere—Tanzanians, Kenyans, Somalis, others in the region, and our own embassy personnel."[36]

"This is a very important guy," former FBI supervisor Pat D'Amuro said during a conversation before Harun was killed. "This is a guy we need to get."[37]

Osama bin Laden, al Qaeda's leader until his death in 2011,
was indicted for his role in the African embassy bombings.
Courtesy of the FBI.

Ayman al-Zawahiri was second in command to bin Laden and replaced him as al Qaeda's leader. Courtesy of the FBI.

Mohammed Atef, also known as Abu Hafs, was the military leader of al Qaeda when the embassy attacks were carried out. He was killed in Afghanistan shortly after 9/11. Courtesy of the FBI.

Fazul Abdullah Mohammed, also known as Harun, was a key al Qaeda leader in East Africa. He was killed at a Somali military checkpoint in a suburb of Mogadishu in 2011. Photo courtesy of the FBI.

Mohamed Rashed Daoud al-'Owhali was a passenger in the truck that delivered the bomb to the American Embassy in Nairobi. He survived the blast and was arrested soon afterward. Courtesy of the U.S. Attorney's Office. Southern District of New York.

K. K. Mohamed helped in the preparation of the bomb used against the American Embassy in Dar es Salaam. He was arrested in South Africa months after the event. Courtesy of the U.S. Attorney's Office, Southern District of New York.

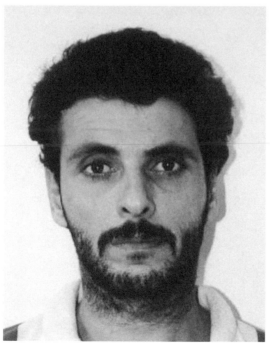

Mohamed Saddiq Odeh was among the al Qaeda operatives who were convicted during the first trial of embassy bombing suspects. He is serving a life sentence without possibility of parole at the federal supermax facility in Florence, Colorado. Courtesy of the U.S. Attorney's Office, Southern District of New York.

Mamdouh Mahmud Salim participated in the embassy bombings, but he was ultimately convicted for the attempted murder of a correctional officer while he was awaiting trial in Manhattan. Courtesy of the U.S. Attorney's Office, Southern District of New York.

Ahmed Khalfan Ghailani was captured in 2004 and held in a series of black prisons before being tried in New York, where he was convicted in 2010 and sentenced to life without possibility of parole. Courtesy of the FBI.

Abu Anas al-Liby is alleged to have helped plan the African embassy bombings. He was grabbed off a street in Tripoli, Libya, by American Special Forces in 2013 and remanded for trial in federal court in New York. Courtesy of the FBI.

Abdullah Ahmed Abdullah, reputed to have once led the East African cell, remains on the FBI's list of most wanted terrorists. His whereabouts are unknown. Courtesy of the FBI.

Saif al-Adel, a member of al Qaeda's ruling and military councils, joined al Qaeda from Ayman al-Zawahiri's Egyptian Islamic Jihad organization. Courtesy of the FBI.

Ahmed Mohamed Hamed Ali served as an al Qaeda trainer in Somalia. Courtesy of the FBI.

Sheikh Ahmed Salim Swedan purchased components used for the manufacture of the embassy bombs, and the vehicle used in the Nairobi attack. He was killed in 2009 in Pakistan. Courtesy of the FBI.

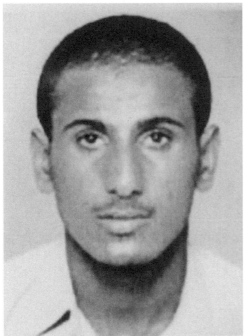

Fahid Mohammed Ally Msalam, Swedan's deputy in East Africa, was killed alongside him in Pakistan. Courtesy of the FBI.

Muhsin Musa Matwalli
Atwah was responsible for
assembling the bombs used
in the embassy attacks.
Courtesy of the FBI.

Mustafa Mohamed
Fadhil participated in the
preparation of the bomb
used against the embassy
in Dar es Salaam. In 2005,
he was removed from the
FBI's list of most wanted
terrorists. He was reportedly
killed in Afghanistan.
Courtesy of the FBI.

Intelligence fails because it is human, no stronger than the
power of one mind to understand another.
—Tim Weiner, *Legacy of Ashes: The History of the CIA*

[16] THE MYTH OF HINDSIGHT

It is impossible to reflect on the embassy bombings without feeling the onrushing doom of 9/11. Naturally enough, when looking back, you try to elicit predictors. Only because you know the outcome, you find them. But imagine you can't foresee what is to come. What, then, is predictable?

In the years since 9/11, it has become widely accepted wisdom that it could have been prevented. Among the first significant public figures to advocate this notion was Richard Clarke. In his 2004 bestseller *Against All Enemies: Inside America's War on Terror*, Clarke wrote with an insider's authority and the credibility of having been an early proponent of proactive measures against bin Laden while serving as a counterterrorism official in the Clinton and Bush administrations. He claimed that the FBI and CIA "had specific information about individual terrorists from which one could have deduced what was about to happen."[1] Earlier in his book, Clarke describes 9/11 as "the 'Big al Qaeda Attack' we had warned was coming and it was bigger than almost anything we had imagined, short of a nuclear weapon."[2] Consider the contradiction: that there was specific information from which what happened could have been deduced; yet, what happened, he concedes, was bigger than almost anything imaginable.

In its final report, the 9/11 Commission came to a damning conclusion: "We found that our government failed in its duty to protect us on that day."[3] However, the prism through which it arrived at this finding was distorted by the very exercise of looking back from a known outcome.

The journalist Tim Weiner offers a sweeping condemnation: 9/11, he wrote, "was a systemic failure of American government—the White House, the National Security Council, the FBI, the Federal Aviation Administration, the Immigration and Naturalization Service, the congressional intelligence committees. It was a failure of policy and diplomacy. It was a failure of the reporters who covered the government to understand and convey its disarray to their readers. But above all it was a failure to know the enemy. It was the Pearl Harbor that the CIA had been created to prevent."[4]

Where the Pearl Harbor analogy breaks down is on the fact that Japan's military might was undisputed. The 9/11 attacks were on a scale beyond the operational capacity al Qaeda had theretofore demonstrated. It stretched the imagination in ways that Pearl Harbor did not.

I believe what really happened was more elemental, less insidious. It was a *normative* failure. The United States was unprepared for 9/11 because, notwithstanding warnings and clues, the country—public and policy makers alike—was predisposed to complacency and averse to inconvenience on the security front. The deep, wide moats of the Atlantic to the east and Pacific to the west; the expansive land-bridge of Canada over the north; and the relatively tame Americas to the south reinforced its long-standing predisposition toward isolationism and its post–Cold War perception of invincibility. These strong psychological factors inclined it to passivity.

In other words, 9/11 could not have been prevented without experiencing the precedent of 9/11. Under the guise of *pre*-diction, the 9/11 Commission, and others, have actually engaged in the deceptive practice of *post*-diction; that is, working backward through the facts from a known outcome to illustrate how it might have been foreseen. From that perspective, all the clues are made to add up because, after all, we know what awaits at the end of the trail.

Roger Cressey, Clarke's deputy and one of those who understood the extreme threat that al Qaeda represented, acknowledged, "It sounds terrible, but we used to say to each other that some people didn't get it—it was going to take body bags."[5] Moreover, it would take lots of body bags, and on American soil. Six from the World Trade Center in 1993 had been insufficient. As had the 200-plus dead in East Africa and seventeen more killed aboard the *Cole*.

The point is not that no mistakes were made. The fact that 9/11 happened proves that the intelligence system did not perform as it was meant to. What I'm suggesting is that without anticipating the imminence of the threat, no agency had adopted a crisis mind-set. Absent that, 9/11 would not be prevented.

"I'm not sure I agree with the idea that we didn't think al Qaeda was going to do something on as large a scale as 9/11," reflected FBI agent Jack Cloonan. "In our heart of hearts, we in the New York office certainly understood, and provided the government a lot of information about al Qaeda using planes as weapons. You could argue that a lot of what we were doing was preventive in nature. Were enough resources brought to bear against al Qaeda to prevent 9/11? In hindsight, clearly not. You would have been hard pressed to get the military to sign off on any action to go after bin Laden before 9/11."[6]

"The East Africa attacks were insulated from the American consciousness simply for having occurred in Africa," said Mary Jo White, who amassed a strong record prosecuting terrorists as U.S. attorney for the Southern District of New York. "There was a palpable change of consciousness in New York following 9/11."[7] The same could be said for Washington.

The 9/11 Commission would chide that "the United States did not, before 9/11 adopt as a clear strategic objective the elimination of al Qaeda."[8] Precisely! And absent that, al Qaeda would not be preempted.

Any failure to prevent 9/11 dates back long before those frantic months and weeks when, as CIA Director George Tenet told the 9/11 Commission, the system began "blinking red"[9] and reports were piling up about planned attacks in Israel or Saudi Arabia or India or Italy or Yemen or Canada, or London, Boston, and New York, or maybe a hostage-taking, or a hijacking, or the storming of an American embassy. The where, when, what, and how of the next attack were unknown. But the who was clear all along. An unpredictable event could not be prevented. A known actor could be interdicted. Doing so, however, required decisive action before the vaguely forewarned plot was carried out.

Indeed, the embassy bombings gave three years' warning, the *Cole* attack one year, that al Qaeda was hell-bent on carrying out its fatwa against America and Americans. As Gary Berntsen, the CIA officer who led the Clandestine Service's efforts to kill bin Laden at Tora Bora in late 2001, wrote, "rarely in history has a great power like ours received two such warnings and failed to act to defend itself."[10]

In April 2001, Ahmad Shah Mahsoud, leader of Afghanistan's Northern Alliance, whom the United States favored as an alternative to the Taliban, met privately with CIA officers in France following a public address to the European Parliament in Strasbourg. He warned that bin Laden was sending twenty-five operatives to Europe for terrorist activities. To which Anthony Summers and Robbyn Swan wrote, preposterously, "The intelligence was not far off target. 'Twenty-five' was close to nineteen, the actual number of terrorists dispatched on the 9/11 mission."[11] Such is the quality of analysis that makes the opaque seem transparent.

On June 22, 2001, all CIA station chiefs were notified of a possible al Qaeda suicide attack against an American target within a few days.[12]

In other words, threats were being tossed about with the loose ease adopted by barroom toughs, with little to distinguish the serious from the fanciful. And none really closely presaged what actually came to pass on 9/11. The 9/11 Commission conceded, "Despite their large number, the threats received contained few specifics regarding time, place, method, or target. Most suggested that attacks were planned against targets overseas; others indicated threats against unspecified 'U.S. interests.' We cannot say for certain whether these reports, as dramatic as they were, related to the 9/11 attacks."[13]

Interpreting these vague, blustery threats—after the fact—as clues to 9/11 is intellectually dishonest. Moreover, it disregards the most impressive part of the entire plot: how the perpetrators maintained exceptional operational security, and upheld their morale and resolve over the course of years. Any one of them could have defected to a life of riches and ease, escaping the certain death that their mission foretold. None of them did.

The intelligence community did recognize that bin Laden was a threat early on. That's why Alec Station was created in 1996. Over the years, the bin Laden Unit discussed options for kidnapping or neutralizing him. None were ever operationalized because of their dubious legality and likelihood of failure resulting in embarrassment.

Cofer Black, head of the CTC, told the House and Senate Intelligence Committees on September 26, 2002, "There was a 'before 9/11' and there was an 'after 9/11.' After 9/11, the gloves came off."[14] Before, there was simply no consensus supporting a concerted effort to decimate al Qaeda and eliminate its leader. Neither the embassy bombings nor the attack on the *Cole* nor the two together—though each was an act of war in its own right—stirred the government to mobilize. The determination to destroy al Qaeda was born of 9/11.

Yet, even then, there were bizarre lapses. As the Taliban crumbled, American Special Forces and CIA agents had bin Laden pinned down in the rugged mountains of Tora Bora in December 2001. Inexplicably, senior American leaders rebuffed urgent appeals from the small contingent on the ground for reinforcements sufficient to assault his stronghold and kill or capture the target. "*When will the bureaucrats back in Washington face the real challenges and respond appropriately?*" lamented Berntsen [italics in original].[15]

In the midst of all the threats that rang hollow was a golden nugget of intelligence that could have sounded an alarm. And it originated from the embassy bombings investigation.

When al-'Owhali divulged to the FBI that the phone number he called immediately after escaping the Nairobi bombing belonged to Ahmed al-Hada in Yemen, he gave away the tell-tale intelligence that ultimately revealed the identity of two key al Qaeda operatives, Khalid al-Mihdhar and Nawaf al-Hazmi. Al-Mihdhar was al-Hada's son-in-law and the NSA had intercepted several calls between them. Despite being identified by the CIA, these two Saudi nationals were able to enter the United States with no more scrutiny than if they were common tourists. Both were among the hijackers who crashed American Airlines flight 77 into the Pentagon on 9/11.

Early in 1999, Al-Mihdhar and al-Hazmi were two of the first recruits for the operation. They were experienced mujahideen who had fought in Bosnia in 1995. Inspired by the example of their mutual friend, Azzam, the driver of the Nairobi truck bomb, they requested a martyrdom mission. They even took the initiative to obtain visas for the United States—in their own names—before ever receiving an assignment.[16]

Intercepts picked up from al-Hada's phone in December 1999 revealed that al-Mihdhar and al-Hazmi, both of whom were unknown to American intelligence at the time, were preparing to travel to Malaysia. Thanks to good investigative work, the CIA succeeded in getting a photocopy of al-Mihdhar's passport, which contained multiple entry visas to the United States. Because the CIA did not tell the FBI, Immigration, or State, no other agency was on the lookout for him.[17]

In January, the two met in Kuala Lumpur with Khallad, the purported mastermind of the *Cole* bombing. The CIA closely observed what proved to be an important al Qaeda meeting, getting a valuable trove of surveillance photos of the participants.

Traveling on to Bangkok, al-Mihdhar and al-Hazmi met with two other suspects in the *Cole* conspiracy, who were on their way to bring money to Khallad from Yemen. They then flew from Bangkok to Los Angeles on January 15, 2000. The connection between the Saudis and Khallad singled them out as obvious persons of interest.

Had the CIA shared this information, the FBI may have learned that these al Qaeda operatives were in the United States. In the event, neither al-Mihdhar nor al-Hazmi were located prior to 9/11.[18] The chance to detect them does seem to have offered a possibility to disrupt the plot.

In June 2000, al-Mihdhar left the United States for Yemen. In June 2001, he applied for, and was granted, a new visa, returning to America on July 4. He was able to come and go because the CIA neither placed him on a watch list nor provided his identity to the FBI on the basis of caveats that its intelligence was not to be shared with law enforcement investigators.[19] The fact that al-Mihdhar and al-Hazmi were never identified to the FBI as persons of interest continues to trouble Ali Soufan to this day: "At a minimum, Khalid al-Mihdhar would not have been allowed to just walk into the United States on July 4, 2001, and Nawaf al-Hazmi, [9/11 plot leader Mohammed] Atta's deputy, would have been arrested. At a minimum."[20]

Part of the confusion, the 9/11 Commission would report, was "the void between the foreign and domestic threat. The foreign intelligence agencies were watching overseas, alert to foreign threats to U.S. interests there. The domestic agencies were waiting for evidence of a domestic threat from sleeper cells within the United States. No one was looking for a foreign threat to domestic targets."[21] The Commission went on, "The terrorists exploited deep institutional failings within our government."[22]

Soufan, who led the *Cole* investigation, disputes this last point: "There was no structural failure. It was as simple as some people failing to pass information to which they had access along proper channels to the agencies that could have done something with it. This is what the 9/11 Commission found. It is what the CIA's own Inspector General found. Had the FBI *Cole* team been given the information linking al-Mihdhar to Khallad, things could have been done to disrupt 9/11." He refuses to speculate on why the information was not shared: "The issue is too critical to engage in speculation. I will speak only to the facts and, in fact, I do not know why."[23]

The Department of Justice inspector general's investigation into the FBI's conduct during the critical period leading up to 9/11 "found no evidence indicating the FBI or any other member of the Intelligence Community had specific intelligence regarding the September 11 plot." It went on to document five missed opportunities when the Bureau could have learned, or followed up, information related to al-Mihdhar and al-Hazmi. The first was when the CIA failed to share its knowledge of the pivotal Malaysia meeting in January 2000, that al-Mihdhar had a multiple-entry visa, or that al-Hazmi, who had also been spotted at the meeting, had arrived in Los Angeles in January 2000, which it learned the following March. The second was when it failed to learn that the pair were in San Diego in early 2000, even though they were renting rooms from a longtime Bureau cooperator. The third came in late December 2000 or early January 2001 when a report from a reliable source linked them to Khallad. Fourth was in the summer of 2001 when the FBI and CIA met to discuss the *Cole*, but still the Agency did not fully disclose the background to the Malaysia meeting, which would have brought the al Qaeda operatives living in California to the FBI's attention. And, finally, in August 2001, when the Bureau did learn that these individuals were in the United States, its search for their whereabouts was not assigned any particular priority.[24] It was just another routine inquiry because, even at this late date, less than a month before 9/11, "this case was 'no bigger' than any other intelligence case."[25]

There's no escaping the fact that the failure to track and make contact with al-Mihdhar and al-Hazmi was a failure with tragic consequences. With no suspicion that something like 9/11 was imminent, however, nobody seemed to appreciate their importance. Indeed, even to the extent that the FBI sought to identify them, "Mihdhar's significance continued to be his potential connection to Khallad and the Cole attack—not that he was operational in the U.S."[26] At the time, it looked more as if something was being planned to take place in Malaysia than America.

Bureau veteran Jack Cloonan is also incredulous about the CIA's handling of the case. "What 9/11 is really all about was the lack of follow-up on these two people, Khalid al-Mihdhar and Nawaf al-Hazmi," he said. He is astonished that the success of covering the Malaysia meeting resulted in nothing actionable. "After the group breaks up in Kuala Lumpur and they go to Thailand, you're telling me you just lost sight of it? You just forgot to put them on the notification list? That's as bad as it gets! . . . It's not structural, it's not organizational—it's about human failure. It's people not doing their job. It's just that simple. And all this other stuff just obscures that fact."[27]

He remains emotional on the subject and it is clearly something that haunts him. "There was some sloppiness there," he says softly, understatedly. "It would never happen today. But this one thing [the failure to pass along the information about al-Mihdhar and al-Hazmi] is just hard to get beyond."[28]

One interesting theory that has been floated is that the CIA may have withheld information because they hoped for the opportunity to recruit the al Qaeda members as penetration agents. Though they are not supposed to operate in the United States, approaching a foreigner to serve as an agent abroad fell conveniently within that domestic-foreign void of which the 9/11 Commission spoke. The Agency could have assessed that pitching them on American soil would be more secure, and more likely to succeed, than to formulate an approach overseas. Since neither man had committed any crime against the United States, the Agency could have reasoned there was no imperative to identify them to the Bureau. Al-Mihdhar reportedly told K. S. M. at one point that he believed he was under surveillance in California.[29] This theory lacks plausibility for the fact that, given such intense scrutiny of the CIA's efforts leading up to 9/11, some documentary evidence of a recruitment proposal should have been unearthed by now.

Another theory is that the two future hijackers were not watch-listed because

Saudi intelligence told the CIA that they were already double agents working against al Qaeda.[30] Prince Turki al-Faisal, longtime head of the General Intelligence Department (GID), claimed that al-Mihdhar and al-Hazmi had been known to his service since 1997. A censored paragraph from Congress's Joint Inquiry, suggested that al-Hazmi disclosed information about the African embassy attacks to the Saudis in 1999.[31] If that was the case, they were obviously triple agents, playing the GID on behalf of bin Laden.

In this swirl of information and misinformation, the usual deep sludge beneath which facts take cover, the significance of the two terrorists was not as apparent before 9/11. One can empathize with the frustration of agents like Soufan and Cloonan, with the what-ifs that will forever plague them. And who can say how their intervention may have served to disrupt 9/11. But for all the sensitivity of investigators attuned to the nuances of their case, convincing decision makers to authorize hard charging remained a challenge because the system was not supportive of charging hard against unrealized threats. Maybe they would have been authorized to conduct close surveillance on al-Mihdhar and al-Hazmi, but who's to say they would have been able to do anything but watch them board American 77 on September 11, 2001.

The closest analogy I can think of relates to clinical drug testing. When a deadly disease runs rampant—AIDS or breast cancer being prime examples—the public clamors for quick and ready access to even the most experimental and unproven pharmaceuticals. But when a drug produces harmful side effects, the public demands more stringent preclinical testing. So it goes with security. In the aftermath of a deadly attack, everyone wonders why the authorities didn't do more. In the absence of an attack, authorities are chastised for being too aggressive and intrusive or of needlessly sowing fear.

It is reassuring to believe that 9/11 was preventable; a relief to presume that, had mistakes been avoided here or there, the catastrophe would have been averted. It raises hope that the next attack can be stopped. But the real thrust and parry of terrorism and counterterrorism is far more complex and ambiguous than that.

Nearly every attack leaves a trail of clues and operational opportunities that can be fully interpreted only in light of knowing the final objective. With regard to the 1993 World Trade Center bombing, the Blind Sheikh was on a terrorist watch list, but was still granted a visa to enter the United States—reportedly by a CIA official in Sudan.[32] Ramzi Yousef landed at JFK on September 1, 1992, with fraudulent documents, but provided his real name and requested political asylum. Following a standard interview, he was given a hearing date and admitted on nothing more than a promise to appear.[33] Thus leaving him free to plot the bombing.

During the course of that investigation, Khalid Sheikh Mohammed's name came up through a wire transfer of $660 into the bank account of one of the coconspirators. He was secretly indicted in early 1996, at which time he was living in Qatar. Discussions about arresting him were held at the NSC. The Qatari government, having just survived a coup attempt, was unwilling to cooperate. An unnamed American official said, "We could not have snatched him. That would not have been either politic or possible."[34] He fled Qatar that same year, apparently tipped off that the Americans were looking for him, and remained at large to plot 9/11. The FBI put K. S. M. on its Most Wanted List in connection with the Bojinka plot and offered a $2 million reward for information leading to his arrest. He was eventually apprehended in Rawalpindi in 2003, after he was betrayed by a cousin once the reward had grown to $25 million.

In the African embassies case, there was the walk-in who described a plot that bore an eerie similarity to what actually occurred. He was dismissed as unreliable. More significantly, Wadih el Hage, an active conspirator in the attack, was interviewed by the FBI and called in front of the grand jury *before* the bombings without impeding the conspirators or shaking their operational discipline.

The American legal system has proven itself better equipped to respond to crimes than to prevent them. This stems from constitutionally protected rights and legal values that most sensibly and effectively restrict the authorities' power to interfere with people's lives. It stems from a philosophical preference for individual liberty over state control. Such is the basis for: protection against random searches; requiring that electronic surveillance be authorized by judicial warrant; why nobody may be compelled to incriminate themselves before police, the courts, or legislative bodies; why the United States has no provision for preventive detention; and why suspects must be informed of the charges against them and brought before a judge within the shortest delay possible.

When I put this premise to Soufan, he strongly disagreed. "Conspiracy trials have proven very effective," he insisted. "Most of those convicted for terrorism haven't actually committed an act of terror, but conspired to do so."[35]

True, but in the majority of these cases, the attack actually occurred, even if perpetrators were convicted on conspiracy charges. I would contend that few conspiracy convictions involved foiled plots before 9/11. Of course, efforts at prevention became far more vigorous afterward, and juries far more credulous regarding prosecutor's arguments concerning a suspect's *intent* to commit acts of violence.

Counterterrorism investigations follow two imperatives. One is national security—to collect intelligence and preempt future attacks. The other is law enforcement—to gather evidence to bring about the apprehension and prosecution of terrorists. The fundamental difference between them is that law enforcement works backward from a crime that has occurred, while intelligence gropes forward, uncertain of what might happen.

From the FBI's perspective, Pat D'Amuro affirmed, "The *primary purpose* of any counterterrorism investigation has always been about prevention; the problem being, you can't really prevent unless you use the criminal tools to disrupt and incarcerate because, if you don't take that cell off the street, that threat does not go away. You need a combination of national security and prosecutorial tools to really succeed."[36]

Two of President Clinton's Presidential Decision Directives (39 of June 1995 and 62 of May 1998) avowed that terrorism was a national security concern.[37] The former directive, entitled "U.S. Policy on Counterterrorism," instructed the CIA to engage in "an aggressive program of foreign intelligence collection, analysis, counterintelligence, and covert action." Furthermore, it warned, "The acquisition of weapons of mass destruction by a terrorist group, through theft or manufacture is unacceptable. There is no higher priority than preventing the acquisition of this capability or removing this capability from terrorist groups potentially opposed to the U.S."[38] It also made the FBI the lead agency for investigating acts of terrorism on American soil or abroad whenever American citizens were among the casualties.

Steve Coll wryly commented, "On paper, at least, American policy was now more forceful and clearly stated than it had been in years. . . . The challenge now was to put the words into practice."[39] In effect, that would not happen until after 9/11. Only then were all the tools in the American arsenal—military, intelligence, law enforcement, diplomacy, and economic influence—employed in a concerted and coordinated strategy to wipe out al Qaeda.

In hindsight, every neglected opportunity to disrupt bin Laden from the time of his declaration of war has become indefensible. Thousands of lives hung in the balance. We now know this for a fact. We know how many—the nearly three thousand that were lost on 9/11, along with more than two hundred who perished in Nairobi and Dar es Salaam.

In hindsight.

[17] AHMED KHALFAN GHAILANI

Ahmed Khalfan Ghailani left Dar es Salaam for Nairobi on August 1, 1998. He checked into the Hilltop Hotel, where he stayed until August 6, when he joined the exodus of al Qaeda operatives. He departed on Kenya Airways flight 310, along with Abdullah Ahmed Abdullah, a leading organizer, for Karachi. From there, he crossed into Afghanistan and made his way to bin Laden's base at the al Farouq training camp. For the next six years, he was lost in the murky terrorist underground.

Ghailani was identified as an accomplice by K. K. Mohamed. Specifically, he was accused of purchasing, along with Sheikh Ahmed Salim Swedan, the Nissan Atlas that the suicide bomber drove into the embassy in Dar, and of obtaining TNT, detonators, fertilizer, and gas cylinders, and using these materials to help assemble the bomb. He was also alleged to have participated in reconnaissance missions against the target and of obtaining a cell phone that enabled the conspirators in Tanzania to communicate with their counterparts in Kenya.[1]

In 2001, he was indicted in the Southern District of New York on 286 charges—224 of which were for murder—related to his involvement in al Qaeda's East Africa plot.

While at the al Farouq camp, he received weapons training and became adept at forging documents. He admitted having met bin Laden and Khalid Sheikh Mohamed. He even lived with one of K. S. M.'s relatives for a time in Pakistan. But, he specified, he never pledged bayat. Bin Laden personally requested his services as a bodyguard. He also cooked for the emir, saying of his fellow guards, "Most of them didn't like to cook."[2]

In March 2001, Ghailani moved into a safe house in Monrovia, Liberia, along with Harun, to run an al Qaeda diamond-trading operation. Within just a couple of months they ran afoul of their superiors when stories of their spending on women and alcohol started to spread. According to a British newspaper, the *Observer*, al Qaeda made as much as $20 million trading diamonds.[3] After 9/11,

U.S. Special Forces reportedly mustered in neighboring Guinea for an operation to snatch them, but it was called off because their identities could not be confirmed.[4] If Ghailani is to be believed, they must have been on to the wrong man, because he claims to have been in Afghanistan on 9/11 and to have narrowly escaped American bombardments of al Qaeda bases on two occasions. Soon after the U.S. ground war began, he said, he retreated to Pakistan.

In June 2004, while trawling through the dense masses of e-mail, web chatter, and other electronic exchanges that flow across the Internet like plankton in the sea, U.S. intelligence homed in on one Musaad Aruchi, a nephew of K. S. M. and cousin of Ramzi Yousef, the first World Trade Center bomber. Aruchi was identified as a hub for exchanges between jihadis. He was traced to Karachi, where Pakistani intelligence arrested him on June 12. Three "unpleasant" days later, he was turned over to the CIA and taken to one of its black prisons.[5]

Aruchi's computer, which authorities seized, contained photos of various landmark sites in the United States, as well as an important cache of phone numbers and e-mail addresses. Analyzing the information, investigators became interested in a twenty-five-year-old technical wizard named Muhammed Naeem Noor Khan, who had attended an al Qaeda camp in 1998. The CIA and NSA directed intense electronic surveillance against Khan, collecting every e-mail and IP address that touched his network.[6] On July 13, he was taken into custody in Lahore.

Pakistani and American interrogators forced him to send urgent e-mails to his contacts around the globe in an effort to flush them out. Dozens were located as responses came in to Khan's computer.[7] Among them, Ghailani.

Under intensive interrogation by the ISI, Khan provided details about Ghailani's whereabouts in the city of Gujrat.[8] When Pakistani police came for him on July 25, he didn't come quietly. It took a fierce gun battle at his apartment that lasted anywhere between eight and sixteen hours, depending on which news outlet you believe, before Ghailani surrendered. With him were thirteen others, including his Uzbek wife, his daughter, and four other children.

Among Ghailani's possessions were a pair of laptops, on which were found detailed surveillance reports of the Citicorp headquarters in New York, the New York Stock Exchange, the Prudential Tower in Newark, and the World Bank and International Monetary Fund buildings in Washington, D.C. However, these documents dated as far back as 2000 and 2001. Acting as if the intelligence was fresh and harkened to an imminent attack—with a presidential election barely five months away and terrorism being a reliable Republican rallying cry—the secretary of Homeland Security announced heightened security measures in the vicinity of these locations on August 1, prompting Howard Dean, the former governor of Vermont and chair of the Democratic National Committee, to remark, "It's just impossible to know how much of this is real and how much of this is politics."[9]

Following his arrest, Ghailani disappeared into the CIA's maze of black prisons, not to resurface until September 2006, when he was transferred to the terrorist internment camp at Guantánamo Bay. Here was a high-value target, on the FBI's list of twenty-two Most Wanted Terrorists, with a $25 million reward on his head, plus he was in possession of troubling plans pertaining to major American targets. While the specifics of his secret detention remain classified, he was certainly subjected to enhanced interrogation techniques, the government's euphemism of choice to describe what in any other setting would be characterized as torture, while in extra-judicial detention. Whatever he may have revealed during questioning, however it may have been extracted, remains classified.

On March 17, 2007, Ghailani appeared before a Combatant Status Review Tribunal at Guantánamo Bay to determine whether he would be designated an enemy combatant against the United States—a variant of prisoner-of-war status—in which case he could be held indefinitely and tried before a military court. He denied any wrongdoing, while conceding that he'd done the things the prosecution alleged. He had, indeed, been present when the Atlas was purchased, but insisted it was Swedan who bought it. Furthermore, as far as he knew, it was all quite innocent. Swedan explained that he needed the refrigerator truck to transport cargo between Mombasa and Somalia. Similarly, he admitted purchasing the TNT, but he had been told that it was to be used at a training camp and for mining diamonds in Somalia. He did buy a phone for an Egyptian friend named Mustapha, but had no idea to whom he made calls. He denied ever scouting targets for attack or knowing that there was a plot afoot to bomb the American embassy.[10] Reportedly, he had already confessed to the FBI that he was told the embassy was the target a week before the attack.[11]

Yes, he lived with a group of friends in Dar, as K. K. Mohamed had said, but he had no idea they were involved in terrorism. Not until he arrived in Afghanistan, he testified, did he learn that these people were part of al Qaeda. Prior to that, he insists, he'd never even heard of such a thing as al Qaeda. Similarly, only once he was in Afghanistan did he learn of bin Laden's war against the United States.[12]

Asked why he had fled Tanzania, he shrugged, "They took me with them," in reference to the friends with whom he was living in Dar.[13]

He told the tribunal that he had tried to go to Afghanistan for military training as early as 1996. What he didn't relate was that he had been detained in Kenya as he attempted to fly out on a false passport. He was released after paying a fine.[14] Asked why he'd wanted the training, he said, "Because I am from Africa. . . . I wanted this for self-defense. Because in Tanzania, we didn't have any problems but our neighbors, Rwanda, Burundi, Congo and other countries. They have problems. . . . I wanted training for myself only, in my country, I couldn't, I didn't like to go to government training in Tanzania, but I like to have military training."[15]

He gave a rather different explanation to the FBI investigators, to whom he "specifically stated that he wanted to learn to fight so that he could kill Jews."[16]

In a final comment to the CSRT, Ghailani said softly, "I would like to apologize to the United States Government for what I did before. In helping them because I helped but although it wasn't—it was without my knowledge what they were doing but I helped them. So I apologize to the United States Government for what I did. And I'm sorry for what happened to those families who lost, who lost their friends and their beloved ones."[17]

Ahmed Ghailani was born in 1974 in Zanzibar. His mother is a nurse midwife. His father ran a small restaurant until his death, when Ghailani was just fifteen, which plunged the family into poverty. A court-appointed psychiatrist, Dr. Gregory Saathoff, reported that his father's death had a "profound impact," leaving him fearful of going hungry. Nonetheless, he refused to beg. He completed high school and studied electronics at a technical school before moving to Dar in 1996, where he lived with a friend whose family owned a clothing store.[18]

His mother insisted that the family was not particularly religious. After he resettled in Dar, Ghailani began to travel to Mombasa where he met people whom he described, in a statement to the FBI, as "serious jihad types."[19] Thus began his immersion in al Qaeda and engagement in the embassy plot.

On June 9, 2009, Ghailani became the first Guantánamo inmate to be transferred to the civilian justice system. He was held at the MCC, and would be tried in the same federal courthouse in Foley Square where previous defendants had answered to charges stemming from the embassy case. The Honorable Judge Lewis Kaplan was selected to preside.

Ghailani was an appropriate candidate for civilian trial because, unlike others who had been swept up after 9/11 and held without charge, advice of rights, or access to counsel, and who had been subjected to treatment that would normally be judged illegal, Ghailani had an outstanding indictment that predated all of this (K. S. M. had also been secretly indicted, but for the Bojinka plot, which did not result in the death of any Americans. The government prefers to prosecute him for the thousands of murders on 9/11). Nonetheless, since he'd been on a tour through the black sites, his trial promised to be an important precedent for subsequent terrorist prosecutions. In particular, it would give a strong indication about the practicality of moving K. S. M. into the civilian system, as President Barack Obama proposed.

Though Obama's administration promised to close the prison facility at Gitmo, the mechanics of how to go about dispensing with its inmates has proven to be an administrative and procedural nightmare. Many are considered extremely dangerous and cannot be repatriated. Nor is it necessarily obvious where they ought to be repatriated to. The issue of whether they are enemy combatants or criminals has yet to be settled.

As well, the government worries over how to protect classified information in a public proceeding. In a military tribunal, where there is less transparency in the presentation of evidence, classified information is more easily safeguarded. As well, a trial within the civilian system raises practical issues regarding security at federal courthouses, particularly in Manhattan, and within civilian penitentiaries. Such problems simply don't exist at an off-shore military installation.

While civil libertarians worry that the less transparent military justice system could be manipulated to accommodate the violation of suspects' rights, civilian prosecutors could be gravely hobbled by the circumstances of the accused's detention and interrogation.

Ultimately, Ghailani's trial would help to define how much the American justice system's faith in itself had been undermined by terrorism. It would undoubtedly present the federal court with occasion to establish its position on the admissibility of statements elicited through enhanced interrogation, which the previous administration's Justice Department had decided were legal and necessary. Judge Sand had suggested, "A government can say that a detainee can be tortured; however, that doesn't change one's constitutional rights."[20]

Fredrick Cohn, who had defended al-'Owhali, predicted, "Judge Kaplan is very smart, very able, and he believes in the ethics of prosecutions. I think the government ought to be, if they're not, very worried. The government may not even try to proffer a bunch of evidence they think they have because they don't want an opinion floating around telling them what shits they are."[21]

And, true enough, the prosecution stated early on that it would not introduce any statements Ghailani made "while in custody of other government agencies."[22] The defense, of course, tried not to let it go at that. In submitting a not guilty plea, Ghailani emphasized, "I have been a victim of the cruel 'enhanced interrogation techniques,' never afforded the right to remain silent nor the right to have an attorney."[23]

Several months into his incarceration at the MCC, Ghailani began refusing to appear in court for pretrial motions. He strenuously objected to the frequent invasive strip searches to which he was subjected—as many as four every time he was brought between the detention center and the courthouse. His attorney, Peter Quijano, expressed to the judge that Ghailani's competence to assist with his defense was compromised "as a result of the residual after effects of the . . . insidious program he was subjected to."[24] A defense psychiatrist concluded, "Nudity serves as a profound 'trigger' for Mr. Ghailani, thrusting him into vivid memories of the interrogation process he endured, as well as a real fear that further maltreatment will occur in the present setting."[25]

It was critical to the defense that he be present once the trial began so that the jury could see him. Quijano was counting on his slight build and youthful countenance to work in his favor. Furthermore, he was African, as opposed to Arab, which made him more relatable to a jury of nine African Americans and three whites.

"He doesn't look like somebody who'd blow up an embassy. He looks like somebody you'd want to take home with you,"[26] said Quijano.

Defending an alleged member of al Qaeda in 2011 was an entirely different prospect than it had been at the first African embassies trial. Al Qaeda had become entangled deep among those primal nerve endings that spark and crackle with fear.

"We had to defuse al Qaeda," said Quijano. "He isn't al Qaeda. We couldn't have him convicted out of fear of al Qaeda."[27]

Quijano had been assigned to the defense as learned counsel because of the prospect that Ghailani would face the death penalty, and remained as lead attorney after the prosecution elected not to pursue this ultimate sentence. He is the type of defender who revels in his role of advocate. A professional whose job gives him a rush. Charming, articulate, there is more than a touch of rogue in his demeanor. He has no cause to champion and no axe to grind. He is confident in the way of a man who feels he has all the tools he needs for getting out of a jam.

Kaplan ruled that there was no reason to doubt the defendant's competence, but that he would regard it as "an open question throughout the proceedings."[20] He also said that it wouldn't be appropriate for him to interfere with the security measures applied by the Bureau of Prisons. Eventually, Ghailani did agree to come to court.

As to the nature of his treatment before being remanded to the Southern District, the judge issued a protective order that prevented the disclosure of anything related to the techniques employed against him. The order extended to communications he was able to have with his lawyers. While attorneys were cleared to see classified materials, they were not allowed to discuss any of the contents with him, unless he raised the issue at his own initiative.

Gregory Cooper, who represented Ghailani for about six months from the time he was arraigned, offered, "The first thing you ask any client is whether he made a particular statement and under what circumstances. The restrictive orders said we couldn't do that because we couldn't disclose what was in the classified documents. I found it was very difficult in terms of how effectively you could represent your client."[29]

In an effort to preempt the trial, the defense submitted a motion to have the charges dismissed on the grounds of "outrageous government conduct," a reference to his treatment at the hands of the CIA. The prosecution responded, "Neither the manner by which a defendant is brought to court for prosecution nor the conditions of his confinement prior to that prosecution are valid grounds for dismissal of an indictment." Judge Kaplan agreed, concluding, "Even if Ghailani was mistreated while in CIA custody and even if that mistreatment violated the due process clause, there would be no connection between such mistreatment and this prosecution."[30]

The first constitutional issue to be adjudicated was a defense motion asserting that Ghailani's right to a speedy trial had been violated on the basis of the nearly six years that had passed since he'd been taken into U.S. custody. Calling it "possibly the most unique and egregious example of a speedy trial violation in American jurisprudence to date," the defense argued for dismissal. They asserted that he had been interrogated as many as one hundred times in an effort to extract intelligence on al Qaeda's history and operations, bin Laden's whereabouts, and the embassy bombings themselves.[31]

In an amicus (friend of the court) brief, the Center on the Administration of Criminal Law (CACL) at New York University argued that the defendant's rights weren't violated because, until he was turned over to the Department of Justice he had been held for purposes other than prosecution, namely intelligence gathering. Therefore, the clock ought not to have been running against prosecutors from the moment he was arrested and while in the custody of other government agencies.

As with many legal principles, the right to a speedy trial is open to interpretation. For example, the notion of "speedy" is left unspecified, thereby giving judges latitude to interpret what constitutes a violation.

Though what Ghailani told the CIA remains classified, Kaplan wrote, "Suffice it to say, the CIA program was effective in obtaining useful intelligence from Ghailani throughout his time in CIA custody." The purpose of this phase of his detention was not prosecutorial, but information gathering. When he was transferred to the custody of the Department of Defense and held at Guantánamo, it wasn't by any means certain that he would be handed over for a civilian proceeding.

Furthermore, the judge ruled a key consideration of the speedy trial provision did not apply, writing, "There is no persuasive evidence that the delay in this prosecution has impaired Ghailani's ability to defend himself in any respect or significantly prejudiced him in any other way pertinent to the speedy trial analysis." Hence, he rejected the motion, ruling that the speedy trial clock did not begin running against the prosecution until he was turned over to the Department of Justice.

Whatever the merits of the Judge's ruling, one would imagine that he felt the pressure to bring the case to trial as opposed to dismissing it on some procedural—or even legal—grounds. Not to suggest that Kaplan was unduly influenced, but when a decision was made at the highest political levels to try Ghailani in the civilian justice system, the implication was that there would be a trial.

"I agree there would always be a subtext for any judge, 'Do you understand what I am doing if I were to grant this motion?'" allows Cooper. "My personal view is that there were certain areas that Judge Kaplan moved quickly past. But that isn't unusual. Where your argument is weakest, don't argue."[32]

Judge Kaplan was called to make a much more contentious and far-reaching ruling concerning whether the prosecution's key witnesses would be permitted to testify. "This is a giant witness for the government," asserted prosecutor Michael Farbiarz. "There's nothing bigger than him."[33]

He was Hussein Abebe, who worked in his family's mining business in Arusha, in central Tanzania. He told Tanzanian police and FBI investigators that he had sold hundreds of pounds of TNT to Ghailani, believing that it was for use in a mining operation. Only later was he to learn that the explosives had been purchased to make the bomb that destroyed the U.S. Embassy.

Though an unwitting participant, Abebe managed to keep his role a secret until August 13, 2006, when he was taken into custody and flown to Zanzibar, where he was held for about a week. According to the FBI, he cooperated with police and expressed his willingness to come to the United States to testify against Ghailani should that ever be necessary, at which point he was freed. Both the Bureau and the Tanzanians deny that Abebe was ever threatened or coerced.

No one disputes that Ghailani first revealed Abebe's identity to the CIA when he was being held without charge and, likely, under the influence of enhanced interrogation. The defense asserted that Abebe should be disqualified as a witness, since the government learned about him only through a statement that would be deemed inadmissible because it was coerced. Hence, anything to which Abebe might testify was so-called fruit of the poisonous tree. This principle contends that if the origin of evidence is tainted, then everything traceable back to that tainted source is contaminated and, consequently, to be excluded.

The prosecution countered, saying that, while unable to deny the first disclosure of Abebe came during Ghailani's CIA interrogations, it could have identified him independently. It was a tough argument to sell, if only because it's impossible to unlearn what has already been learned and it is impossible to prove that a path other than that which was pursued would have led to the same destination.

Having already ruled, and accepted, that the CIA's interest in holding Ghailani differed from that of the prosecution, Judge Kaplan said, "If the government is going to coerce a detainee to provide information to our intelligence agencies, it may not use that evidence to prosecute the detainee for a criminal offense."[34]

This was a critical ruling that will ricochet into any subsequent cases ever to be brought against suspects (including K. S. M.) who had been denied their basic rights and subjected to enhanced interrogation. It gave notice that the federal court was not going to compromise judicial principle for what the government thought was expedient when dealing with terrorists. Kaplan let it be known that, while the court might not be able to impede the use of torture to obtain intelligence, it could and would exclude its fruits from evidence. The ruling established a powerful precedent regarding the executive branch's decision to sanction torture.

The "Constitution is the rock upon which our nation rests," he said. "We must follow it not only when it is convenient, but when fear and danger beckon in a different direction. To do less would diminish us and undermine the foundation upon which we stand."[35]

Kaplan ruled that Abebe could not testify, a potentially staggering blow to the prosecution. He wrote that "the Court does not have the requisite high level of confidence that the government inevitably would have obtained [Abebe's] testimony absent Ghailani's statements." He went on to say that the link was "direct and close." And he found it "not clear that [Abebe] truly would be the volunteer that the government claims," believing that his agreement to testify was based on fear of the consequences.[36]

In law, it's not what you know happened, it's what can be proved to have happened. Prosecutor Farbiarz was keenly aware that he was going to have to prove his case with just fragments of what he believed he knew about the defendant's actions. He anticipated how, without being able to present evidence of Ghailani's direct connection to the TNT, his link to a truck and gas cylinders would not have the same impact.

Anticipating what he was up against, Farbiarz said, "I expect the defense will say: 'Look, he's buying a truck with a friend; he doesn't know what it's going to be used for. He's buying gas tanks, helping a friend; he doesn't know where this is going.'"[37]

Another key piece of evidence that would never be presented before the jury was a statement that Ghailani made to the FBI over the course of four days of interviews at Gitmo in 2007 that prosecutors referred to as tantamount to a "confession."[38]

And what about everything that he had been up to during his years on the lam? Certainly admitting to having been bin Laden's bodyguard was powerful circumstantial evidence of membership in al Qaeda.

Cooper shrugs this off: "The assumption of what he did—that he was bin Laden's bodyguard—leads to further assumptions. Any claim of his position after he left Tanzania is based upon information released by the government. Where did that information come from? Who's to say he wasn't a bottle-washer? To elevate him to a position close to bin Laden is leaping."[39]

Unless the government was prepared to contend with questions about how information was extracted from Ghailani, it had no alternative but to avoid any evidence taken following his capture.

"If I'm a prosecutor, do I want a jury to hear the kinds of things that were done in order to get somebody to talk?" asked Cooper. "The last thing I want is for one juror to be repulsed by what was done."[40]

Ultimately, Ghailani's trial would turn as much on what was admitted as on what was not, which was what the government feared all along. They anticipated that the courts would not apply lesser standards of constitutionality with regard to terrorism defendants. The prosecution was reduced to presenting the jury nothing but the evidence gathered prior to Ghailani's arrest.

The trial of Ahmed Khalfan Ghailani was originally scheduled to convene on September 13, 2010, the first Monday following the anniversary of 9/11. In perceptual terms, that tragic day seemed more immediate than nine years past, and the tenth anniversary was spoken of in ominous terms as "looming." An undercurrent of anxiety over the next attack still pervades media coverage of the 9/11 commemorations. This is one of those rare cases where it needn't bleed to lead; just hold out the threat, the promise. Like the Blair witch, one doesn't need to see violence—or even a witch, for that matter—only a jittery suggestion. Al Qaeda had us convinced the next attack was on its way. Ghailani would enter the courtroom through this emotional haze.

The defense requested a delay, fearing the flood of reminders of that still raw date might prejudice their case. Judge Kaplan concurred, and the trial opened on October 12, 2010.

The jury was introduced to Dr. Jekyll and Mr. Hyde versions of the defendant. Steve Zissou, opening for the defense, said Ghailani was "neither a member of al Qaeda nor does he share their goals."[41] Nicholas Lewin, for the prosecution, said Ghailani did what he did "because he and his accomplices were committed to al Qaeda's overriding goal, killing Americans."[42] Peter Quijano argued Ghailani was "used as a dupe."[43] Harry Chernoff condemned him as a "mass murderer."[44]

The prosecution presented what evidence they could to connect Ghailani to components of the bomb and the truck that would carry it to the target. And, of course, this put him in direct contact with other members of al Qaeda.

The defense gave the jury a very different person. It portrayed Ahmed as a go-getter, working hard in Dar es Salaam's bustling Kariakoo market area, where commerce is a chaotic free-for-all. Buyers and sellers frantically sought each other out, often using middlemen to make connections. If somebody is looking for something, nobody asks why. The hustlers just scramble to find it.

Someone might tell Ahmed that they needed a gas cylinder, for example. Or some fertilizer. They needed a truck. And he'd be off, scouring the market for sellers. Success meant commissions. Quijano told the court that Ahmed thought he was simply engaging in normal business transactions. That was how he survived.

"He knew his way around that environment, anything you need, he could get," explained Quijano with admiration.[45]

"Why would anyone question buying anything?" he asked incredulously. "It's not like you're buying a gun. You're buying commercial items in a commercial temple that was Kariakoo."[46]

He wasn't part of any al Qaeda conspiracy, the defense insisted. He was a dupe. He didn't know there was any plot to blow up the American embassy. He was trying to survive, to get from one day to the next.

The prosecution rebutted: "Any dupe with half a conscience, after the attacks, would say, 'I know who did it.'"[47]

The jury took these contrasting portraits of the defendant with them when they retired to their deliberations.

On the third day, a female juror asked Judge Kaplan to remove her, saying that she was alone in her position and felt as though she was being attacked by the eleven other members of the panel. It was not revealed whether this lone juror was arguing for acquittal or conviction. Both sides were left to wonder whether they had been so effective as to convince all but her or that their case was hanging by the thin strand of her unwillingness to compromise.

Quijano puzzles over what was transpiring between the jurors. He is incredulous that this juror, an African American woman in her forties with little formal education, could have influenced all the others to vote for acquittal. Clearly the verdict was some sort of compromise.[48] He saw it as a *Twelve Angry Men* scenario in which the majority favored acquittal across the board, but were convinced to go along with at least one conviction.

Cooper, who was no longer on the case at this point, takes a different approach, laughing, "I sort of say this with a smile, but my theory of jury selection has always been, find the nut. All I need is one person who's off the wall, who will either drive the other eleven crazy or just won't listen to them." He goes on to quote the legendary Ohio State football coach Woody Hayes who argued against using the forward pass because only three things could happen and two of them were bad (incompletion or interception). The same applies to a trial. "Three things can happen and two of them are bad (conviction or mistrial). But of the two, I'll take a mistrial, because if you get a mistrial, you aren't convicted."[49]

The judge refused to declare a mistrial, instructing, instead, that the jury continue their discussions.

They did as he ordered, and two days later emerged with a unanimous verdict.

An operation of the magnitude of the embassy bombings involves few actual killers, but very many conspirators, each of whom performed his assigned task, knowing only as much as was needed, thereby protecting the broader plot from the defection of any one individual. For a jury to find an accused conspirator guilty of murder, it must link his role in the conspiracy to the deaths at the end of a chain of events.

Of 285 charges, the jury found Ghailani guilty on but a single count of conspiracy to destroy government buildings and property. It was a startling outcome.

"Our entire case turned on a single question: Did he know?" Quijano explains. "We never denied that he did what the government alleged. A friend came to him for help finding a truck. He's a hustler in Kariakoo, that's what he does. So, he knows a trucker. He introduced the two to earn a commission. That doesn't make him part of a conspiracy to bomb anything. The jury could not have acquitted on so many counts if they didn't accept our version."[50]

At sentencing, the government demanded the maximum, life imprisonment without possibility of parole, arguing that the court take into consideration evidence to which it was privy but that had not been made known to the jury.[51] The defense requested leniency in light of his having been found not guilty on the overwhelming majority of charges and the suffering he endured at the hands of the CIA.

If Judge Kaplan dropped the full weight on Ghailani, it wouldn't matter how many charges he'd been convicted of. Any one carried the possibility of life without parole. The question, really, was whether the judge might be swayed by the vast number of charges on which he'd been found not guilty. Might he not be influenced in his decision by the seeming contradiction in the verdict? Somehow, the jury concluded that he was a willing conspirator in an effort to destroy government buildings and property, but not in the conspiracy to murder anyone within those buildings or on the property. Nor was he found culpable for any of the deaths that resulted from the destruction of those buildings and property.

When Ghailani returned to court for sentencing on January 25, 2011, he listened as the judge characterized the act for which he was found guilty as "a cold-blooded killing and maiming of innocent people on an enormous scale." He concluded, "Mr. Ghailani knew and intended that people would be killed as a result of his own actions and of the conspiracy that he joined."[52]

Thus, he imposed the maximum allowable sentence: life without possibility of parole. The same as if he had been convicted on any greater number of counts.

Quijano was disappointed by the sentence, "I believed there was something fundamentally unfair with a defendant being given a life sentence for one, non-mandatory life sentence count, after being acquitted of every mandatory life count—all of the counts which specifically dealt with the bombing of the embassies and murder. There is something wrong when a suspect is found innocent on 284 of 285 counts, yet receives the exact same punishment as if the verdict had been the reverse."

"Ghailani is bitter over the outcome," Quijano goes on. "He felt cheated by the sentence. Clearly, there was an inconsistency in finding him guilty of conspiring to destroy property."[53]

The verdict was greeted with shock and dismay among those who believed Ghailani's guilt a foregone conclusion. The outcome was taken as the strongest possible argument that terrorists ought not to be tried in civilian court. It's as if they held Ghailani responsible for his own torture and, thus, for the inadmissibility of key evidence that would have made his guilt far more apparent to the jury.

Was some ticking time bomb, to use the favorite metaphor of the proponents of enhanced interrogation, defused because Ghailani was tortured? Not that we know. The most unnerving intelligence of which the public is aware related to surveillance reports that predated his arrest by several years. True, these sent homeland security authorities into such a tizzy that they immediately scrambled up the now-infamous color-coded alert chart that the Bush-era Department of Homeland Security implemented to keep the nation abreast of the imminence of danger. Of course, he also identified the most damning witness against him—Abebe, who sold him the TNT for the bomb. However, this was not time sensitive and the inadmissibility of this evidence nearly cost the prosecution its case.

The government was so spooked by how close Ghailani came to acquittal that it reacted by reversing course with regard to K. S. M. and deciding that he would face a military tribunal. A rather drastic reaction, unless the evidence for his role in 9/11 was in jeopardy of being ruled inadmissible. The common perception that he was the mastermind behind that atrocity is of little value if it cannot be demonstrated to the rigorous evidentiary standards upheld by federal court.

But what if the verdict was, as Quijano insists, the result of the jury genuinely believing that Ghailani did not know about the bomb plot? After all, the defendant comes to court presumed innocent and the prosecution has to prove his guilt beyond a reasonable doubt.

"If you judge the process on the basis of the outcome, all you end up with is a show trial," said Quijano. "It was up to the government to prove its case."[54]

It doesn't take a court to confirm that Ghailani was undoubtedly a participant in the conspiracy to destroy the American embassy in Dar es Salaam and a member of al Qaeda and its broader scheme to kill Americans wherever and whenever possible. The reason the jury had reasonable doubt in this case can be attributed directly to the government's egregious conduct in questioning Ghailani.

Once the state's conduct shocked the conscience of the court, the prosecution was in deep trouble. Said Pat D'Amuro, the former senior FBI supervisor who was among the first investigators on the bombing case, "Nobody thought about the end game with these individuals. Once you go down this path, how can you bring these people before an American court of law? So what do you do with them? Will they disappear off the face of the earth? Are you going to send them to countries where, we know, after six months of house arrest, they'll be released?"[55]

It wasn't just a case of not thinking things through, it was a function of inordinate obsession with the ticking time bomb.

"They thought they were going to get hit again. They convinced themselves that they were facing a ticking time bomb," said Roger Cressey, the former head of the National Security Council's Terrorist Threats Sub-Group.[56] Before 9/11, there was no particular expectation that al Qaeda could escalate its war against America. Afterward, the government took for granted that 9/11 was prelude to something grander, more spectacular.

When a suspect was taken into custody, it was deemed necessary to extract intelligence as quickly as possible. The premise being that torture works quickly. The fact that K. S. M. was reportedly waterboarded 183 times suggests otherwise.

Ron Suskind defined it as the Cheney Doctrine: "Even if there's just a one percent chance of the unimaginable coming due, act as if it is a certainty. It's not about 'our analysis,' as Cheney said. It's about 'our response.' This doctrine—the one percent solution—divided what had largely been indivisible in the conduct of American foreign policy: analysis and action. Justified or not, fact-based or not, 'our response' is what matters. As to 'evidence,' the bar was set so low that the word itself almost didn't apply."[57] This practice of taking supposition as certainty and frightened conjecture as analysis would inevitably lead to excess.

The ticking time bomb has been grossly exaggerated. Actionable intelligence is extremely perishable. Al Qaeda emphasizes long-term objectives over instant gratification. It adheres to well-established principles of operational security—at which it is extremely good. Its cells are strictly compartmentalized. Upon learning of the arrest of one of its members, the cell would consider itself compromised and abandon or adjust imminent operations. A terrorist training manual that British police discovered during a search of Abu Anas al-Liby's residence in Manchester in 2000 warned operatives to expect torture if captured and instructed them to resist interrogation for forty-eight hours in order to give anyone they might betray ample opportunity to escape.[58]

There's nothing original about this. In *The Battle of Algiers*, Gilo Pontecorvo's 1965 classic film about the struggle between Algerian nationalists and French forces, insurgents are instructed by their leaders that they need hold out only for twenty-four hours, giving their comrades enough time to flee. Interestingly, the Department of Defense was so impressed by the realism of Pontecorvo's film that it was screened at the Pentagon in August 2003.[59] Apparently this was one of its lessons not taken to heart.

Thus, even those who contend that torture is an effective instrument ought to acknowledge that it offers, at best, a very narrow window of opportunity.

A training manual unearthed from the bunker of al Qaeda's military leader Abu Hafs, following his death in an aerial bombing in November 2001, told recruits that they would face torture, dismemberment, and certain death if taken prisoner.[60] Long before these documents were discovered, FBI Agent Jack Cloonan acknowledged that his source, Jamal al-Fadl, "was taught that the American government would torture him if we got our hands on him. All we ever did was get him fat, dumb, and happy. We smuggled out twenty-two members of his family, took care of him, paid $750,000 for a heart transplant for his kid. So, every preconceived notion he had about us turned out to be wrong."[61]

When you defy expectations, you throw your adversary off balance and gain a distinct advantage. When you show mercy to a man who anticipates cruelty, and respect when he expects contempt, he is filled with relief and gratitude. These emotions are more likely to elicit genuine cooperation than the pain he has been girding himself to endure.

As for our common defense, we reject as false the choice between
our safety and our ideals.
—Barack Obama, Inaugural Address, January 20, 2009

[18] ANWAR AL-AWLAKI

Anwar al-Awlaki was killed in a drone strike on September 30, 2011, in Marib
province, Yemen. No incident more clearly illustrates the normative shift between
America's pre- and post-9/11 approach to terrorism than the decision to target
him with lethal force, despite his being a U.S. citizen, despite his residing in a
country against which the United States was not at war, and despite his never
having been indicted for a single crime.

Born in 1971 in New Mexico, where his father was studying, al-Awlaki spent
his formative years in his ancestral Yemen before returning to the United States
to study civil engineering in Colorado, which profession he abandoned to take
up religion. While preaching at a mosque in San Diego, he became acquainted
with Khalid al-Mihdhar and Nawaf al-Hazmi, two of the 9/11 hijackers. The FBI
referred to him as the latter's "spiritual advisor" and he was interviewed several
times in the days following 9/11.[1] Some investigators believe he was more deeply
connected to the plot than they were ever able to prove. An unidentified FBI
agent told the 9/11 Commission that "if anyone had knowledge of the plot, it
would have been" al-Awlaki because "someone had to be in the U.S. and keep the
hijackers spiritually focused."[2] He certainly demonstrated the requisite passion
for jihad to fulfill that role.

Convinced that the war on terror was an excuse for a war against Muslims—
and perhaps concerned over the attention he drew from law enforcement—he
left America and settled in London, where his rhetoric became increasingly
vitriolic. In 2004, he returned to Yemen, where he became prominent within al
Qaeda in the Arabian Peninsula. With his fluent English, his sermons broadcast
over the Internet attracted a wide following in the West. He was identified as
a source of inspiration for several terrorists, but not as a direct participant in
their schemes. The suicide bombers who attacked the London public transit
system on July 7, 2005, were devotees of his lectures. The so-called Toronto 18,
who were arrested on June 2, 2006, before they were able to carry out their plan

to bomb a number of locations around Canada's largest city and behead the prime minister, watched his videos as part of their training. Several men who were arrested on May 8, 2007, for planning attacks against Fort Dix, New Jersey, took their inspiration from him. Major Nidal Hasan, a U.S. Army psychiatrist, who killed thirteen people during a shooting rampage at the Fort Hood, Texas, military base on November 5, 2009, had exchanged e-mails with al Awlaki. Still, the FBI concluded, "there is no information to indicate . . . Hasan had any co-conspirators or was part of a broader terrorist plot."[3] A twenty-one-year-old British woman in London listened to more than one hundred hours of al-Awlaki's sermons before stabbing Stephen Timms, a member of Parliament, on May 14, 2010. Faisal Shahzad, a Pakistani-American, who failed in his attempt to set off a car bomb in the middle of Times Square on May 1, 2010, was also a follower.

Al-Awlaki was most directly implicated in the case of the Nigerian jihadi Umar Farouk Abdulmutallab, who tried unsuccessfully to ignite his explosives-filled underwear aboard Northwest flight 253 as it approached Detroit from Amsterdam on Christmas Day 2009. The Department of Justice contended in a sentencing document presented at his trial that Abdulmutallab went to Yemen seeking out al-Awlaki, who told him he "would find a way for defendant to become involved in jihad," and that it was al-Awlaki who "accepted defendant for a martyrdom mission." Ultimately, it was he who "gave it final approval, and instructed Defendant Abdulmutallab on" the mission. Al-Awlaki "gave defendant operational flexibility, Awlaki instructed defendant that the only requirements were that the attack be on a U.S. airliner, and that the attack take place over U.S. soil."[4] He was also believed to have been behind a foiled effort to explode package bombs on cargo aircraft bound for the United States from overseas on October 29, 2010.

Given that he had been accused of direct responsibility or being an active part of a criminal conspiracy in only the Northwest and cargo bomb plots, no deaths were directly attributable to his actions. Nevertheless, President Obama authorized the U.S. military to track down and kill him in February 2010 (following secret briefings to Congressional oversight bodies).[5] Possessing the power to inspire terrorism, the eloquence to motivate others to perform acts of violence, had become sufficient to be painted with a hot infrared target.

Contrast this with bin Laden in the wake of the embassy attacks. He bore direct responsibility—and had been indicted—for more than two hundred capital crimes. He had no claim to the protections afforded by American citizenship. And yet there was no consensus that he ought to be pursued, by either legal or military instruments. This is a clear example of the stark life and death distinction across the pre- and post-9/11 divide. The order against al-Awlaki was decisive and without ambiguity and was, consequently, carried out.

By 2010, it was no longer acceptable to take notice of threats, monitor them until they came to fruition, and apprehend the perpetrators after they struck. Now, it is understood that they must be neutralized in advance. What conclusion is there to reach other than that the bombing of the embassies in Africa failed to outrage and anguish? It was tolerable. Only once bin Laden committed the intolerable—9/11—was the nation outraged and its leadership mobilized to fight. Post-9/11, no weapons at the president's disposal were too extreme to deploy against the al Qaeda threat. Where it was once unthinkable to engage the military to go after bin Laden in Afghanistan, it was absolutely practicable to deploy into Yemen to eliminate al-Awlaki.

The current climate is impatient with limitations on the state's right to proceed aggressively against people it designates a threat. When Obama called al-Awlaki's death "a major blow to al-Qaeda's most active operational affiliate" and "another significant milestone in the broader effort to defeat al-Qaeda and its affiliates," he was generally taken at his word. Such is the current norm, "a shift away from detention and interrogation for the sake of intelligence towards killing with no questions asked."[6]

While running for the presidency, Obama had been highly critical of the Bush policies of enhanced interrogation, detention without due process, and preference for military tribunals. There is no hypocrisy here. It is analogous to empowering police officers to use deadly force under prescribed circumstances when confronting violent suspects, while prohibiting them from beating secured prisoners. By taking an individual into custody—whether in the United States or on a foreign battlefield—one assumes responsibility for that person's care. When war has been openly declared by a stateless entity that takes refuge in several locales where arrest is often not a realistic option, that entity's leaders can no longer rely upon immunity from attack anywhere in the world.

Notwithstanding the decision to target al-Awlaki, Obama affirmed, "America does not take strikes when we have the ability to capture individual terrorists; our preference is always to detain, interrogate, and prosecute."[7]

Civil rights advocates had challenged the legality of killing al-Awlaki. In August 2010, the American Civil Liberties Union and the Center for Constitutional Rights, acting on behalf of his father, went to the district court in the District of Columbia seeking an injunction against the government. Beyond the specific intent of gaining respite for al-Awlaki, the plaintiffs argued, generally, that "targeting individuals for killing who are suspected of crimes but have not been convicted—without oversight, due process or disclosed standards for being placed on the kill list—also poses the risk that the government will erroneously target the wrong people."[8] Properly elucidating the absurdity of the claim, William Shawcross wrote, "They seemed to be asserting a constitutional right not to be caught while conspiring to commit murder."[9]

In his opinion, delivered on December 7, 2010, Judge John Bates dismissed the action on the grounds that al-Awlaki's father lacked legal standing to bring the suit and that it raised political questions that were beyond the court's purview, while conceding that "these threshold questions of jurisdiction may seem less significant than the questions posed by the merits of plaintiff's claims." He sounded regretful, ruling, "Because these questions of justiciability require dismissal of this case at the outset, the serious issues regarding the merits of the alleged authorization of the targeted killing of a U.S. citizen overseas must await another day or another (non-judicial) forum."[10]

Much emphasis was placed on al-Awlaki's being an American citizen, but, as Attorney General Eric Holder would emphasize, "it is clear and logical that United States citizenship alone does not make such individuals [i.e. those who threaten the United States from abroad] immune from being targeted."[11]

The most vexing question is why a government requires judicial authority to direct electronic surveillance against targets but not to actually terminate their lives.

Judge Bates allowed, "To be sure, this Court recognizes the somewhat unsettling nature of its conclusion—that there are circumstances in which the Executive's unilateral decision to kill a U.S. citizen overseas is 'constitutionally committed to the political branches' and judicially unreviewable."[12] Nonetheless, that's the position in which the court found itself, given that the Constitution places military and foreign policy decisions outside the judiciary, within the executive and legislative branches of government.

As litigious as American society is, the government does little, if anything, without obtaining a favorable legal brief. Holder made his first public statement about the administration's decision to employ lethal force against al-Awlaki when he spoke at the Northwestern University School of Law in Chicago on March 5, 2012.

"It is entirely lawful—under both United States law and applicable law of war principles—to target specific senior operational leaders of al Qaeda and associated forces. This is not a novel concept." Holder vehemently denied that al-Awlaki was assassinated. "Assassinations are unlawful killings. Here, . . . the U.S. government's use of lethal force in self-defense against a leader of al Qaeda or an associated force who presents an imminent threat of violent attack would not be unlawful—and therefore would not violate the Executive Order banning assassination or criminal statutes."

He went on, "The Constitution does not require the President to delay action until some theoretical end-stage of planning—when the precise time, place, and manner of an attack become clear. Such a requirement would create an unacceptably high risk that our efforts would fail, and that Americans would be killed." In other words, it is no longer necessary to wait until body bags are being filled to take decisive action. The mere chance that nobody died aboard Northwest 253 could not negate al-Awlaki's intent to commit mass murder. He added, "This is an indicator of our times—not a departure from our laws and our values."[13]

A year after his Northwestern address, Holder expanded on the criteria for using lethal force in a foreign country against an American national: "(1) the U.S. government has determined, after a thorough and careful review, that the individual poses an imminent threat of violent attack against the United States; (2) capture is not feasible; and (3) the operation would be conducted in a manner consistent with applicable law of war principles." He pointed out, "Anwar al-Aulaqi [sic] plainly satisfied all of the conditions."[14] Imagine had these conditions been in place after bin Laden declared war in 1996, or, at least, after he demonstrated his capabilities in 1998, rather than just in the hectic days following 9/11. History could have been forestalled.

President Obama has taken direct responsibility for approving every person put on America's "kill list." He is reported to have called the decision to kill al-Awlaki "an easy one."[15] Selecting targets in the first instance is carried out by more than 100 national security advisors. A short list goes to the White House, where the president signs off on each strike. The process is conducted with consideration for the moral and practical implications of, in effect, passing a death sentence. Critics suspect "that Mr. Obama has avoided the complications of detention by deciding, in effect, to take no prisoners alive."[16]

Michael Hayden, director of the CIA under President Bush, commented, "This program rests on the personal legitimacy of the president, and that's not sustainable. . . . Democracies do not make war on the basis of legal memos locked in a D.O.J. safe."[17] Indeed, the law is intended to remove absolute arbitrariness from the process.

Politically, the killing of al-Awlaki could be explained by invoking the specter of another 9/11 (as it is whenever government action is criticized). After the African embassies, or even after the *Cole*, no such dire consequences were imagined. To suggest a hypothetical bombing against another American installation, whether in Bamako or Kampala, would not have rallied much support. Neither would the promise of preventing another *Cole*, as if a mighty billion-dollar war machine needed such protection against a caveman. The fear of "another 9/11" trumps a lot of reservations.

American and allied law enforcement agencies have performed dangerous arrest operations all around the world, taking into custody the likes of Ramzi Yousef, Khalid Sheikh Mohamed, and Ahmed Ghailani. With al-Awlaki and bin Laden, the military employed deadly force. Flexibility and timing are key in combating a stateless enemy. There is no territory to claim or occupy, there is only a mobile and diffuse command and control structure to eradicate.

Flexibility, variability, and reliance on the full arsenal at its disposal exemplify the current U.S. counterterrorism strategy. Thus, while a drone strike was deemed the most appropriate means for neutralizing al-Awlaki, a snatch-and-grab raid was employed to apprehend Abu Anas al-Liby, who had eluded capture for fifteen years. A computer expert, he was alleged to have conducted surveillance against the embassy in Nairobi and was among the last high-ranking al Qaeda members wanted for the bombings to remain at large. There was a $5 million bounty on his head.

On October 5, 2013, he was returning home from morning prayer in Tripoli, Libya, when he was surrounded and taken into custody by members of the U.S. Army's Delta Force. He was spirited to the USS *San Antonio*, which was cruising nearby in the Mediterranean.

Al-Liby (real name Nazih Abdul Hamed al-Ruqai) fought with the Afghan mujahideen in the 1980s, joining bin Laden in Sudan in 1993. When bin Laden returned to Afghanistan in 1996, al-Liby took political asylum in Britain, which is where he was living when the embassy bombings occurred. His wife claimed to CNN that he ceased to be a part of al Qaeda from the time he settled in the United Kingdom.[18]

Of course, whether or not he had ceased to participate in jihadi activity is of no relevance to the charges against him, nor does any change of heart invalidate the indictment under which he was taken into custody. It may, of course, determine whether or not he cooperated with intelligence officers who questioned him immediately after his capture.

In 1999, he'd been picked up by Scotland Yard, but ultimately released for lack of evidence. In May 2000, British police raided his Manchester apartment, where they found the terrorist training manual previously mentioned, which has become known as the Manchester Manual.[19] Divided into eighteen "lessons," it discusses how to contend with interrogation and torture; principles of military organization; intelligence gathering; kidnapping and assassinating enemies, including foreign tourists; using explosives and other weaponry; operational security; and forging documents.

Spooked by the raid, al-Liby fled back to Afghanistan, and lived in Kabul until the American invasion following 9/11, at which point he left for Pakistan before moving on to Iran. As the Iranians would not mistake al Qaeda members for friends, al-Liby, along with his entire family, was held in detention there for nearly a decade. Upon his release, he returned home to Libya, where he settled with his wife and four children. CNN reported that he had been seen around Tripoli more than a year before his capture.[20]

When he made his initial appearance in federal court in New York in mid-October 2013, al-Liby entered a plea of not guilty. He is scheduled to go on trial, along with Khalid al-Fawwaz and Adel Abdel Bary, in November 2014.

A democracy must never forget. There is no pardon, there is no forgiveness
for those who carry out a deliberate attack on civilians.
—Jean-Louis Bruguière, former French counterterrorism magistrate

[19] THE DEATH OF OSAMA BIN LADEN

Those videos of a disheveled Osama bin Laden hunkered down in his window-
less bunker in Abbottabad, Pakistan, brought to mind the quip made by Defense
Secretary Harold Brown about Iran's supreme leader Ayatollah Khomeini during the Iran hostage crisis, when U.S. officials feared Khomeini was prepared
to martyr himself for his faith: "A man with a martyr complex rarely lives to be
seventy-nine."[1] Though far short of seventy-nine when he met his fate, the fifty-
four-year-old Osama's post-9/11 behavior was that of a man desperate to save
his own skin. According to Ayman Saeed Abdullah Batarfi, a Yemeni doctor
who treated al Qaeda fighters on the front line in Afghanistan as they fled the
American onslaught, bin Laden was "mainly preoccupied with his own escape.
'He did not prepare himself for Tora Bora,' Batarfi said, 'and to be frank he didn't
care about anyone but himself.'"[2] Rather than standing his ground and fighting
to his death back in 2001, he chose to survive by retreating into Pakistan and,
eventually, to a compound from which he dared not emerge, living as a hermit
for as long as five years, cut off and of dubious relevance.

On December 14, 2001, bin Laden had signed his last will at Tora Bora, in
which he instructed his children not to continue with al Qaeda. "If it is good,
then we have had our share; if it is bad, then it is enough,"[3] he wrote.

One wonders at this odd, melancholy expression. Of doubt? Of regret? Hard
to believe either crept up on so single-minded a fanatic. Was it a father's natural
instinct to have his children enjoy a better, easier life? What was it—beyond the
prospect of death, which he supposedly welcomed—that could cause him to contemplate that his life's work was possibly bad? Did he see the monstrous bunker-
busters exploding around him with devilish fury as a sign of God's displeasure?

Was he sorry that he had pushed too far? After all, he came away from the
embassies and *Cole* attacks unscathed. Had he imagined he could escalate without
ever facing the consequences of a full-press American response? Or was he tired
and awakening to the realization that terrorists, unlike dictators, could never
find a restful exile?

He could wax poetic about the death of his supporters and profane on the death of his enemies, but he seemed less certain of what awaited his own passing. That he, himself, had a character trait about which he was contemptuous—namely, fear of death—is not so uncommon. Self-loathing is a common characteristic in extreme megalomaniacs.

On May 1, 2011, with precision shots to the head and chest, members of the U.S. Navy's elite SEAL Team Six terminated the criminal case against Osama bin Laden inside his Abbottabad compound. The audacious operation that resulted in his death demonstrated American relentlessness and courage, two qualities bin Laden had chided them for lacking.[4]

One of the SEALs on the mission heaped a warrior's contempt on bin Laden for his failure to grab a nearby firearm and defend himself with his last breath: "He hadn't even prepared a defense. He had no intention of fighting. . . . In all of my deployments, we routinely saw this phenomenon. The higher up the food chain the targeted individual was, the bigger a pussy he was."[5]

Bin Laden's body was bundled aboard a helicopter and flown to the USS *Carl Vinson*, an aircraft carrier waiting in the middle of the Arabian Sea. It was given Muslim rites and dumped into the ocean, where it vanished without a trace.

Had they taken him alive, he would have been charged subject to the indictment for his role in the embassy bombings. Upon careful analysis of the available options, Robert Dannenberg, the CIA's head of counterterrorism operations, had said that arresting al Qaeda's leader was never really a practicable option. "We wanted to make sure that we didn't find ourselves in a situation where we were obliged to capture, not kill bin Laden. . . . We would much rather give him the five-hundred-pound bomb on his complex and pick up his DNA someplace than put him on trial."[6]

During a preparatory briefing for the raid, SEAL team member Mark Owen recounts that the question of whether or not it was a "kill mission" was raised. A lawyer made it clear that the operation wasn't an assassination, saying, "If he is naked with his hands up, you're not going to engage him."[7] It seems clear that the very slightest twitch of a threat justified the use of deadly force. And, under the circumstances, it is difficult to conceive how the raiders could not find themselves at sufficient risk to engage the target.

For better or worse (and the argument is convincingly made both ways) the prospect that bin Laden would one day stand trial in the Southern District of New York had been obviated. The charges against him were formally dismissed in a Manhattan courtroom on June 17.

Confirming bin Laden's death, President Obama announced, "Justice has been done."[8] Kenya's President Mwai Kibaki echoed this sentiment: "His killing is an act of justice."[9]

The news was greeted with satisfaction, relief, and raucous crowds in front of the White House and at Ground Zero in New York. A critical milestone in the conflict with al Qaeda had been achieved.

Surprisingly, the news of bin Laden's death did not provoke any intense vitriol or explosive demands for revenge from those parts of the world sympathetic to his cause. "The decision to bury him at sea was a stroke of genius," marveled Jack Cloonan. "There's a sense of finality to it that took the breath out of a lot of people."[10] There was poetry in his absolute disappearance. Even the refusal to produce a photo of the corpse failed to raise a chorus of conspiracy theorists insisting that he was still alive. The entire affair was handled in such a fashion as to create the perfect void.

Intelligence retrieved from Osama's compound indicated that he was still actively developing operations, including plans to assassinate Obama and General David Petraeus, who was in charge of American forces in Afghanistan and soon to be appointed Director of the CIA, some kind of extravaganza for the tenth anniversary of 9/11, and an attack on American trains.[11] Whether he still exercised enough command, control, and communication to direct operations is open to debate.

Though only time will tell for sure, al Qaeda should not easily recover from the loss of its most charismatic and inspirational figure. Even in hiding, he remained a powerful unifying force right up until his death. Without him, the various factions that have found it effective to brand themselves as al Qaeda may opt for independence or fragment involuntarily.

Writing at least two years before the event, the onetime leader of the East Africa cell, Harun, cautioned against equating Osama's death with the end of al Qaeda: "[The Zionists and Americans] should understand that the death of Usama bin Laden does not mean that Islam and jihad come to an end. No, a thousand times no. Muslims superior to Usama bin Laden died . . . all are heroes who departed [this transient world], but Islam is eternal."[12] For him, al Qaeda had already morphed from a group to an idea that had permeated the Muslim conscience. Moreover, he equated this idea with the fundamental tenets of Islam. One can certainly imagine Osama's name being dredged up from obscurity a hundred years from now as a source of inspiration by some aggrieved terrorist, sending Western analysts scurrying back into the archives to refresh their short memories about who he was.

John Yoo, the Office of Legal Council attorney who drafted the infamous memo that laid out the guidelines for lawful torture on behalf of the White House during the Bush administration, was quick to weigh in: "President Obama can take credit, rightfully for the success . . . but he owes it to the tough decisions taken by the Bush administration," claiming that the killing of bin Laden was somehow a vindication for enhanced interrogation.[13] However, the evidence is, at most, inconclusive and contradictory. Piecing together the public record, it appears that intelligence leading the United States to bin Laden came from a variety of sources over the course of years.

The critical information was the identification of his most trusted courier, known as Abu Ahmed al-Kuwaiti. Through a combination of surveillance techniques, American intelligence was able to track al-Kuwaiti to the walled compound in Abbottabad. Meticulous analysis suggested that bin Laden might— estimated probabilities among the intelligence people involved varied between 60 and 90 percent certainty—be holed up there, as well. Assessing the risk as commensurate to the reward, even at the low end of the probability scale, Obama ordered the SEALs to conduct the raid.

Some of the information that helped them close in on al-Kuwaiti may or may not have been elicited under the influence of torture. Certainly—based on what we know today—there was no single extraordinary revelation that directed American forces to Abbottabad. Rather, it was from careful pursuit of a variety of investigative leads and diligent analysis that it was discovered. Even Jose Rodriguez, head of the CIA's clandestine services at the time, and an unequivocal defender of the enhanced interrogation program, concedes that K. S. M., the captive who was most likely to know Osama's whereabouts, resisted saying anything that could betray bin Laden's hideaway, despite nine and a half days of sleep deprivation and one-hundred-and-eighty-three waterboarding sessions.

"That was the one secret he was going to take to the grave," Rodriguez declared.[14] Of course, the rationale for enhanced interrogation is that the suspect's desperation to stop the punishment supposedly conquers his will to keep secrets. Admitting that K. S. M. could withhold this most critical of all pieces of intelligence is to, tacitly, agree that the techniques designed to break the suspect failed.

Rodriguez explained that waterboarding—the diabolical practice of restraining the subject on an inclined board, covering his face with a cloth, and pouring a stream of water over his nose and mouth to simulate the sensation of drowning—was performed under a strictly controlled formula. Henri Alleg, a French journalist who was arrested by French paratroopers in Algiers in 1957, was subjected to waterboarding and vividly described the experience: "The rag was soaked rapidly. Water flowed everywhere: in my mouth, in my nose, all over my face. But for a while I could still breathe in some small gulps of air. I tried, by contracting my throat, to take in as little water as possible and to resist suffocation by keeping air in my lungs for as long as I could. But I couldn't hold on for more than a few moments. I had the terrible impression of drowning, and a terrible agony, that of death itself, took possession of me. In spite of myself, all the muscles of my body struggled uselessly to save me from the suffocation. In spite of myself, the fingers of both my hands shook uncontrollably."[15]

As the CIA employed the technique, each pour lasted, on average, only ten seconds. "Khalid Sheikh Mohamed would use his fingers to count the number of seconds because he knew that in all likelihood we would stop at ten. This doesn't sound like a person who is afraid of dying," Rodriguez said.[16]

The inherent contradiction—and the shortcoming of torture as applied by the Americans—is that it depends on the suspect's uncertainty as to how far the torturer is prepared to go. A tough guy—and Rodriguez called K. S. M. "one of the toughest killers out there"[17]—can endure a great deal when he is convinced it will not surpass a certain point. Thus, it wasn't so much whether K. S. M. feared death as his certainty that his tormenters were not going to kill him. Consequently, he did not have to take the secret of bin Laden's whereabouts to the grave, but only as far as the limits of his interrogator's abuse.

"This program [enhanced interrogation] wasn't about hurting anybody," Rodriguez insisted; "this program was about instilling a sense of hopelessness and despair in the terrorist so that he would conclude on his own that he was better off cooperating with us."[18] Clearly, the subject's understanding of the limits to which the torturer is willing to go would temper his sense of hopelessness and despair, thus strengthening his resolve to withstand and withhold.

The attacks of 9/11 shook America's faith in itself, in its justice system. "Rather than seeing the American legal system as the country's greatest strength, it was instantly regarded as a burden," wrote Jane Mayer.[19]

The foundation of the Anglo-American legal system rests on two extraordinarily brilliant concepts of justice: the presumption of innocence and reasonable doubt. They have an elegant symbiosis, seeming to favor the defendant, but really serving as a bulwark of fairness. The first, as defined by the venerable *Black's Law Dictionary*, is the "fundamental principle that a person may not be convicted of a crime unless the government proves guilt beyond a reasonable doubt, without any burden placed on the accused to prove innocence."[20] This is an utterly counterintuitive notion. The jury has before it an individual accused of a crime. Not someone plucked off the street at random (or so we trust, at any rate). But one against whom the police have gathered enough evidence to feel confident about laying a charge. The state solemnly proclaims, this is the guilty person. Nonetheless, the jury is to put that aside and think of the defendant as innocent until presented with enough proof to, in effect, convince them otherwise and declare him guilty "beyond a reasonable doubt."

That fabulously ambiguous standard, defined by *Black's* as "the doubt that prevents one from being firmly convinced of a defendant's guilt, or the belief that a defendant is not guilty."[21]

After more than three months of hearing evidence, the jury in the trial of al-'Owhali, Odeh, el Hage, and Mohamed was instructed on the presumption of innocence by Judge Sand as follows: "The presumption of innocence was with each defendant when the trial began and remains with him even now as I speak to you, and will continue with each defendant into your deliberation. It is not removed with respect to a defendant and with respect to a particular count unless and until you are convinced the government has proved that defendant's guilt beyond a reasonable doubt on that count."

He went on, "What is reasonable doubt? The words almost define themselves. It is a doubt based upon reason and common sense. It is a doubt that a reasonable person has after carefully weighing all the evidence. It is a doubt that would cause a reasonable person to hesitate to act in a matter of importance in his or her personal life. Proof beyond a reasonable doubt must therefore be proof of such a convincing character that a reasonable person would not hesitate to rely and act upon it in the most important of his affairs. A reasonable doubt is not a caprice or whim. It is not a speculation or a suspicion. It is not an excuse to avoid the performance of an unpleasant duty. And it is not sympathy."[22]

Isn't it fascinating how, in a profession obsessed with quibbling over definitions and distinctions between synonymous concepts, *the* critical element in distinguishing guilt from innocence is reduced to the vicissitudes of nothing more certain than the common sense and reason of twelve randomly selected jurors? Which puts me in mind of the old lawyer's joke, "I wouldn't want to be judged by twelve people who aren't smart enough to get out of jury duty."

Every sovereign country on earth employs a legal system, but how many are worthy of public trust? Arbitrary arrest and summary conviction are so often the rule. Confessions are often extracted by the most brutal means, without regard for their veracity. Witnesses are intimidated and evidence tampered with. Defendants are presumed guilty. The capacity of defense counsel to present their case is constrained, both by their complicity with the state and fear of the consequences of daring to question its authority and integrity.

What legitimizes legal proceedings is less about the prosecution than the defense, for in the independence and vigor of the defense do we see the proof of a fair trial. The reason we mostly believe in the verdicts of American courts is our confidence that the defendants had benefit of counsel with the liberty to advocate on their behalf, without fear or favor. And that the court adjudicates without passion or prejudice. And, on top of all that, the ultimate determination of guilt or innocence is freely rendered by a jury of the defendant's peers, randomly selected from the jurisdiction wherein the crime was perpetrated.

To side with law and order demands respect for the principles and ideals the system embodies in their entirety. The concept of law and order is not a knee-jerk belief that every defendant is guilty. Rather, it is the belief in the right to a fair trial and to the scrupulous application of the rule of law and the procedures of the justice system. For the measure of a trial is in its conduct, not the outcome. To presume guilt is to undermine the process and to introduce bias where justice calls for impartiality.

Robert Jackson, the chief U.S. prosecutor at the Nuremberg war crimes trials, made the point: "You must put no man on trial under the forms of judicial proceeding, if you are not willing to see him freed if not proven guilty. If you are determined to execute a man in any case, there is no occasion for a trial; the world yields no respect to courts that are merely organized to convict."[23] Certainly, in the emotionally charged aftermath of World War II, the full scope of Nazi horrors just freshly revealed, the blood still seeping under the bootprints of occupying Allied troops, resisting a rush to judgment demanded supreme discipline. After all, was not the guilt of those in the dock painfully obvious? And wouldn't their acquittal have been disastrous to the Allies' broad objective of eradicating the old regime and transforming German society? Yes and yes. Still, the Allies ran the risk with confidence in the quality of the evidence and their ability to construct a compelling case against those accused.

The Israeli judiciary faced a comparable dilemma when Adolf Eichmann, who had been kidnapped by intelligence officers from Buenos Aires, was brought before a court in Jerusalem in April 1961 to face judgment for his role in the Holocaust. The presumption of innocence was, Hannah Arendt reported, "an obvious fiction. If he had not been found guilty before he appeared in Jerusalem, guilty beyond any reasonable doubt, the Israelis would never have dared, or wanted, to kidnap him."[24] Nonetheless, of the court's capacity to rule objectively, the presiding judge said, "It cannot be denied that the memory of the Nazi holocaust stirs every Jew, but while this case is being tried before us it will be our duty to restrain these feelings, and this duty we shall honor."[25]

This discussion gets to the fundamental problem with abusing suspects: it presumes guilt or, at the very least, guilty knowledge. A suspect is tortured with a certain preconceived—if often woefully ill-defined—expectation of how he ought to respond. A torture session violates the time-honored principles of a good interrogation. Brute force is adopted as a substitute for knowledge. Emotional outburst is a poor substitute for methodical patience. Rejection of the captive as a fellow human being eliminates the prospect for genuine cooperation. The subject's failure to confess can be met only with more and greater brutality.

When the interrogator insists, "Tell us about the attacks that are going to be launched," "I don't know" is not an acceptable answer, because the questioning assumes that he does know. "There are none" is equally unacceptable because of the interrogator's certainty that attacks are imminent.

The difference between resistance and the sought-after response, according to the torturer's logic, is pain and suffering. Or, more euphemistically, discomfort. Intensification is the magic key to success. And, experience reveals, everyone can be brought to a point of being willing to talk. Because, it is evident, talking will bring relief. Specifically, saying what the interrogator wants to hear. Which is not one and the same with revealing the truth.

A terrorist is a human being, however heinous. Looking him in the eye, the interrogator never loses sight of this. An interrogation, as intimate and manipulative as a seduction, is an opportunity to converse, to build a rapport, and to understand what will entice a suspect to give up what you want. The threat of harsh punishment, whether implicit or explicit, is never totally withdrawn, thus making the promise of support and friendship all the more appealing. Unlike the crude application of brute force that has found favor in American counterterrorism, a successful interrogation isn't exclusively the product of fear and intimidation, but other strong human motivators: the hope of refuge and the possibility of redemption. And moreover, the opportunity for the suspect to find a receptive ear, a person genuinely interested in what he has to say. An opportunity to explain himself; to pontificate on his cause. For the true believer wants nothing better than to spread the word.

Under the Bush administration it was decided that hardened terrorists were immune to such techniques and that interrogators were best off wringing information from them. That talking to them was a waste of time. After all, terrorists, to their mind, must be impervious to human consideration.

FBI Agent Ali Soufan, a Muslim and native Arab speaker, had the advantage of being able to speak to al Qaeda suspects in their own language and with the confidence of one who shared familiar cultural reference points. He was incredulous when so-called—or self-proclaimed—expert contractors moved in to take over from himself and his FBI and Naval Criminal Investigative Service (NCIS) colleagues during the *Cole* investigation. These contractors were not former police or intelligence officers. They presented themselves as behavioral specialists. When Soufan asked them of their experience with interviewing Middle Easterners, they had little to offer. After all, there are very few opportunities to gain practical experience as an interrogator outside the police, intelligence, or military services. Yet, somehow, these people sold themselves to anxious bureaucrats as more expert.[26]

In contrast to the experience of the FBI was the CIA's position "that had adherents among an army of self-styled amateurs on interrogation in the U.S. government, from the Oval Office on down. No one has time to build 'relationships'—a word that was repugnant to those who viewed al Qaeda operatives as evil incarnate."[27]

It has been proven time and again that the same approach that has coaxed evidence from countless sociopaths is highly effective against terrorists, who are often—within their own particular context—people of principle with a definite moral compass. This accounts for how many people gave voluntary statements in the years leading up to 9/11. I have yet to meet an FBI agent who believes the power to physically abuse a prisoner is an advantage.

"Once captured, al Qaeda members behaved the same as other [criminals]," Soufan said.[28] They were susceptible to the usual mix of inducements, flattery, small courtesies, and the underlying threat that their conditions could always worsen.

"But, there is no silver bullet," he goes on. "Every individual cooperates for their own reason. The common psychology among Islamic terrorists is their suspension of critical thinking. They must do this in order to belong. They embrace the thoughts presented to them by the counterculture. Which doesn't mean they're stupid, only that they are willing to live entirely within their own logical paradigm."[29]

Joe Billy, the FBI supervisor who served on the Dar es Salaam deployment, recognized a fascinating paradox in the character of the terrorists. "On the one hand, it takes enormous balls to carry out a suicide attack. On the other, these guys are extremely impressionable and demand constant fortification. You have this tough terrorist operative, but they are so very impressionable. Their minds can be twisted to where they'll commit this horrendous act. But, you can get them to talk just like anyone else under interrogation. It just doesn't take much to push them in a particular direction."[30]

Pat D'Amuro is unequivocal in his abhorrence for torture. His opposition is part practical—it doesn't work—but, as well, moral—it is in violation of the Constitution that federal officers are sworn to defend. Ken Piernick is adamant: "In the Bureau, we take very seriously absolute respect for the Constitution and the rights that are afforded people, whether foreign or domestic. Certainly, we can push right up to the edge of the line, and you take advantage of everything we have, but you don't violate the law or their rights. Period."[31]

As was the case with al-'Owhali, a skilled interrogator, armed with facts accumulated through other investigative avenues, taking nothing on faith, letting no statement pass without a follow-up *why* or *how, when* or *where*, is able to whittle away at lies, pushing the subject toward the truth. He is attentive to the inconsistent or the illogical. Convincing the suspect that his story isn't making sense, he cajoles him into saying more. The more he says, the more the investigator has to work with. Eventually, in most cases, accurate information is revealed.

D'Amuro says, "Terrorists are taught interrogation techniques and how to stall. Still, it's just a matter of keeping them talking. When you catch them in a lie, they tend to talk even more. A good Muslim is not supposed to lie, so catching them, and having evidence to back it up, can be exploited."[32]

Anything you say may be used against you. To which mandatory caution the suspect usually thinks not "I'd better not speak," but, *I can say something that may exonerate me.*

He who is tortured may eventually comply, but will never confide. He may succumb, but won't collaborate. Neither party will ever trust the other. It is a basic truth of human relations that a person talks to those who are looked upon as friends. A torturer will never be anything but an enemy.

Moreover, torture will further inflame those upon whom it is wielded. The tortured do not easily forget their torment and humiliation. From the holding cage in the Cairo courtroom where he was tried in connection with the assassination of President Sadat, Ayman al-Zawahiri, who now leads al Qaeda, cried out, "We are here in this jail after fourteen months. So where is democracy? Where is freedom? Where is human rights? Where is justice? Where is justice? We will never forget! We will never forget what these criminals have done!"[33] However dangerous he was when he went in, there is no question he emerged even more so and more deeply committed to his cause.

John Yoo, the Bush-era White House lawyer, mused, "Why is it so hard for people to understand that there is a category of behavior not covered by the legal system?"[34]

Probably because it is absolutely untrue and a rather shocking thing for a government lawyer to believe. Long experience and the accumulation of precedents amply prove that the American legal system is remarkably adaptable. And that its procedures and protocols, respect for human dignity, do not impede its effectiveness, nor do they give unfair advantage to the accused or impose undue burdens on the government in exercising its power. The government fears knowing someone is a terrorist but lacking the evidence to prove it. The civil libertarian response is to remind that the burden is on the government to prove that which it believes it knows.

Treating the terrorists who blew up the African embassies as criminal defendants was an effective exercise. Judge Sand, it was affirmed by every defense attorney with whom I spoke, was scrupulous in maintaining impartiality.

"It was a pleasure, a beautiful experience, really, to try this case with Judge Sand, who is one of the great American jurists," effused Odeh's attorney, Edward Wilford. "Now, I didn't agree with every ruling he made, of course, but he did the best that he could to ensure a fair trial. I think the prosecution was above-board. You can't ask for anything more than that."[35]

Late in the trial, Sand told the court, "I want to say something for the record what the lawyers are well aware of, but maybe is not so well known, and that is that defendants in this case have been granted virtually every request that they have made for funding, for investigators, for paralegals, for interpreters—you name it. If there was a colorable claim of need, it has been granted."

This was critical to the defenders, most of whom were independent practitioners and, therefore, severely outgunned by the government's resources, which included an army of associates, paralegals, investigators, and clerical staff, freeing up the lawyers to concentrate on their task. It was a huge advantage in such a complex case, where even the logistics were daunting. For example, classified documents could be viewed only in a designated room at Foley Square, necessitating that the lawyers work together for long hours in close quarters, away from the comfort of their own offices.

Intimidated leaders, shaken and confused by the carnage of 9/11, doubted the system was up to the task of finding and punishing the perpetrators and of safeguarding against future attacks. All its intricate rules and procedures felt like unnecessary—moreover, self-imposed—impediments. Precedents seemed inadequate for judging the unprecedented. Guaranteed rights were nothing but pods in a street-corner shell game, wielded by hustling defense lawyers to quick-shuffle terrorists through the system to freedom.

Scott Brown, Republican senator from Massachusetts, said, "Some people believe our Constitution exists to grant rights to terrorists who want to harm us. I disagree."[36] This statement, which probably elicited cheers from the senator's conservative audience, is patently absurd. The Constitution exists to protect the rights of all, who are presumed innocent. It holds no mercy for those found guilty of the worst offenses. Never in the history of the United States has its Constitution impeded the work of the criminal justice system. It has made prosecutorial work more exacting, as is its intent.

Those who advocate shortcuts that deny an individual's rights, those who decry informing suspects that they do have rights, presume to know who is guilty and like to point to suspects who seem obviously culpable beyond any reasonable doubt—bin Laden or K. S. M. All the while, they take for granted the law they might someday face would be applied with fairness and respect because, after all, they are innocent. It would, in their minds, always be wild-eyed fanatics with turbans and long beards, brandishing swords dripping with fresh blood that would be rousted in the night and locked away in camps without recourse to lawyers and due process. In their minds, it would always be thus.

And because they are sure they will only ever be imperiled by these mad fanatics, they are content to empower government bureaucrats to decide whose rights can be violated, and to formulate the surreal legalese that has come to define what level of abuse is legitimate and what crosses beyond the pale to be properly defined as torture. The public has been either unimpressed or too frightened to notice that all eight defendants—including five embassy bombers—tried under docket 93 CR 180, which was initiated following the first World Trade Center attack in 1993, have been convicted.[37]

When Attorney General Holder filed a superseding indictment against K. S. M. in federal court in the Southern District of New York on December 14, 2009, he set off a firestorm of outraged protest from those who insisted that it was an inappropriate venue in which to try him. There were legitimate concerns that Foley Square would become a target were he ever to appear there. Even if nothing came to pass, the cost of the process, including fortress-like security around lower Manhattan, was estimated at $1 billion.[38] On April 4, 2011, Holder succumbed to pressure and dismissed the federal charges, announcing that K. S. M. would be tried before a military tribunal. It was as though he were conceding that certain crimes and particular defendants could not be accommodated by a justice system that had been honed and refined along strong girders of unshakable principles for centuries. It was a dangerous admission by the country's top law officer.

On April 4, 2012, K. S. M. and four others were charged before the Office of Military Commissions with terrorism, hijacking, conspiracy, murder, and destruction of property in violation of the laws of war. If convicted, they could face the death penalty. The ACLU decried "prosecuting the most important terrorism trials of our time in a second-tier system of justice . . . set up to achieve easy convictions and hide the reality of torture, not to provide a fair process."[39]

Another fear was that K. S. M. would use the opportunity of a trial to spout al Qaeda propaganda. Speaking generally about terrorism cases, the former U.S. Attorney for the Southern District of New York, Mary Jo White said, "Often, for the defendant, the trial is a continuation of the assault. Generally, they welcome it as a forum for making a public statement."[40] Upsetting as that might be, it isn't entirely clear what fear this holds for the United States.

White argues for the efficacy of the military tribunal system from a concern over protecting confidential intelligence sources. "As you go up the al Qaeda chain of command, this becomes a greater concern because you're likely dealing with more delicate sources." Given her own success in prosecuting terrorists, she surprised me by saying, "Law enforcement is not necessarily the most effective model for dealing with terrorists. We need to be able to produce evidence without jeopardizing national security. There can be a fair and robust regime outside the civilian courts, and we shoot ourselves in the foot by doubting the credibility of the military commissions. Due process can absolutely be respected in that forum. This is a war and there exists a group of people that you can't charge for fear of compromising sources and methods."[41]

On the surface, the outcome of the Ahmed Ghailani trial, in which he was acquitted on all but one charge, was interpreted as proof that the criminal court system is unreliable. However, the end result was the same as had he been found guilty on any greater number of counts—imprisonment for life without possibility of parole.

Being the first instance of a former detainee of the CIA black prisons and Guantánamo Bay to come before a federal court, the Ghailani case was widely considered a precedent-setter for K. S. M.'s eventual process. The court established that it would not admit evidence acquired through torture. Hence, if K. S. M. first confessed to being the mastermind of 9/11 following waterboarding, the prosecution could well be jeopardized.

The enthusiasm for sanctioning abuses has been misrepresented as resolve to let nothing stand in the way of protecting the national security; an admirable sacrifice of inhibitions by men who have never actually engaged in violence, proof of their toughness and character. One sees this in leaders who have never stood in harm's way. George Bush, for example, was less enthusiastic about experiencing combat in Vietnam than he was to issue orders for the invasion of Iraq. He cavalierly authorized American soldiers and intelligence officers to torture in the interest of extracting information that he glibly assured was saving lives without revealing who, where, or when.

Bush reveled in Old West notions of law and order. He tossed off sound bites about getting bin Laden "dead or alive" and "smoking him out" of the caves he was presumed to be hiding in. He must have loved it when CTC head Cofer Black promised him that al Qaeda terrorists would "have flies walking across their eyeballs."[42] Colin Powell, Bush's first secretary of state, who had actually been in combat during his long and distinguished military career, told one of the president's friends, "He has these cowboy characteristics, and when you know where to rub him, you can really get him to do some dumb things. You have to play on those swaggering bits of self-image. [Vice President Dick] Cheney knew exactly how to push all his buttons."[43] John Kerry, the Democratic nominee who faced Bush in the 2004 presidential elections, and a decorated Vietnam War veteran, told the Democratic National Convention in July 2003, "In these dangerous days, there is a right way and a wrong way to be strong. Strength is more than tough words."[44]

Cheney spoke with relish about the need "to work sort of the dark side, if you will."[45] On that side was abuse, brutality, and the abrogation of American and international law. Of course, Bush and Cheney were spared the unpleasantness of working there themselves. They would merely discuss expediency and review memos. It would be an entirely different experience for the people ordered to do their bidding. As one CIA officer with knowledge of enhanced interrogation said, "When you cross over that line of darkness, it's hard to come back. You lose your soul. You can do your best to justify it, but it's well outside the norm. You can't go to that dark a place without it changing you."[46]

The 9/11 attacks changed America, infusing daily life with an unfamiliar sense of vulnerability. It raised the stakes for political leaders, who had heretofore been spared tough decisions by terrorism's fundamental irrelevance to the vast majority of the electorate. Terrorism, like shark attacks and airplane crashes, became feared beyond all probability of its occurrence. What had been left to law enforcement and intelligence professionals finally seized the attention of politicians.

"People who are living in fear are willing to give up rights for the feeling of safety," said Edward Wilford, Mohamed Odeh's defense attorney. "Since 9/11, I've seen a contraction of the objective mind-set. People's feelings have been galvanized, not against terrorists, but against people accused of terrorism. It furthered my resolve to stand in the trench, to fight for the protections that the Constitution affords. Because there was an immediate clamoring to cut back on everybody's rights. Once we start doing that, we've lost something. So many freedoms we take for granted have already been infringed upon."[47]

Fear makes us reactionary. When we feel threatened, anthropology trumps philosophy, and instinct propels us to seek safety. Little thought is wasted on the well-being of others. We are grateful for those in authority—a president, a vice president, a secretary of Homeland Security—who assure us that they have the magic formula to protect us. We are inclined to grant them the authority to do what they insist is necessary. Expediency rules. But our system is more resilient than we give it credit for. Perhaps because we are constantly being worried that it is in jeopardy. The national security can be invoked to guard legitimate secrets; or to camouflage the absence of substance. Secrecy is not necessarily a source of strength. But it is almost always a source of power.

The world is now faced with the equally believable
possibilities of an African Renaissance or an African Anarchy.
—Gérard Prunier, *Africa's World War*

[20] AFRICA

When Africa is not neglected, it is most frequently exploited. It is a land where
men without scruples have always gotten away with murder.

"Africa is too peripheral to the contemporary interests of the so-called world
community to actually be part of it," writes Gérard Prunier, the renowned Africa
scholar from the University of Paris. "The September 11 crisis and its vast consequences only accelerated the process of Africa's international marginalization."[1]

Marginalization is of course a process that al Qaeda and its affiliates are prac-
ticed at taking advantage of, having done it in Afghanistan and Sudan and Yemen,
and now in Somalia and Mali and across the Maghreb.

"Africa represents a region of threat that is not properly assessed. It is my view
that now is the time to focus on Africa. It is not widely shared, but I'm quite
sure," Jean-Louis Bruguière says with quiet certainty. He spent thirty years at the
forefront of France's often-violent battles against terrorists as an investigating
magistrate, a position that has no equivalent in the United States. He wielded
the power to order investigations; authorize searches, seizures, and wiretaps; issue arrest warrants; and even incarcerate suspects. Among the triumphs of his
celebrated career was the arrest of Carlos the Jackal, the world's most notorious
terrorist before bin Laden, and the conviction, in absentia, of six Libyan agents
for the most deadly terrorist attack in French history: the 1989 bombing of a
passenger jet, UTA flight 772, killing 171 people over Niger.

In 2007, Bruguière warned the Senate Committee on Homeland Security
and Government Affairs[2] of a new terrorist menace rooted in North Africa,
with strong tentacles reaching south across the Sahel into the sub-Saharan region. Originally called the Algerian Salafist Group for Preaching and Fighting
(known by the French acronym GSPC), it swore formal allegiance to al Qaeda
in 2006 and adopted the moniker al Qaeda in the Islamic Maghreb (AQIM).
At the time, its leader, Abu Musab Abdul Wadud, said al Qaeda "is the only
organization qualified to gather together the mujahideen."[3] It has been respon-

sible for bombing a U.N. building in Algiers, attacking the Israeli embassy in Mauritania, kidnapping and killing several Westerners, and fomenting unrest in those countries—Niger, Mali, Nigeria, Chad—where ethnic tensions, usually between Muslims and Christians, fester. The Maghreb—like Yemen, the Horn of Africa, and the Pakistan-Afghanistan frontier—has all the conditions terrorists look for in a haven: poorly defined and uncontrolled borders, open spaces where governments exercise minimal sovereignty, and desperate people who can be convinced that violence, with its appealing simplicity, promises a quick solution to myriad problems.

Bruguière would be proven right five years later when Mali became a major battleground in the war on terror. His analysis was based on the fact that, from its initial operationalization as a terrorist organization, al Qaeda has been an African institution. It planned its first attacks from Khartoum, inspired by America's intervention in Somalia, and spilled its first blood in Kenya and Tanzania.

The travel writer Jeffrey Tayler, who undertook a 4,000 mile trek across Chad, northern Nigeria, Niger, Mali, and Senegal the year following 9/11, paints a dire picture of the future: "emaciated hordes fleeing south from the encroaching desert, swamping settled communities and provoking their ire and violent resistance; renewed civil war; the further spread of Islamic and probably even Christian extremism . . . ; the infiltration of foreign terrorist groups and criminal gangs; and the rise of Western-backed dictators who promise to stamp them out."[4] As the body count inevitably mounts, he warns, "The imams will tell the survivors whom to blame."[5] You can be sure that it won't be the putative defenders of the faith.

Among those who had been held hostage by AQIM was Robert Fowler, the Canadian ambassador and former deputy minister of defense, who was kidnapped in Niger while on a mission as the U.N. secretary-general's special envoy. He was spirited off to a series of makeshift camps in eastern and northern Mali, where he was held for more than four months in 2008–2009. After this extended period of observation and interaction with AQIM militants, he wrote, "I have never met a more single-minded and committed set of individuals. . . . By almost any modern standards their ideas were naïve and unsophisticated in the extreme, to say nothing of dangerous and just a little anti-social. Their version of Islam was simplistic and dramatically dated. But there must be no doubt about the depth of their faith and their absolute commitment to what they perceived to be its fundamental principles. . . . These self-styled soldiers of God demonstrated over and over again the extent to which they are prepared to use extreme brutality to achieve their ends, but their viciousness appeared to be neither arbitrary nor casual. Their every act was considered and needed to be justifiable in terms of their chosen path of *jihad*."[6] Furthermore, he added, "I know of no argument that would convince them to abandon their chosen path."[7]

Conditions in Mali were further complicated in May 2012 when separatist elements in the north took advantage of political upheaval in Bamako by declaring the independent Republic of Azawad, which includes the cities of Timbuktu and Gao, which it deemed would be governed according to Islamic law. AQIM and other extremist groups have been welcomed to the region. Though no member of the international community has recognized their "state," the central government's loss of de facto control could give AQIM and its fellow travelers a secure base from which to operate.

General Carter Ham, Commander of the United States Africa Command, told an audience at the Homeland Security Policy Institute at George Washington University in December 2012, "As each day goes by, al Qaeda and other organizations are strengthening their hold in northern Mali. There is a compelling need for the international community, led by Africans, to address that."[8]

France, which retains an interest in its former colonial territories, sent troops into Mali beginning January 11, 2013 in support of the central authorities. The French defense minister, Jean-Yves Drian, claimed that the Islamists were within three to four days of reaching Bamako had they not intervened.[9] Notwithstanding the questionable legitimacy of the new rulers in the capital, they are certainly preferred to al Qaeda affiliates.

The Islamist leader, Oumar Ould Hamaha bellowed that France had "opened the gates of hell for all the French."[10] AQIM's threat was not born of the conflict in Mali. Reports indicate that at least six AQIM-affiliated cells were dismantled over the past several years in France.[11]

Based in lawless Somalia, al Shabab represents a significant menace in East Africa. Its worst attack to date came on July 11, 2010, when suicide bombers attacked locations around Kampala, where people had gathered to watch the World Cup—at a restaurant and on a rugby pitch where outdoor television screens had been set up. More than seventy people were killed. Uganda was targeted because of its participation in an African Union peacekeeping mission in Somalia.

On October 16, 2011, Kenya, compelled to react to the kidnapping of three Westerners from its territory near the Somali frontier within a month, launched an offensive against al Shabab. Its troops crossed into Somalia with the support of the Somali government, which likely appreciated the show of force in the southern regions where it exerts little control. Kenyan forces advanced some eighty miles in a single day, prompting al Shabab to deny responsibility for the kidnappings, while threatening to "strike at the heart of your [Kenyan] interests," chillingly adding, "Kenya has peace, its cities have tall buildings and business is booming there."[12] In June 2012, the Obama administration acknowledged for the first time that U.S. military forces were engaged in "direct action" on the ground against al Shabab.[13]

On September 14, 2012, Kenyan police thwarted an al Shabab terror plot when it raided an apartment in Eastleigh, the same neighborhood where the embassy bombing conspirators once congregated, seizing a cache of weapons and explosives and arresting two individuals. An alert was issued for eight suspects who were still at large. At least four bombers were supposed to detonate suicide vests at churches and other public places in Nairobi, Nanyuki, and Kisumu, while other terrorists lay in wait to attack survivors and first responders in a hail of machine gun fire. The vests were similar in design to those used in the Kampala attacks.[14] Then came the nearly week-long siege at Nairobi's Westgate Shopping Centre, commencing September 21, 2013, that left more than sixty dead and shook the entire capital. Al Shabab planned this operation carefully, renting a retail space within the mall, which allowed them to amass an arsenal without drawing attention until they were ready to strike. It was a vicious attack that demonstrated the group's ruthlessness and utter lack of discrimination in selecting targets.

Much havoc has been wrought in religiously divided Nigeria in the name of al Qaeda-linked Boko Haram. On August 26, 2011, it claimed responsibility for a suicide truck bomb detonated at the U.N. headquarters in Abuja. Boko Haram has conducted myriad shootings and bombings in northern Nigeria and claimed responsibility for bombing the National Police Headquarters in June 2011. However, at least one analyst claims that "there is no proof that a well-organized, ideologically coherent terrorist group called Boko Haram even exists today." Jean Herskovits, a professor of African history and politics at the State University of New York, suggested that it is a flag of convenience flown by disconnected groups posing as a coordinated movement, and invoked by the Nigerian government in order to taint all civil unrest as terrorism. Similar to what has happened with al Qaeda, "Boko Haram has evolved into a franchise."[15] However coordinated or not, it has been responsible for more than seventeen hundred deaths in the four years since roughly 2009, with the cumulative effect of Islamic extremists in northern Nigeria being able to destabilize the nation.

As Steve Coll so colorfully put it, "individuals can strap on the Al Qaeda football jersey, as it were, and declare membership without ever meeting another member; they may do that and subsequently meet some regional specialist who can help them with technical or tactical issues; or they may travel to the Afghanistan-Pakistan border and connect with members tied to the central leadership. All of these scenarios are probably best thought of as Al Qaeda-related, but not necessarily Al Qaeda-directed."[16]

"Conservative estimates are that eighteen thousand to twenty thousand individuals went through the training camps in Afghanistan," said Pat D'Amuro. "All the splinter groups that popped up after 9/11 makes the job more difficult because we've got to collect intelligence on all these different groups."[17]

Even before bin Laden's death further weakened his organization's centralization of command and control, Bruguière offered, "The term *al Qaeda* is really quite irrelevant. It is now more of a loose conglomerate of militants or individuals, acting on their own or in small cells, but not with a centralized connection to bin Laden. This makes it more difficult to understand and to anticipate what may emerge."[18]

Drop these increasingly amorphous groups into the chaos of Africa and you have all the accelerant necessary to ignite a powder keg of grievance and disaffection.

The developed world has exhibited a shameful out-of-sight out-of-mind attitude toward Africa's dead—one palpable source of grievance. It helped al Qaeda conspire and operate with impunity for nearly a decade since abu Ubaydah recognized Africa as an opportune base and moved to Kenya to establish the East Africa cell. It may seem like a lessening of intensity in its jihad against the United States if al Qaeda is consigned to the periphery, but this is no solution, as it has proven capable of using peripheral locations as bases from which to launch devastating attacks.

For all the continent's poverty, the International Monetary Fund has projected that seven African states (Ethiopia, Mozambique, Tanzania, Congo, Ghana, Zambia, and Nigeria) will be among the ten fastest growing economies between 2011 and 2015.[19] The prospects for such impressive growth and development will multiply the points of intersection between African and foreign interests. It could well be at these load-bearing joints where it will be decided whether Africa initiates its renaissance or falls to anarchy.

CONCLUSION

The effects of an act of terrorism are not measured by the immediate body count. The full misery lies in the malign trauma hanging in its aftermath, the corrosive mushroom cloud of collective fear that blooms up thickly and wafts far beyond the explosion. Ordinary people, physically distant from the point of impact, must be emotionally transported to the scene and infected with looking-over-the-shoulder disquiet at death's stalking. Anxious governments must be persuaded to divide the world into suspects and victims, while left unable to distinguish the one from the other.

For all the blood spilled that dark day in Africa, and tears shed ever after, little impression was left on the American conscience despite the embassy bombings being the worst act of terrorism ever directed against American targets (though not the deadliest in terms of American casualties). The attacks occurred in too obscure a part of the world, at a place few imagined they might ever find themselves. They sparked little more than the passing clucks of sympathy emitted for half a dozen international tragedies that blip through any twenty-four-hour news cycle.

Without popular outrage—an emotion, history teaches, not much distinct from widespread panic—it was easy for U.S. policy makers to defer decisive action and ignore those few dedicated bin Laden hunters in the law enforcement and national security communities who were arguing that al Qaeda posed a grave threat to the country.

Not until the spectacular tragedy of September 11, 2001, would the name Osama bin Laden resonate throughout the land. The dark genius of 9/11 was twofold. First, the delay between the planes striking the north and south towers of the World Trade Center afforded enough time for the media to get in place to broadcast the latter strike live, thereby maximizing the number of witnesses. Second, the mundane circumstances of the victims were easily relatable: passengers aboard routine commercial flights; working people going about their business in large office towers. For those reasons, we all reacted very personally to 9/11, the way we shudder when we learn that someone near our own age has suddenly been stricken with cancer. And, through our imagination, the experience became our own.

The the historian John Lukacs observed, "Whatever we know, or think we know, of the future is hardly anything but the projection (and often an exaggeration) of some things we see occurring at the present."[1] Which was exactly the trap before 9/11—when complacency reigned—and after—when fear rose to its apex, with exaggerated projections of the bows remaining in al Qaeda's quiver. Choking on the dust that shrouded Manhattan, unable to look across its skyline without seeing those missing towers, it was natural to imagine Islamic fundamentalism triumphant. In bin Laden's serene confidence we perceived our own defeat.

But Gilles Kepel, a scholar of the Middle East at the Institut d' études politiques de Paris, recognized something different. Writing soon after 9/11, he asserted, "September 11 was an attempt to reverse a process in decline, with a paroxysm of destructive violence."[2] He went on, "Terrorism does not necessarily express the true strength of the movement to which it claims to belong. Despite the devastation it can cause—even such shocking devastation as the entire world witnessed on September 11—desperate terrorist acts do not translate easily into political victory and legitimate power."[3]

Al Qaeda is capable of perpetrating violence, but not of consolidating it to any purpose. As Nelly Lahoud says, "Al Qaeda offers an antiestablishment concept, but nothing in the way of a solution or alternative. It came into being to wage jihad, but has never identified anything for after the jihad."[4] Even though it offered no coherent governing plan, it did promise, in terms as vague as they were utopian, a sweeping theocracy encompassing all the lands where Islam had ever been dominant; rather as if some latter-day English zealot aspired to assert dominion to the farthest reaches over which the British Empire once reigned supreme.

Over the succeeding decade, al Qaeda's influence has diminished in the face of American resolve to defend itself, as well as its own failure at mass appeal. President Bush's promise that radical Islam would join fascism, Nazism, and totalitarianism in "history's unmarked grave of discarded lies"[5] may have been fulfilled when bin Laden's death coincided with the so-called Arab spring of 2011 that saw revolts against dictators across the Middle East and North Africa without the slightest reference to al Qaeda. Regimes in Tunisia, Libya, and, most significantly Egypt, fell in the face of mass uprisings. That bin Laden's replacement, Ayman al-Zawahiri, had failed for years as the leader of Egyptian Islamic Jihad to get to Hosni Mubarak, while those amorphous street activists brought him down in a matter of weeks was both an embarrassment and a revelation that al Qaeda exerted no political influence.

With the victory of the Muslim Brotherhood candidate, Mohammed Morsi, in Egypt's first democratic presidential election the possibility of a fundamentalist resurgence or of a more pragmatic iteration of political Islam did emerge. However, in July 2013, barely a year after the election, Egypt's military stepped in and deposed Morsi in what was either a coup or an expression of popular will in the face of widespread dissatisfaction with an ineffective and unresponsive government, depending on one's perspective. It would be foolhardy to suppose that any conclusions can be drawn about a situation that is so volatile and fluid, beyond reiterating that al Qaeda's leadership, nowhere to be seen or heard, is proving itself incapable of exploiting political unrest.

With regard to its War on Terrorism, the United States runs the risk of falling into the same frightened stasis that marked its attitude during the last decades of the Cold War, when the perception of Soviet might was so ingrained among policy makers and intelligence agencies that its inherent fragility and inability to sustain its empire went unnoticed. Today, the fear of terrorism is so endemic that the inclination has been to understate how badly al Qaeda has been degraded.

In a speech delivered in May 2013, President Obama acknowledged, "Today, the core of al Qaeda in Afghanistan and Pakistan is on the path to defeat. Their remaining operatives spend more time thinking about their own safety than plotting against us." Consequently, the time has come to "define our efforts not as a boundless 'global war on terror,' but rather as a series of persistent, targeted efforts to dismantle specific networks of violent extremists that threaten America." He conceded, "A perpetual war—through drones or Special Forces or troop deployments—will prove self-defeating, and alter our country in troubling ways."[6] This was a reasoned assessment, in contrast with President Bush's triumphal appearance on the deck of the USS *Abraham Lincoln* in front of a banner proclaiming "Mission Accomplished" almost exactly ten years earlier (on May 1, 2003).

The war is not against terror, which is a tactic. It is against those who would employ it. When we assess our progress more objectively sometime in the future, we may well see that uprooting al Qaeda from its home base in Afghanistan within months of 9/11 had a decisive effect on curtailing its capabilities. Though a nonstate actor need not exercise sovereignty, it must have territory from which it can stage and to which it can retreat. Al Qaeda has been denied that essential component in its arsenal. So long as it is denied a base, it will always be pushed to the defensive.

The shock and fear reverberating from 9/11 cracked the bedrock principles of American justice. In the helter-skelter of the ensuing invasion of Afghanistan, the decade-long hunt for Osama, the war against Iraq, and the acceptance that torture could be valid and due process void, the clarity of America's values was obscured in a haze of fright.

When American lawmakers decided that the homeland could not be defended without suspending individual rights, when they mocked the principles of due process, they ignored the landmark investigation into the African embassy bombings and the ensuing trials. This case stands as an important precedent in the annals of terrorism jurisprudence and a clear example of how the American judicial system is capable of contending with terrorists without capitulating to measures that would shock the conscience of the court and, in another era, the public.

"This was a case of great magnitude, for America was on trial, too, in terms of the sanctity and propriety of our system of jurisprudence," said Edward Wilford. "We had taken these individuals from other countries and brought them to America for trial, and the vast majority of the murdered were African. But the attack was against American territory, against our regime."[7] Thus, the implications of the proceedings were powerfully magnified.

And the judicial system proved worthy of its responsibilities to be fair and transparent: the prosecution lived up to its burden of proof; the defense was carried out with vigor. The prosecution was supported by the testimony of key human sources recruited by tried-and-true methods. Confessions were obtained through skilled interrogations, not by torture, whether at the hands of Americans or even less squeamish third parties. Those who were convicted are securely confined in U.S. prisons, though not without one horrific instance of brutal violence.

Legal formalities didn't seem ferocious enough in the wake of 9/11. Even the prospect of the death penalty was too tame, as if al Qaeda members couldn't be killed enough for what they'd done. President Bush told Vice President Cheney, "We're going to find out who did this and kick their ass."[8] Guys don't get their asses kicked in a courtroom, but out in the field. This is the kind of frontier imagery, the "dead or alive," "with us or against us," approach that characterized the Bush attitude toward terrorism.

After 9/11, the nonsense that protecting freedoms necessitates that they be violated gained traction and took hold with politicians excited to tough talk and quick to abandon their moral obligation to the Constitution. It is in this context that the story of the African embassies is an important reminder of the genius of the American justice system.

Defense attorney Laura Gasiorowski said, "9/11 destabilized our concept of justice. It changed what Americans were willing to sacrifice in the name of security."[9]

Looking back at this case is useful for reinforcing how the American legal system is, in fact, robust and that its rules and procedures have struck an admirable balance between protecting the innocent and punishing the guilty, providing a framework that enables investigations to proceed effectively while respecting human dignity. And to do so in the face of events unforeseeable and, yes, terrifying.

The African embassies case straddles that divide between when police were sent to arrest terrorists and soldiers to kill them; between due process and black prisons; between federal court proceedings and military tribunals. Between a fleeting post–Cold War moment of apparent American invincibility and an exaggerated perception of vulnerability. Between certainty that its capitalist, consumerist, democratic society held the secret to fulfilling aspirations that all humans hold in common and confusion over what people want.

The attacks of 9/11 changed the world beyond what was warranted. Those changes were not imposed by al Qaeda. They were implemented by American officials, elected and appointed, who let panic and disarray overwhelm their duty to defend and uphold the Constitution in any and all circumstances. After all, none of the atrocities of 9/11, nor the conspiracies preceding them, were legal on 9/10. Existing laws were adequate; there was no need for a Patriot Act and certainly no justification for the implication that opposition to what the government proposes is unpatriotic. As defense attorney David Baugh pointed out in court, "We don't take an oath to a flag or even a government, we take an oath to a philosophy that protects him [the accused]."

The government's actions were fueled by the growing conceit that 9/11 could—and *should*—have been prevented and by its conviction that even more devastating attacks were imminent. Fundamental rights—including the centuries-old principle of habeas corpus, the foundation of fair and transparent legal proceedings—were swept aside and replaced by convoluted opinions that sanctioned torture. And it became a matter of patriotism to go along.

We ought to approach every conflict with the certain knowledge that it will eventually end. If we did that, we'd proceed with more humility. Such an attitude is what enabled the Allies to quickly rehabilitate their Axis adversaries and reintegrate them into the community of nations after the fierce fighting and atrocities against civilian populations of World War II. It can be done without leaving any ambiguity as to who has the authority and the power to dictate terms. And it applies not just to institutions, but to people. After all, the Nazis were effectively purged from government and Nazism from the German polity. We will be well served to keep in mind that those who purport to speak for a people, a nation, or a religion, more often than not speak only for themselves.

So which exaggerated projections based upon the present are we to avoid? Do we believe that our apparent upper hand against al Qaeda signals their defeat? Or do we agonize that the enemy continues to probe for vulnerabilities to exploit?

It does not serve society to aggressively pursue wars that have already been won. At the same time, national security is achieved through vigilance. One of the challenges of relating to people of vastly different culture and values is that our points of reference and interpretations of history have little in common, and that can be a difficult obstacle to overcome.

Among the most significant points of divergence between ourselves and Islamic extremists is in how differently we conceive time. No further proof is needed than our illusion that 9/11 was long ago, evident when officials congratulate one another for every week, month, year that passes without a catastrophic attack. Said FBI agent Joe Billy, "You have to look at this in decades. The embassy bombings happened yesterday in their minds. It's one piece in a continuing, long-term conflict. We need to view this in decades and centuries."[10] One thing bin Laden never suffered was impatience.

Time, for al Qaeda, stands still. Islam's "catastrophes of yesterday are present as the wounds of today. This belief that all events, no matter how long ago, have moral meaning and urgency, that six-hundred-year-old wrongs can somehow be righted, is the mark of a mind that believes God is near, insistent upon action, and ready to intervene."[11]

The continuous nature of the age-old battle they are waging nurtures grudges and justifies the broadest interpretation of collective guilt. Al Qaeda operates according to the "belief that their struggle is an integral part of Islam's more than 1,400-year historical continuum in which the central feature is the defence of Islam against Christian aggression . . . which Allah has not only blessed, but has also directed to be waged as part of the price of entering paradise,"[12] wrote CIA analyst Michael Scheuer.

The only honest conclusion is to admit that we cannot know the future. We cannot even know how far it lurks ahead of the present. We are destined to be vulnerable, fragile, and susceptible to error. We cannot plan for every contingency, nor can we protect against every threat. What 9/11 did reveal is just what a nation will do under the influence of fear. It will torture, it will violate rights, it will circumvent the rule of law. The African embassies case demonstrated what American justice can accomplish within the framework of legality. Americans can take courage in their country's essential commitment to justice, knowing that nothing al Qaeda has done necessitates changing its values. The enduring challenge will be to resist the temptation to explain the future as an exaggeration of the present.

ACKNOWLEDGMENTS

This book was a very long time in the writing. During the course of my research, I was privileged to interview many of the participants in this case. I want to sincerely thank all of those who shared their knowledge and insights: Anthony Barkow, Joe Billy, Jean-Louis Brugière, Jack Cloonan, Frederick Cohn, Gregory Cooper, Pat D'Amuro, Joshua Dratel, Scott Fenstermaker, Laura Gasiorowski, Sheila Horan, Nelly Lahoud, Kenneth Piernick, Peter Quijano, Leonard B. Sand, Sam Schmidt, Ali Soufan, David Stern, Mary Jo White, and Edward Wilford. I can honestly say that each conversation had an influence on my thinking about the case. For that I am grateful. Whether or not I agree with what I was told, I aspired to faithfully report on opinions held by others. I, alone, bear responsibility for the end result that is this book.

Michael Carin graciously read the manuscript and made an invaluable contribution. Beverley Slopen, my literary agent, was responsible for getting it into print.

I very much appreciate the support I have received from the Canada Council for the Arts, without which I would not have been able to complete this project.

APPENDIX

The Twenty-Two Suspects Indicted for the Bombing of
the American Embassies in Kenya and Tanzania

Osama bin Laden Founder and leader of al Qaeda. Killed in a raid on his hideout by
   U.S. Navy SEALs in Abbottabad, Pakistan, May 1, 2011.

Ayman al-Zawahiri The leader of Egyptian Islamic Jihad, he became al Qaeda's
   number two when he joined forces with bin Laden. Took over al Qaeda upon bin
   Laden's death.

Mohammed Atef, aka Abu Hafs, aka Taysir Replaced Abu Ubaydah al Banshiri as head
   of al Qaeda's military council in 1996. Killed in a U.S. bombing raid against his
   home outside Kabul, Afghanistan in mid-November 2001.

Abdullah Ahmed Abdullah, aka Abu Mohammed al-Masri, better known as
   Saleh Replaced Abu Ubaydah as head of the East Africa cell, and was part of al
   Qaeda's ruling council, Identified by al-'Owhali as the leader behind both the
   Nairobi and Dar attacks. He remains on the FBI's list of Most Wanted Terrorists.

Abu Anas al-Liby (real name Nazih Abdul Hamed al-Ruqai) Helped conduct
   surveillance of potential targets in Nairobi. Arrested and questioned by British
   police in Manchester in 1999. Released due to insufficient evidence, he evaded
   surveillance and fled England for Afghanistan. He was arrested in Tripoli by U.S.
   forces on October 5, 2013, and is held in American custody.

Saif al-Adel A member of al Qaeda's ruling council, as well as the military council,
   where he reported to Abu Hafs. He gave military and intelligence training to al
   Qaeda members and to Somali jihadis. He has been variously reported to be in
   Waziristan or Iran. He remains on the FBI's list of Most Wanted Terrorists.

Mamdouh Mahmud Salim, aka Abu Hajer al-Iraqi A member of al Qaeda's ruling
   council, he engaged in business activities, travelled and purchased equipment on
   its behalf. He worked for various bin Laden companies in Sudan. Convicted of
   attempted murder of a corrections officer while awaiting trial for his role in the
   embassy bombings. Serving a life sentence without possibility of parole at the
   federal penitentiary in Florence, Colorado.

Muhsin Musa Matwalli Atwah, aka Abdel Rahman al-Muhajer Made the bombs used against the embassies. Went on to become al Qaeda's chief bomb maker. He was killed in a helicopter raid by Pakistani forces on a village in Waziristan in April 2012. His death was confirmed the following October by the United States following DNA testing.

Khalid al-Fawwaz An early leader of the East Africa cell before moving from Nairobi to London, where he set up al Qaeda's media information office, known as the Advice and Reformation Committee. He was arrested in London and, following a long legal battle, was extradited to the United States in October 2012, where he awaits trial in the Southern District of New York.

Ibrahim Eidarous Began organizing a cell of the Egyptian Islamic Jihad in Azerbaijan in 1995. Moved from Baku to London in 1997, where he helped provide false passports to EIJ members and disseminated al Qaeda messages to the media. Was arrested in London in September 1998. Diagnosed with leukemia in 2002, he was released from prison and given house arrest in 2008. He died later that year.

Adel Abdel Bary Appointed head of the London cell of Egyptian Islamic Jihad in May 1996 by al-Zawahiri. He provided false passports to other EIJ members and disseminated claims of responsibility for its actions to the media. Arrested in the United Kingdom 1999 and extradited to the United States in October 2012, he awaits trial in the Southern District of New York.

Wadih el Hage Bin Laden's personal secretary in Khartoum before being sent to Nairobi, where he ran al Qaeda fronts while the embassy attacks were being planned. Convicted on perjury and conspiracy charges for his role in the attack. Currently serving a life sentence without possibility of parole at the federal penitentiary in Florence, Colorado.

Fazul Abdullah Mohammed, aka Harun One of the senior al Qaeda participants in the embassy bombing plot and a leader in East Africa after this attack. Killed by Somali soldiers at a checkpoint in Mogadishu on June 7, 2011.

Ahmed Mohamed Hamed Ali, aka Ahmed al-Masri (the Egyptian) Served as a trainer in Somalia. Reportedly killed in a drone strike in Pakistan in 2011.

Mohamed Saddiq Odeh Participated in the conspiracy to destroy the American embassies. Convicted in 2001 and sentenced to life imprisonment without possibility of parole. He is held at the federal penitentiary in Florence, Colorado.

Mohamed Suleiman al-Nalfi Created, and led, a Sudanese jihadi group in 1989 at the behest of Abu Ubaydah. He helped to prepare for bin Laden's relocation to Khartoum in 1991 and to establish Taba Investments. In late 2000, he was lured from Sudan to Kenya, where he was taken into U.S. custody. He was held in secret for four months before being charged in a Kenyan court, where he was sentenced to ten years and a month in prison.[1]

Mohamed Rashed Daoud al-'Owhali Convicted in 2001 for his role in trying to blow up the U.S. Embassy in Nairobi. Sentenced to life imprisonment without possibility of parole. He is held at the federal penitentiary in Florence, Colorado.

Mustafa Mohamed Fadhil Recruited K. K. Mohamed and helped him prepare explosives for the bomb in Dar es Salaam. Killed in Afghanistan around 2005.

Khalfan Khamis Mohamed Participated in the Dar es Salaam bombing. Arrested in South Africa. Convicted in 2001. Currently serving a life sentence without possibility of parole at the federal penitentiary in Florence, Colorado.

Abu Talha al-Sudani Planned the 2002 attacks against an Israeli owned hotel and Israeli passenger jet in Mombasa with Harun. Al Sudani operated primarily out of Somalia and took over leadership of the East Africa cell after Harun fled to Afghanistan. He would later be suspended from al Qaeda and set up his own jihadi operation in Somalia. He was killed in early January 2007 in an ambush carried out jointly by American, Kenyan, and Ethiopian forces.

Ahmed Khalfan Ghailani Arrested in Gujrat, Pakistan in 2004. Was interrogated by the CIA and eventually incarcerated at Guantánamo Bay, Cuba. Was transferred to the Southern District of New York for trial in 2009. He is serving a life sentence without the possibility of parole at the federal penitentiary in Florence, Colorado.

Sheikh Ahmed Salim Swedan Swedan was involved in preparations for the Dar es Salaam bombing, purchasing the suicide vehicle and bomb components. He rose to head al Qaeda operations in Pakistan. Killed January 1, 2009, in an American drone attack on a safe house in Waziristan, Pakistan.

Fahid Mohammed Ally Msalam Helped to prepare the Dar es Salaam attack. Went on to serve as deputy to Sheikh Ahmed Salim Swedan in Pakistan, and was killed alongside him in an American drone attack in Waziristan on January 1, 2009.

NOTES

[1] DARK DAY IN AFRICA

1. Nelly Lahoud, *Beware of Imitators: Al-Qa'ida through the Lens of Its Confidential Secretary* (West Point, NY: The Combating Terrorism Center at West Point, 2012), 9, http://www.ctc.usma.edu/wp-content/uploads/2012/06/CTC-Beware-of-Imitators -June2012.pdf.

2. This and all further quotations that are not endnoted come from the transcript of the United States of America v. Usama bin Laden et al. (98 CR 1023). It was decided not to note each of these references so as to reduce the number of interruptions the reader would encounter.

3. James C. McKinley Jr., "Security Flaws Left Embassy in Nairobi Open to Attack," *New York Times*, September 9, 1998.

4. Testimony given, United States of America v. Usama bin Laden et al.

5. Lahoud, *Beware of Imitators*, 56–57.

6. Personal interview with Ken Piernick, November 3, 2009.

7. John E. Lange, "Dar es Salaam: Confronting the Crisis," *State*, October 1988, 21.

8. Personal interview with Ken Piernick, November 3, 2009.

9. Tim Weiner, "Bombings in East Africa: The Investigation; Sophisticated Terrorists Pose Daunting Obstacle," *New York Times*, August 13, 1998.

10. Personal interview with Pat D'Amuro, September 24, 2009.

11. Personal interview with Mary Jo White, September 24, 2009.

12. Personal interview with Fredrick Cohn, September 22, 2009.

[2] OSAMA'S WAR

1. Personal interview with Joe Billy, September 22, 2010.

2. Steve Coll, *The Bin Ladens: An Arabian Family in the American Century* (New York: Penguin Press, 2008), 67.

3. Ibid., 153.

4. Michael Scheuer, *Through Our Enemies' Eyes: Osama bin Laden, Radical Islam, and the Future of America*, rev. ed. (Washington, DC: Potomac Books, 2006), 33.

5. Coll, *The Bin Ladens*, 258.

6. Scheuer, *Through Our Enemies' Eyes*, 125

7. Ibid., 124.

8. Coll, *The Bin Ladens*, 381.

9. John Miller, Michael Stone, with Chris Mitchell, *The Cell: Inside the 9/11 Plot, and Why the FBI and CIA Failed to Stop It* (New York: Hyperion, 2002), 159.

10. Lawrence Wright, *The Looming Tower: Al-Qaeda and the Road to 9/11* (New York, Vintage Books, 2006), 186.

11. Peter L. Bergen, *Holy War, Inc.: Inside the Secret World of Osama bin Laden* (New York: The Free Press, 2001), 80.

12. Indictment, United States of America v. Usama bin Laden et al., S(9) 98 Cr. 1023 (LBS).

13. Wright, *The Looming Tower*, 193.

14. USA v. Usama bin Laden et al., S(7)98CR1023.

15. National Commission on Terrorist Attacks, *The 9/11 Commission Report* (New York: W.W. Norton, 2004), 60.

16. Scheuer, *Through Our Enemies' Eyes*, 147.

17. Mark Bowden, *Black Hawk Down* (New York, Signet, 2000), 7.

18. Bowden, *Black Hawk Down*, 429.

19. Bowden, *Black Hawk Down*, 133.

20. Ali H. Soufan with Daniel Freedman, *The Black Banners: The Inside Story of 9/11 and the War against al-Qaeda* (New York: W.W. Norton, 2011), 345.

21. Barry Rubin and Judith Colp Rubin, eds., *Anti-American Terrorism and the Middle East: A Documentary Reader* (Oxford: Oxford University Press, 2002), 155.

22. Daniel Benjamin and Steven Simon, *The Age of Sacred Terror* (New York: Random House, 2002), 118.

23. Benjamin and Simon, 121.

24. Soufan and Freedman, *The Black Banners*, 328.

[3] THE EAST AFRICA CELL

1. Lawrence Wright, *The Looming Tower: Al-Qaeda and the Road to 9/11* (New York: Vintage Books, 2006), 262.

2. Peter L. Bergen, *The Osama bin Laden I Know: An Oral History of al Qaeda's Leader* (New York: Free Press, 2006), 82.

3. Personal interview with Nelly Lahoud, September 18, 2011.

4. Quoted in Michael Scheuer, *Osama bin Laden* (New York: Oxford University Press, 2011), 116.

5. Personal interview with Joe Billy, September 22, 2010.

6. National Commission on Terrorist Attacks, *9/11 Commission Report* (New York: W.W. Norton, 2004), 58.

7. Daniel Benjamin and Steven Simon, *The Age of Sacred Terror* (New York: Random House, 2002), 131.

8. Michael Scheuer, *Through Our Enemies' Eyes: Osama bin Laden, Radical Islam, and the Future of America*, rev. ed. (Washington, DC, Potomac Books, 2006), 189.

9. Ibid., 148.

10. Personal interview with Sam Schmidt, September 22, 2009.

11. Indictment, United States of America v. Usama bin Laden et al., S(9) 98 Cr. 1023 (LBS).

12. Michael Scheuer, *Osama bin Laden* (New York: Oxford University Press, 2011), 93.

13. Benjamin Weiser and Susan Sacks, "U.S. Sees Brooklyn Link to World Terror Networks," *New York Times*, October 22, 1998.

14. Steven Emerson, *American Jihad: The Terrorists Living among Us* (New York: The Free Press, 2002), 134.

15. John Miller, Michael Stone, with Chris Mitchell, *The Cell: Inside the 9/11 Plot, and Why the FBI and CIA Failed to Stop It* (New York: Hyperion, 2002), 148–49.

16. Simon Reeve, *The New Jackals: Ramzi Yousef, Osama bin Laden and the Future of Terrorism* (London: Carlton Books, 1999), 60.

17. Quoted in Wright, *The Looming Tower*, 201.

18. Richard A. Clarke, *Against All Enemies: Inside America's War on Terror* (New York: Free Press, 2004), 134.

19. Weiser and Sacks, "U.S. Sees Brooklyn Link."

20. Emerson, *American Jihad*, 137.

21. USA v. Usama bin Laden, et al.

22. Benjamin Weiser, "U.S. to Offer Detailed Trail of bin Laden in Bomb Trial," *New York Times*, January 13, 2001.

23. James Risen and Benjamin Weiser, "Unheeded Warnings: A Special Report; Before Bombings, Omens and Fears," *New York Times*, January 9, 1999.

24. Wright, *The Looming Tower*, 276–77.

25. Personal interview with Josh Dratel, September 23, 2009.

26. Personal interview with Pat D'Amuro, September 24, 2009.

27. Miller et al., *The Cell*, 203.

28. Benjamin Weiser, "A Bin Laden Agent Left Angry Record of Gripes and Fears," *New York Times*, December 2, 1998.

29. Ibid.

30. Ibid.

31. Wright, *The Looming Tower*, 302.

32. George Tenet with Bill Harlow, *At the Center of the Storm: My Years at the CIA* (New York: HarperCollins, 2007), 108.

[4] FATWA

1. Richard A. Clarke, *Against All Enemies: Inside America's War on Terror* (New York, Free Press, 2004), 142.

2. National Commission on Terrorist Attacks, *9/11 Commission Report* (New York: W.W. Norton, 2004), 110.

3. Daniel Benjamin and Steven Simon, *The Age of Sacred Terror* (New York: Random House, 2002), 133.

4. National Commission on Terrorist Attacks, *9/11 Commission Report*, 60.

5. Ibid., 60.

6. Peter L. Bergen, *Holy War, Inc.: Inside the Secret World of Osama bin Laden* (New York: The Free Press, 2001), 102.

7. National Commission on Terrorist Attacks, *9/11 Commission Report*, 67.

8. As reproduced in Barry Rubin and Judith Colp Rubin, eds., *Anti-American Terrorism and the Middle East: A Documentary Reader* (Oxford, Oxford University Press, 2002), 139.

9. In ibid., 141.

10. Anthony Summers and Robbyn Swan, *The Eleventh Day: The Full Story of 9/11 and Osama bin Laden* (New York: Ballantine Books, 2011), 261.

11. Richard A. Clarke, *Against All Enemies: Inside America's War on Terror* (New York, Free Press, 2004), 148.

12. Ibid., 135.

13. National Commission on Terrorist Attacks, *9/11 Commission Report*, 59.

14. Benjamin and Simon, *The Age of Sacred Terror*, 243.

15. National Commission on Terrorist Attacks, *9/11 Commission Report*, 109.

16. Mark Mazzetti, "C.I.A. Closes Unit Focused on Capture of bin Laden," *New York Times*, July 4, 2006.

17. Steve Coll, *The Bin Ladens: An Arabian Family in the American Century* (New York, Penguin Press, 2008), 477–78.

18. Personal interview with Jack Cloonan, September 19, 2011.

19. Benjamin Weiser, "U.S. to Offer Detailed Trail of Bin Laden in Bomb Trial," *New York Times*, January 13, 2001.

20. James Risen and Benjamin Weiser, "Unheeded Warnings: A Special Report; Before Bombings, Omens and Fears," *New York Times*, January 9, 1999.

21. Ibid.

22. John Miller, Michael Stone, with Chris Mitchell, *The Cell: Inside the 9/11 Plot, and Why the FBI and CIA Failed to Stop It* (New York, Hyperion, 2002), 205.

23. Raymond Bonner and James Risen, "Nairobi Embassy Received Warning of Coming Attack," *New York Times*, October 23, 1998.

24. Raymond Bonner, "Tanzania Charges Two in Bombing of American Embassy," *New York Times*, September 22, 1998.

25. Ibid.

26. Bonner and Risen, "Nairobi Embassy Received Warning of Coming Attack."

27. Ibid.

28. "Tanzania Bomb Suspect Said to Know Bin Laden," *New York Times*, October 2, 1998.

29. Bonner and Risen, "Nairobi Embassy Received Warning of Coming Attack."

30. Ibid.

31. Ibid.

32. Personal interview with Ken Piernick, November 3, 2009.

33. Miller et al., *The Cell*, 206.

34. Tim Weiner, "Bombings in East Africa: The Investigation; Reward Is Offered and Clues Studied in Africa Blasts," *New York Times*, August 11, 1998.

35. Quoted in Jane Mayer, *The Dark Side: The Inside Story of How the War on Terror Turned into a War on American Ideals* (New York: Anchor Books, 2009), 114.

36. Risen and Weiser, "Unhecded Warnings."

37. See *African Embassy Bombings: An Online NewsHour Special Report*, PBS NewsHour, www.pbs.org/newshour/bb/africa/embassy_bombing/index.html.

38. Risen and Weiser, "Unheeded Warnings."

39. Quoted in Peter L. Bergen, *The Longest War: The Enduring Conflict between America and al-Qaeda* (New York: Free Press, 2011), 95–96.

40. Rubin and Rubin, *Anti-American Terrorism and the Middle East*, 150.

41. Personal interview, Pat D'Amuro, September 24, 2009.

42. Lawrence Wright, *The Looming Tower: Al-Qaeda and the Road to 9/11* (New York, Vintage Books, 2006), 198–99.

43. Ibid., 193.

44. Ibid., 194.

45. Michael Scheuer, *Through Our Enemies' Eyes: Osama bin Laden, Radical Islam, and the Future of America*, rev. ed. (Washington, DC: Potomac Books, 2006), 101–2.

46. Miller et al., *The Cell*, 161. Salim drew this notion from the teachings of Ibn Tamiyyah (1268–1323), who had made this assertion.

47. Ibid., 187.

48. National Commission on Terrorist Attacks, *9/11 Commission Report*, 340.

49. Wright, *The Looming Tower*, 306.

50. Ibid., 5.

51. Clarke, *Against All Enemies*, 154.

52. National Commission on Terrorist Attacks, *9/11 Commission Report*, 102.

53. Clarke, *Against All Enemies*, 154.

54. Steve Coll, *Ghost Wars: The Secret History of the CIA, Afghanistan, and Bin Laden, from the Soviet Invasion to September 10, 2001* (New York, Penguin Books, 2004), 383.

55. Bergen, *Holy War, Inc.*, 107.

56. Philip Shenon, "Bombings in East Africa: The Security Costs; Envoy's Requests for Safer Building Refused, U.S. Says," *New York Times*, August 13, 1998.

57. James C. McKinley Jr., "Security Flaws Left Embassy in Nairobi Open to Attack," *New York Times*, September 9, 1998.

58. Ibid.

59. Risen and Weiser, "Unheeded Warnings."

60. Ibid.

61. Ibid.

62. Ibid.

63. *Report of the Accountability Review Boards: Bombings of the US Embassies in Nairobi, Kenya and Dar es Salaam, Tanzania on August 7, 1998*, January 8, 1999, www.fas.org/irp/threat/arb/board_nairobi.html.

64. Madeleine Albright, with Bill Woodward, *Madam Secretary* (New York: Hyperion, 2003), 465–66.

65. National Commission on Terrorist Attacks, *9/11 Commission Report*, 340.

66. Michael Scheuer, *Through Our Enemies' Eyes: Osama bin Laden, Radical Islam, and the Future of America*, rev. ed. (Washington, DC: Potomac Books, 2006), 209.

67. Daniel Benjamin and Steven Simon, *The Age of Sacred Terror* (New York: Random House, 2002), 351.

68. National Commission on Terrorist Attacks, *9/11 Commission Report*, 149.

69. Terry McDermott and Josh Meyer, *The Hunt for KSM: Inside the Pursuit and Takedown of the Real 9/11 Mastermind, Khalid Sheikh Mohammed* (New York: Little Brown, 2012), 102.

70. Ibid., 105.

71. Ibid., 117–18.

[5] THE DEPLOYMENT

1. Personal interview with Joe Billy, September 22, 2010.

2. Personal interview with Ken Piernick, November 3, 2009.

3. Personal interview with Pat D'Amuro, September 24, 2009.

4. Personal interview with Sheila Horan, October 18, 2009.

5. Raymond Bonner, "Bombings in East Africa: The Aftermath; Envoy Rejects Accusations Americans Acted Selfishly," *New York Times*, August 13, 1998.

6. Tim Weiner, "Bombings in East Africa: The Investigation; Sophisticated Terrorists Pose Daunting Obstacle," *New York Times*, August 13, 1998.

7. Scheuer, *Through Our Enemies' Eyes*, 139.

8. Simon Reeve, *The New Jackals: Ramzi Yousef, Osama bin Laden and the Future of Terrorism* (London: Carlton Books, 1999), 200.

9. Personal interview, November 3, 2009.

10. Scheuer, *Through Our Enemies' Eyes*, 211.

11. Ibid., 212.

12. Personal interview with Sheila Horan, October 18, 2009.

13. Personal interview with Ken Piernick, November 3, 2009.

14. Personal interview with Ken Piernick, November 3, 2009.

15. Raymond Bonner, "Bombings in East Africa: The Search; As Rescuers' Final Hope Fades, Investigators Toil Begins," *New York Times*, August 11, 1998.

16. Personal interview with Ken Piernick, November 3, 2009.

17. Philip Shenon with James C. McKinley, Jr., "Bombings in East Africa: The Witnesses; Kenyan Guard at Gate Says He Halted Bombers' Truck," *New York Times*, August 11, 1998.

18. Tim Weiner and Raymond Bonner, "Bombings in East Africa: The Investigation in Kenya; F.B.I. Reports Finding Pieces of Bomb Truck," *New York Times*, August 14, 1998.

19. Personal interview with Sheila Horan, October 18, 2009.

20. Personal interview with Joe Billy, September 22, 2010.

21. James C. McKinley Jr., "Bombing in East Africa: The Overview; Bombs Rip Apart 2 U.S. Embassies in Africa; Scores Killed; No Firm Motive or Suspects," *New York Times*, August 8, 1998.

22. Personal interview with Ken Piernick, November 3, 2009.

23. Personal interview with Pat D'Amuro, September 24, 2009.

24. Personal interview with Sheila Horan, October 18, 2009.

25. Benjamin Weiser, "Kenya Statements in Terrorism Case Allowed by Judge," *New York Times*, January 30, 2001.

26. Benjamin Weiser, "Bombing Suspect Threatened His Interrogators, They Testify," *New York Times*, December 13, 2000.

27. Ibid.

28. Personal interview with Sheila Horan, October 19, 2009.

29. Weiser, "Kenya Statements in Terrorism Case Allowed by Judge."

30. Personal interview with Laura Gasiorowski, September 20, 2011.

31. Personal interview with Fredrick Cohn, September 22, 2009.

32. Ali H. Soufan with Daniel Freedman, *The Black Banners: The Inside Story of 9/11 and the War against al-Qaeda* (New York: W.W. Norton, 2011), 88.

33. Lawrence Wright, *The Looming Tower: Al-Qaeda and the Road to 9/11* (New York, Vintage Books, 2006), 315.

34. Soufan and Freedman, *The Black Banners*, 258.

35. Ibid., 192.

36. Benjamin Weiser, "Embassy Suspect Warned U.S. of Yemen Attack, Papers Show," *New York Times*, January 18, 2001.

37. Weiser, "Embassy Suspect Warned U.S. of Yemen Attack."

38. Jane Mayer, *The Dark Side: The Inside Story of How the War on Terror Turned into a War on American Ideals* (New York: Anchor Books, 2009), 168–69.

39. Personal interview, November 3, 2009.

[6] MOHAMED SADDIQ ODEH

1. Peter L. Bergen, *Holy War, Inc.: Inside the Secret World of Osama bin Laden* (New York: The Free Press, 2001), 113.

2. David Johnston, "U.S. Says Suspect Does Not Admit Role in Bombings or Ties to Saudi," *New York Times*, August 18, 1998.

3. Gary Berntsen and Ralph Pezzullo, *Jawbreaker: The Attack on bin Laden and Al-Qaeda: A Personal Account by the CIA's Key Field Commander* (New York: Three Rivers Press, 2005), 25.

4. Personal interview with Joe Billy, September 22, 2010.

5. Personal interview with Sheila Horan, October 18, 2009.

6. Personal interview with Pat D'Amuro, September 24, 2009.

7. Tim Weiner, "Bombings in East Africa: The Investigation; Sophisticated Terrorists Pose Daunting Obstacle," *New York Times*, August 13, 1998.

8. David Johnston, "U.S. Hopes Arrest in Embassy Blasts Will Break Case," *New York Times*, August 17, 1998.

9. Sachs was removed because he was already assigned another capital case and the rules state that a lawyer can be appointed only one capital case at a time, oweing to the severe work load.

10. Benjamin Weiser, "Bombing Defendant Said to Claim Coercion," *New York Times*, September 5, 1998.

11. Ibid.

12. Benjamin Weiser, "Asserting Coercion, Embassy Bombing Suspect Tries to Suppress Statements," *New York Times*, July 13, 2000.

13. Ibid.

14. James C. McKinley, Jr., "After the Attack: In Kenya; In-Laws Say Bomb Suspect Led a Quiet, Religious Life," *New York Times*, August 26, 1998.

15. James C. McKinley, Jr., "Hotel Janitors Don't Recall Bomb Materials in Kenya," *New York Times*, August 20, 1998.

[7] THE RETALIATION

Larry Beinhart's *American Hero* (New York: Ballantine, 1993) was the basis for the film *Wag the Dog*, which became a cultural touchstone of the era, and has been a point of reference ever since.

1. Tim Weiner, "Bombings in East Africa: The Investigation; Reward Is Offered and Clues Studied in African Blasts," *New York Times*, August 11, 1998.

2. "President Bill Clinton Statement on Embassy Bombing," *New York Times*, August 8, 1998.

3. Steve Coll, *Ghost Wars: The Secret History of the CIA, Afghanistan, and Bin Laden, from the Soviet Invasion to September 10, 2001* (New York, Penguin Books, 2004), 144.

4. Ibid., 409.

5. Henry A. Crumpton, *The Art of Intelligence: Lessons from a Life in the CIA's Clandestine Service* (New York: Penguin Press, 2012), 156.

6. Daniel Benjamin and Steven Simon, *The Age of Sacred Terror* (New York: Random House, 2002), 358.

7. Steve Coll, *Ghost Wars*, 428–29.

8. Ibid., 424–25.

9. Richard A. Clarke, *Against All Enemies: Inside America's War on Terror,* New York, Free Press, 2004, 204.

10. National Commission on Terrorist Attacks, *9/11 Commission Report* (New York: W.W. Norton, 2004), 137.

11. Ibid,, 117.

12. George Tenet with Bill Harlow, *At the Center of the Storm: My Years at the CIA* (New York: HarperCollins, 2007), 115.

13. Ibid., 116.

14. Jon Lee Anderson, "Force and Futility," *New Yorker*, May 16, 2011, 98.

15. Peter I. Bergen, *Holy War, Inc.: Inside the Secret World of Osama bin Laden* (New York: The Free Press, 2001), 121.

16. Anderson, "Force and Futility," 98.

17. Lawrence Wright, *The Looming Tower: Al-Qaeda and the Road to 9/11* (New York, Vintage Books, 2006), 323.

18. Quoted in Terry McDermott and Josh Meyer, *The Hunt for KSM: Inside the Pursuit and Takedown of the Real 9/11 Mastermind, Khalid Sheikh Mohammed* (New York: Little Brown, 2012), 153, citing their own copy of the document.

19. Bergen, *Holy War, Inc.*, 123–24.

20. Benjamin and Simon, *The Age of Sacred Terror*, 351–57.

21. National Commission on Terrorist Attacks, *9/11 Commission Report*, 118.

22. Clarke, *Against All Enemies*, 204.

23. Gary Berntsen and Ralph Pezzullo, *Jawbreaker: The Attack on bin Laden and Al-Qaeda, a Personal Account by the CIA's Key Field Commander* (New York: Three Rivers Press, 2005), 291.

24. Peter L. Bergen, *Manhunt: The Ten-Year Search for bin Laden from 9/11 to Abbottabad* (Toronto: Doubleday Canada, 2012), 48.

25. Michael Scheuer, *Osama bin Laden* (New York: Oxford University Press, 2011, 116–18).

26. Ibid., 116.

27. Peter L. Bergen, *The Longest War: The Enduring Conflict between America and Al-Qaeda* (New York: Free Press, 2011), 90.

28. Personal interview with Sheila Horan, October 18, 2009.

29. The several investigations of Clinton's alleged transgressions while in the White House and as governor of Arkansas are recounted at length in Louis J. Freeh, *My FBI: Bringing Down the Mafia, Investigating Bill Clinton, and Fighting the War on Terror* (New York, St. Martin's Press, 2005), 245ff.

30. Personal interview, November 3, 2009.

31. Bergen, *Holy War, Inc.*, 126.

32. Michael Scheuer, *Through Our Enemies' Eyes: Osama bin Laden, Radical Islam, and the Future of America*, rev. ed. (Washington, DC: Potomac Books), 2006, 311.

33. Benjamin and Simon, *The Age of Sacred Terror*, 153.

34. Wright, *The Looming Tower*, 319–20.

35. Benjamin and Simon, *The Age of Sacred Terror*, 280.

36. Quoted in Bergen, *The Longest War*, 41.

[8] KHALFAN KHAMIS MOHAMED

1. Personal interview with David Stern, September 21, 2010.

2. Ibid.

3. Ibid.

[9] THE DEFECTORS

1. Personal interview with Jack Cloonan, September 19, 2011.

2. Ali H. Soufan with Daniel Freedman, *The Black Banners: The Inside Story of 9/11 and the War against al-Qaeda* (New York: W.W. Norton, 2011, 71).

3. Personal interview with Jack Cloonan, September 19, 2011.

4. Ibid.

5. Personal interview with Sam Schmidt, September 22, 2009.

6. Personal interview with Ali Soufan, September 22, 2011.

7. Personal interview with Jack Cloonan, September 19, 2011

8. Lawrence Wright, *The Looming Tower: Al-Qaeda and the Road to 9/11* (New York, Vintage Books, 2006), 217–18.

9. Personal interview with Josh Dratel, September 23, 2009.

10. Wright, *The Looming Tower*, 224.

11. Personal interview with Jack Cloonan, September 19, 2011.

12. Tim Weiner, "Bombings in East Africa: The Investigation; Reward Is Offered and Clues Studied in African Blasts," *New York Times*, August 11, 1998.

13. Ali H. Soufan with Daniel Freedman, *The Black Banners: The Inside Story of 9/11 and the War against al-Qaeda* (New York: W.W. Norton, 2011), 124.

14. Personal interview with Jack Cloonan, September 19, 2011.

15. Personal interview with Sam Schmidt, September 22, 2009.

16. Personal interview with Josh Dratel, September 23, 2009.

17. Benjamin Weiser, "Bin Laden Linked to Embassy Blast by an ex-Soldier," *New York Times*, October 21, 2000.

18. Ibid..

19. Personal interview with Pat D'Amuro, September 24, 2009.

20. Personal interview with Ali Soufan, September 22, 2011.

21. Personal interview with Jack Cloonan, September 19, 2011.

22. Wright, *The Looming Tower*, 204–5.

23. Peter L. Bergen, *Holy War, Inc.: Inside the Secret World of Osama bin Laden* (New York: The Free Press, 2001), 130.

24. Bergen, *Holy War, Inc.*, 130.

25. Wright, *The Looming Tower*, 205.

26. John Miller, Michael Stone, with Chris Mitchell, *The Cell: Inside the 9/11 Plot, and Why the FBI and CIA Failed to Stop It* (New York, Hyperion, 2002), 143.

27. Ibid., 143–44.

28. United States v. Ali Mohamed s(7)98cr.1023(LBS), http://cryptome.org/usa-v-mohamed.htm.

29. Daniel Benjamin and Steven Simon, *The Age of Sacred Terror* (New York: Random House, 2002, 130–31).

30. Weiser, "Bin Laden Linked to Embassy Blast by an ex-Soldier."

31. Wright, *The Looming Tower*, 359.

32. Quoted in Benjamin and Simon, *The Age of Sacred Terror*, 27.

33. Indictment, United States of America v. Usama bin Laden et al., S(9) 98 Cr. 1023 (LBS).

34. Benjamin Weiser, "U.S. Charges Ex-Soldier, Calling Him Plotter with Bin Laden," *New York Times*, May 20, 1999.

35. United States v. Ali Mohamed.

36. Personal interview with Jack Cloonan, September 19, 2011.

37. Personal interview with Pat D'Amuro, September 21, 2010.

38. Personal interview with Jack Cloonan, September 19, 2011.

39. Ali H. Soufan with Daniel Freedman, *The Black Banners: The Inside Story of 9/11 and the War against al-Qaeda* (New York: W.W. Norton, 2011), 77–78.

40. Benjamin Weiser, "Government Says Attack on Guard Was Part of Escape Plan," *New York Times*, December 21, 2000.

[10] WADIH EL HAGE

1. Personal interview with Sam Schmidt, September 22, 2009.

2. Personal interview with Judge Leonard Sand, September 21, 2009.

3. Personal interview with Josh Dratel, September 23, 2009.

4. Personal interview with Josh Dratel, September 23, 2009.

5. Personal interview with Jack Cloonan, September 19, 2011.

6. Ali H. Soufan with Daniel Freedman, *The Black Banners: The Inside Story of 9/11 and the War against al-Qaeda* (New York: W.W. Norton, 2011), 27.

7. Ibid., 38.

8. Personal interview with Mary Jo White, September 24, 2009.

[11] THE DAY IN COURT

1. Personal interview with Mary Jo White, September 24, 2009.

2. Personal interview with Leonard Sand, September 21, 2009.

3. Personal interview with Fredrick Cohn, September 22, 2009.

4. Personal interview with Laura Gasiorowski, September 20, 2011.

5. Personal interview with Fredrick Cohn, September 22, 2009.

6. Personal interview with David Stern, September 21, 2010.

7. Personal interview with Edward Wilford, September 25, 2009.

8. Personal interview with Fredrick Cohn, September 22, 2009.

9. Personal interview with David Stern, September 21, 2010.

10. Personal interview with Edward Wilford, September 25, 2009.

11. Personal interview with Leonard Sand, September 21, 2009.

12. Personal interview with Fredrick Cohn, September 22, 2009.

13. Personal interview with David Stern, September 21, 2010.

14. Personal interview with Laura Gasiorowski, September 20, 2011.

15. Personal interview with Sam Schmidt, September 22, 2009.

16. Ibid.

17. Personal interview with Fredrick Cohn, September 22, 2009.

[12] LIFE AND DEATH

1. Personal interview with David Stern, September 21, 2010.

2. Personal interview with Fredrick Cohn, September 22, 2009.

3. Ibid.

4. Benjamin Weiser, "U.S. Asks British to Deliver Suspected bin Laden Aide," *New York Times*, September 29, 1998.

5. Ali H. Soufan with Daniel Freedman, *The Black Banners: The Inside Story of 9/11 and the War against al-Qaeda* (New York: W.W. Norton, 2011), 101–2.

6. Lawrence Wright, *The Looming Tower: Al-Qaeda and the Road to 9/11* (New York, Vintage Books, 2006), 265.

7. Personal interview with Laura Gasiorowski, September 20, 2011.

8. Personal interview with Laura Gasiorowski, September 20, 2011.

9. Personal interview with David Stern, September 21, 2009.

10. United States v. Salim, Court of Appeals, Second Circuit 04–2643-cr. http://caselaw.findlaw.com/us-2nd-circuit/1333967.html.

11. I first heard this from Judge Leonard B. Sand, during personal interview, September 21, 2009.

12. Reported in Susan F. Hirsch, *In the Moment of Greatest Calamity: Terrorism, Grief, and a Victim's Quest for Justice*, (Princeton, NJ: Princeton University Press, 2006), 287.

13. See Glenn Kessler, "File the Bin Laden Phone Leak under Urban Myth," *Washington Post*, December 22, 2005, A2.

14. Personal interview with Josh Dratel, September 23, 2009.

[13] SALIM

1. "Bonn Says Sudanese Faces U.S. Extradition," *New York Times*, September 21, 1998.

2. Benjamin Weiser, "U.S. Charges Bin Laden Suspect in Larger Plot," *New York Times*, October 1, 1998.

3. Quoted in Susan Saulny, "Inmate Spared Life Sentence in the Stabbing of an Officer," *New York Times*, September 26, 2003.

4. US v. Salim, Court of Appeals, Second Circuit 04–2643-cr. http://caselaw.findlaw.com/us-2nd-circuit/1333967.html.

5. Quoted in Benjamin Weiser, "Reputed bin Laden Adviser Gets Life Term in Stabbing," *New York Times*, August 31, 2010.

6. Personal interview with Josh Dratel, September 23, 2009.

7. Personal interview with Sam Schmidt, September 22, 2009.

8. Personal interview with Edward Wilford, September 25, 2009.

[14] SUPERMAX

1. Personal interview with Leonard Sand, September 21, 2009.
2. Personal interview with Josh Dratel, September 23, 2009.
3. Personal interview with Sam Schmidt, September 22, 2009.
4. Jeff Tietz, "Slow-Motion Torture," *Rolling Stone*, December 6, 2012, 58–66.
5. Personal interview with David Stern, September 21, 2010.
6. Personal interview with Joe Billy, September 22, 2010.
7. Personal interview with David Stern, September 21, 2010.
8. Personal interview with Fredrick Cohn, September 22, 2009.
9. Ibid.

[15] HARUN

1. Nelly Lahoud, Beware of Imitators: Al'Qa'ida through the Lens of Its Confidential Secretary (West Point, New York: The Combating Terrorism Center at West Point, June 4, 2012), http://www.ctc.usma.edu/wp-content/uploads/2012/06/CTC-Beware-of -Imitators-June2012.pdf.
2. Donald G. McNeil Jr., "Assets of a Bombing Suspect: Keen Wit, Religious Soul, Angry Temper," *New York Times*, October 6, 1998.
3. Lahoud, *Beware of Imitators*, 33.
4. Ibid., 36.
5. Personal interview with Ali Soufan, September 22, 2011.
6. Superseding indictment.
7. McNeil, "Assets of a Bombing Suspect."
8. "Deposition of Haroun Fazul's Wife," transcript, available at PBS *Frontline*, http://www.pbs.org/wgbh/pages/frontline/shows/saudi/fazul/depo.html.
9. Ibid.
10. McNeil, "Assets of a Bombing Suspect."
11. Haroun Fazul's letter to his brother Omar, available at PBS *Frontline*, http://www.pbs.org/wgbh/pages/frontline/shows/saudi/fazul/letter.html.
12. Personal interview with Pat D'Amuro, September 21, 2010.
13. McNeil, "Assets of a Bombing Suspect."
14. Ibid.
15. Personal interview with Pat D'Amuro, September 21, 2010.
16. "Deposition of Haroun Fazul's Wife."
17. Lahoud, *Beware of Imitators*, 25.
18. Jonathan Fighel, *Al Qaeda—Mombassa Attacks 28 November 2002* (Herzliya, Israel: International Institute for Counter-Terrorism, June 13, 2011), www.ict.org.il /Articles/tabid/66/Articlsid/942/currentpage/2/Default.aspx.

19. "31 plots listed in Khalid Sheikh Mohammed's confession," *International Herald Tribune*, March 15, 2007, www.iht.com/articles/ap/2007/03/16/america/NA-GEN-US-Terrorist-Confession-List.php.

20. Lahoud, *Beware of Imitators*, 87.

21. Jeffrey Gettleman and Eric Schmitt, "U.S. Kills Top Qaeda Leader in Southern Somalia," *New York Times*, September 15, 2009.

22. Fighel, *Al Qaeda—Mombassa Attacks*.

23. Dexter Filkins, "Terror in Africa: Attacks in Mombasa; Kenyans Hunting Clues to Bombing; Toll Rises to 13," *New York Times*, November 30, 2002.

24. Fighel, *Al Qaeda—Mombassa Attacks*.

25. Lahoud, *Beware of Imitators*, 60.

26. David Ignatius, "A Lion in Winter," *Washington Post*, March 18, 2012, www.washingtonpost.com/opinions/osama-bin-laden-a-lion-in-winter/2012/03/18.

27. Lahoud, *Beware of Imitators*, 55.

28. Personal interview with Nelly Lahoud, September 21, 2011.

29. Lahoud, *Beware of Imitators*, 29.

30. "Key al Qaeda Operative Killed in U.S. Strike, Somalia Says," CNN, September 15, 2009, www.cnn.com/2009/WORLD/africa/09/15/somalia.strike/index.html.

31. Gettleman and Schmitt, "U.S. Kills Top Qaeda."

32. Lahoud, *Beware of Imitators*, 94.

33. Mugumo Munene, "Nairobi Bomb Blast Mastermind Is Dead," *Daily Nation* (Nairobi), June 11, 2011.

34. Jeffrey Gettleman, "Somalis Kill Mastermind of 2 U.S. Embassy Bombings," *New York Times*, June 12, 2011, A1.

35. Lahoud, *Beware of Imitators*, 98.

36. Secretary of State Hillary Rodham Clinton, "Death of Harun Fazul," press statement, www.state.gov/secretary/rm/2011/06/165942.htm.

37. Personal interview with Pat D'Amuro, September 21, 2010.

[16] THE MYTH OF HINDSIGHT

1. Richard A. Clarke, *Against All Enemies: Inside America's War on Terror* (New York, Free Press, 2004), 237.

2. Clarke, *Against All Enemies*, 17.

3. National Commission on Terrorist Attacks, *9/11 Commission Report* (New York: W.W. Norton, 2004), x.

4. Tim Weiner, *Legacy of Ashes: The History of the CIA* (New York, Anchor Books, 2008), 555.

5. Jane Mayer, *The Dark Side: The Inside Story of How the War on Terror Turned into a War on American Ideals* (New York: Anchor Books, 2009), 24.

6. Personal interview with Jack Cloonan, September 19, 2011.

7. Personal interview with Mary Jo White, September 24, 2009.

8. National Commission on Terrorist Attacks, *9/11 Commission Report*, 108.

9. Ibid., 259.

10. Gary Berntsen and Ralph Pezzullo, *Jawbreaker: The Attack on bin Laden and Al-Qaeda, a Personal Account by the CIA's Key Field Commander* (New York: Three Rivers Press, 2005), 311.

11. Anthony Summers and Robbyn Swan, *The Eleventh Day: The Full Story of 9/11 and Osama bin Laden* (New York: Ballantine Books, 2011), 313.

12. National Commission on Terrorist Attacks, *9/11 Commission Report*, 255–56.

13. Ibid., 262–63.

14. Quoted in Mayer, *The Dark Side*, 43.

15. Berntsen and Pezzullo, *Jawbreaker*, 309.

16. National Commission on Terrorist Attacks, *9/11 Commission Report*, 155.

17. Ali H. Soufan with Daniel Freedman, *The Black Banners: The Inside Story of 9/11 and the War against al-Qaeda* (New York: W.W. Norton, 2011), 291.

18. Lawrence Wright, *The Looming Tower: Al-Qaeda and the Road to 9/11* (New York, Vintage Books, 2006), 387–88.

19. National Commission on Terrorist Attacks, *9/11 Commission Report*, 267–69.

20. Soufan and Freedman, *The Black Banners*, 296.

21. National Commission on Terrorist Attacks, *9/11 Commission Report*, 263.

22. Ibid., 265.

23. Personal interview, September 22, 2011.

24. Office of the Inspector General, *A Review of the FBI's Handling of Intelligence Information Related to the September 11 Attacks (November 2004)*, publicly released June 2006, www.justice.gov/oig/special/s0606/final.pdf, 223–24.

25. Ibid., 305.

26. Ibid., 303.

27. Mayer, *The Dark Side*, 17–18.

28. Personal interview with Jack Cloonan, September 19, 2011.

29. Summers and Swan, *The Eleventh Day*, 386–87.

30. Ibid., 399–400.

31. Ibid., 398.

32. Soufan and Freedman, *The Black Banners*, 47.

33. Simon Reeve, *The New Jackals: Ramzi Yousef, Osama bin Laden and the Future of Terrorism* (London: Carlton Books, 1999), 139–40.

34. Terry McDermott, "The Mastermind: Khalid Sheikh Mohammed and the making of 9/11," *New Yorker*, September 13, 2010, 48.

35. Personal interview with Ali Soufan, September 22, 2011.

36. Personal interview with Pat D'Amuro, September 24, 2009.

37. National Commission on Terrorist Attacks, *9/11 Commission Report*, 108.

38. Quoted in Steve Coll, *Ghost Wars: The Secret History of the CIA, Afghanistan, and Bin Laden, from the Soviet Invasion to September 10, 2001* (New York, Penguin Books, 2004), 318.

39. Ibid.

[17] AHMED KHALFAN GHAILANI

1. Combatant Status Review Tribunal, www.defense.gov/news/transcript_ISN10012.pdf.

2. Benjamin Weiser, "Conspirator's Path from Poverty as Boy in Zanzibar to bin Laden's Side," *New York Times*, January 2011, A19.

3. Amelia Hill, "Bin Laden's $20m African 'Blood Diamond' Deals," *Observer*, October 20, 2002, www.guardian.co.uk/world/2002/oct/20/alqaida.terrorism?INTCMP=SRCH.

4. Rory Carroll, "West African Leaders 'in al-Qaida Plot,'" *Guardian*, December 30, 2002, www.guardian.co.uk/world/2002/dec/30/alqaida.terrorism?INTCMP=SRCH.

5. Ron Suskind, *The One Percent Doctrine: Deep Inside America's Pursuit of Its Enemies Since 9/11* (New York: Simon & Schuster, 2006), 317.

6. Ibid., 318.

7. Ibid., 325.

8. Peter Taylor, "The Crucible," *Guardian*, August 8, 2005, www.guardian.co.uk/world/2005/aug/08/pakistan.terrorism?INTCMP=SRCH.

9. Suskind, *The One Percent Doctrine*, 325–26.

10. Combatant Status Review Tribunal.

11. Weiser, "Conspirator's Path from Poverty," A19.

12. Combatant Status Review Tribunal.

13. Ibid.

14. Weiser, "Conspirator's Path from Poverty."

15. Combatant Status Review Tribunal.

16. Weiser, "Conspirator's Path from Poverty."

17. Combatant Status Review Tribunal.

18. Weiser, "Conspirator's Path from Poverty."

19. Ibid.

20. Personal interview with Leonard Sand, September 21, 2009.

21. Personal interview with Fredrick Cohn, September 22, 2009.

22. Benjamin Weiser, "Terrorism Trial May Point Way for 9/11 Cases," *New York Times*, November 23, 2009.

23. Benjamin Weiser, "A Plea of Not Guilty for Guantánamo Detainee," *New York Times*, June 9, 2009.

24. Benjamin Weiser, "Mental State of Suspect May Be Issue in Terror Case," *New York Times*, December 18, 2009.

25. Benjamin Weiser, "Psychologist Says Strip-Searches Traumatized Embassy Bombings Suspect," *New York Times*, May 5, 2010.

26. Benjamin Weiser, "Ghailani's Lawyers Detail Terror Defense Strategy," *New York Times*, January 17, 2011.

27. Personal interview with Peter Quijano, September 19, 2011.

28. Weiser, "Mental State of Suspect."

29. Personal interview with Gregory Cooper, September 22, 2010.

30. Benjamin Weiser, "No Dismissal in Terror Case on Claim of Torture in Jail," *New York Times*, May 10, 2010.

31. Benjamin Weiser, "Suspect Cites Trial Delay in Seeking Dismissal," *New York Times*, December 1, 2009.

32. Personal interview with Gregory Cooper, September 22, 2010.

33. Benjamin Weiser, "Witness in 1998 Bombings Is Identified at a Hearing," *New York Times*, September 19. 2010.

34. Benjamin Weiser, "Judge Says Key Figure in Embassies Bombing Case Isn't Credible," *New York Times*, October 14, 2010.

35. Benjamin Weiser, "Judge Bars Major Witness from Terrorism Trial," *New York Times*, October 6, 2010.

36. Written opinion submitted by Judge Kaplan, August 17, 2010, and Weiser, "Judge Says Key Figure."

37. Benjamin Weiser, "Missing from Trial: Detainee Statements," *New York Times*, October 4, 2010.

38. Ibid.

39. Personal interview with Gregory Cooper, September 22, 2010.

40. Ibid.

41. Benjamin Weiser, "Trial of Man Once Held at Guantánamo Opens," *New York Times*, October 12, 2010.

42. Ibid.

43. Benjamin Weiser, "Ex-Detainee's Defense Calls Him Qaeda Dupe in Its Closing," *New York Times*, November 9, 2010.

44. Benjamin Weiser, "Prosecution Closes in Trial of Detainee," *New York Times*, November 8, 2010.

45. Personal interview with Peter Quijano, September 19, 2011.

46. Weiser, "Ex-Detainee's Defense Calls Him Qaeda Dupe."

47. Ibid.

48. Personal interview with Peter Quijano, September 19, 2011.

49. Personal interview with Gregory Cooper, September 22, 2010.

50. Personal interview with Peter Quijano, September 19, 2011.

51. Benjamin Weiser, "Life Sentence Is Requested in Bomb Case," *New York Times*, January 27, 2011.

52. Benjamin Weiser, "Ex-Detainee Gets Life Sentence in Embassy Blasts," *New York Times*, January 23, 2011.

53. Personal interview with Peter Quijano, September 19, 2011.

54. Ibid.

55. Personal interview with Pat D'Amuro, September 24, 2009.

56. Jane Mayer, *The Dark Side: The Inside Story of How the War on Terror Turned into a War on American Ideals* (New York: Anchor Books, 2009), 4.

57. Suskind, *The One Percent Doctrine*, 62.

58. Ali H. Soufan with Daniel Freedman, *The Black Banners: The Inside Story of 9/11 and the War against al-Qaeda* (New York: W.W. Norton, 2011), 116.

59. Charles Paul Freund, "The Pentagon's Film Festival," *Slate*, August 27, 2003, http://slate.msn.com/id/2087628/.

60. Suskind, *The One Percent Doctrine*, 114.

61. Personal interview with Jack Cloonan, September 19, 2011.

[18] ANWAR AL-AWLAKI

1. Scott Shane and Souad Mekhennet, "Imam's Path from Condemning Terror to Preaching Jihad," *New York Times*, May 8, 2010, www.nytimes.com/2010/05/09/world/09awlaki.html?pagewanted=1.

2. Shane and Mekhennet, "Imam's Path from Condemning Terror."

3. FBI statement quoted in David Johnston and Scott Shane, "U.S. Knew of Suspect's Tie to Radical Cleric," *New York Times*, November 9, 2009, www.nytimes.com/2009/11/10/us/10inquire.html.

4. United States v. Umar Farouk Abdulmutallab, Sentencing Memorandum, 2:10-cr-2005-NGE-DAS, document # 130, U.S. District Court for the Eastern District of Michigan.

5. As revealed in a declassified admission that the United States was responsible for killing al-Awlaki, released in a letter from Attorney General Eric Holder to the Chairman of the Committee on the Judiciary, May 22, 2013, www.scribd.com/doc/143070298/Letter-from-Attorney-General-Eric-Holder-on-Americans-killed-in-counterterrorism-operations.

6. William Shawcross, *Justice and the Enemy: Nuremberg, 9/11, and the Trial of Khalid Sheikh Mohammed* (New York: PublicAffairs, 2011), 109.

7. Remarks by the President at the National Defense University, Fort McNair, Washington, May 23, 2013, www.whitehouse.gov/the-press-office/2013/05/23/remarks-president-national-defense-university.

8. Center for Constitutional Rights, "Al-Aulaqi v. Panetta," http://ccrjustice.org/targetedkillings.

9. Shawcross, *Justice and the Enemy*, 173.

10. Nasser Al-Aulaqi, on his own behalf and as next friend of Anwar Al-Aulaqi, v. Barack H. Obama, in his official capacity as President of the United States; Robert M. Gates, in his official capacity as Secretary of Defense; and Leon E. Panetta, in his official capacity as Director of the Central Intelligence Agency, Civil Action No. 10–1469 (JDB), http://ccrjustice.org/files/15(1)-Al-Aulaqi%20USG%20PI%20Opp%20&%20MTD%20Brief_09-25-10.pdf.

11. Letter from Attorney General Eric Holder to the Chairman of the Committee on the Judiciary, May 22. 2013, www.scribd.com/doc/143070298/Letter-from-Attorney-General-Eric-Holder-on-Americans-killed-in-counterterrorism-operations.

12. Nasser Al-Aulaqi, on his own behalf and as next friend of Anwar Al-Aulaqi, v. Barack H. Obama.

13. U.S. Department of Justice, "Attorney General Eric Holder Speaks at Northwestern University School of Law," www.justice.gov/iso/opa/ag/speeches/2012/ag-speech-1203051.html.

14. Letter from Attorney General Eric Holder to the Chairman of the Committee on the Judiciary.

15. Jo Becker and Scott Shane, "Secret 'Kill List' Proved a Test of Obama's Principles and Will," *New York Times*, May 29, 2012, www.nytimes.com/2012/05/29/world/obamas-leadership-in-war-on-al-qaeda.html?pagewanted=all.

16. Becker and Shane, "Secret 'Kill List.'"

17. Ibid.

18. www.cnn.com/video/data/2.0/video/us/2013/10/06/bpr-terror-suspect-in-custody.cnn.html.

19. The complete text of the Manchester manual can be found at www.combat-terror.com/library/al%20Qaeda%20Manual.pdf.

20. Tim Lister and Paul Cruickshank, "Senior al Qaeda Figure 'Living in Libyan Capital,'" September 27, 2012, http://security.blogs.cnn.com/2012/09/27/exclusive-senior-al-qaeda-figure-living-in-libyan-capital/?iref=allsearch.

[19] THE DEATH OF OSAMA BIN LADEN

Bruguière is quoted in Jay Cheshes, "France's Legendary Terror Cop," www.salon.com/news/feature/2002/01/03/bruguiere/.

1. Mark Bowden, *Guests of the Ayatollah: The Iran Hostage Crisis: The First Battle in America's War with Militant Islam* (New York, Grove Press, 2006), 379.

2. Peter L. Bergen, *The Longest War: The Enduring Conflict between America and al-Qaeda* (New York: Free Press, 2011), 75.

3. Quoted in David Remnick, "Exit bin Laden," *New Yorker*, May 16, 2011, 35.

4. There are, at the time of this writing, several accounts of the raid against the Abbottabad compound that ended with bin Laden's death. The first was Nicholas Schmidle, "Getting Bin Laden," *New Yorker*, August 8, 2011, 34–45. The most detailed is to be found in Mark Owen with Kevin Maurer, *No Easy Day: The Firsthand Account of the Mission That Killed Osama bin Laden* (New York: Dutton, 2012). A somewhat contradictory story is presented in Phil Bronstein, "The Shooter," *Esquire*, March 2013, 132–41, 203–8. This latter version was called "complete B-S" by another SEAL participant in the raid in Peter Bergen, "Who Really Killed bin Laden?" March 27, 2013, www.cnn.com/2013/03/26/world/bergen-who-killed-bin-laden/index.html?hpt=hp_c2, Thus, anyone depending on published sources must note the degree of uncertainty in the public record about how the raid unfolded.

5. Owen and Maurer, *No Easy Day*, 249

6. Peter L. Bergen, *Manhunt: The Ten-Year Search for bin Laden from 9/11 to Abbottabad* (Toronto, ON: Doubleday Canada, 2012), 77.

7. Owen and Maurer, *No Easy Day*, 177.

8. The full text of President Obama's remarks were published by the *New York Times* on May 2, 2011, at www.nytimes.com/2011/05/02/world/middleeast/02obama-text.html?_r=1&ref=asia.

9. Jeffrey Gettleman, "For Many Africans, Bin Laden's Death Was a Long Time Coming," *New York Times*, May 2, 2011.

10. Personal interview with Jack Cloonan, September 19, 2011.

11. Schmidle, "Getting bin Laden," 43

12. Nelly Lahoud, *Beware of Imitators: Al-Qa'ida through the Lens of Its Confidential Secretary* (West Point, New York: The Combating Terrorism Center at West Point, June 4, 2012), 69, http://www.ctc.usma.edu/wp-content/uploads/2012/06/CTC-Beware-of-Imitators-June2012.pdf.

13. Scott Shane and Charlie Savage, "Bin Laden Raid Revives Debate on Value of Torture," *New York Times*, May 3, 2011.

14. Jose Rodriguez, quoted in "Hard Measures, Hooked," *60 Minutes*, CBS-TV, April 29, 2012.

15. Henri Alleg, *The Question*, translated by John Calder (New York: George Braziller, 1958), 60–61.

16. Jose Rodriguez, quoted in "Hard Measures, Hooked," *60 Minutes*, CBS-TV, April 29, 2012.

17. Ibid.

18. Ibid.

19. Jane Mayer, *The Dark Side: The Inside Story of How the War on Terror Turned into a War on American Ideals* (New York: Anchor Books, 2009), 52.

20. *Black's Law Dictionary*, 8th ed. (St. Paul, MN: Thomson West, 2004), 1225.

21. Ibid., 1293.

22. United States of America v. Usama bin Laden, et al, S(7) 98 Cr. 1023.

23. Quoted in William Shawcross, *Justice and the Enemy: Nuremberg, 9/11, and the Trial of Khalid Sheikh Mohammed* (New York: PublicAffairs, 2011), 15.

24. Hannah Arendt, *Eichmann in Jerusalem: A Report on the Banality of Evil* (New York: Penguin Books, 1964), 209.

25. Ibid., 208–9.

26. Soufan discussed this during our personal interview, September 22, 2011 and in his book, *The Black Banners*.

27. Ron Suskind, *The One Percent Doctrine: Deep Inside America's Pursuit of Its Enemies Since 9/11* (New York: Simon & Schuster, 2006), 115.

28. Personal interview with Ali Soufan, September 22, 2011.

29. Ibid.

30. Personal interview with Joe Billy, September 22, 2010.

31. Personal interview with Ken Piernick, November 3, 2009.

32. Personal interview with Pat D'Amuro, September 21, 2010.

33. Peter L. Bergen, *The Osama bin Laden I Know: An Oral History of al Qaeda's Leader* (New York: Free Press, 2006), 65.

34. Mayer, *The Dark Side*, 153.

35. Personal interview with Edward Wilford, September 25, 2009.

36. Quoted in Jane Mayer, "The Trial," *New Yorker*, February 15 and 22, 2010, 53.

37. Benjamin Weiser, "In Federal Court, a Docket Number for Global Terror," *New York Times*, April 11, 2011, A18.

38. Mayer, "The Trial," 53.

39. "Khalid Sheikh Mohammed, 4 Others Charged in 9/11 Attacks," CNN Wire, April 4, 2012, www.cnn.com/2012/04/04/us/khalid-9–11-charges/.

40. Personal interview with Mary Jo White, September 24, 2009.

41. Ibid.

42. Anthony Summers and Robbyn Swan, *The Eleventh Day: The Full Story of 9/11 and Osama bin Laden* (New York: Ballantine Books, 2011), 177.

43. Quoted in Mayer, *The Dark Side*, 125.

44. Quoted in Suskind, *The One Percent Doctrine*, 324.

45. Quoted in Mayer, *The Dark Side*, 9.

46. Mayer, *The Dark Side*, 174.

47. Personal interview with Edward Wilford, September 25, 2009.

1. Gérard Prunier, *Africa's World War: Congo, the Rwandan Genocide, and the Making of a Continental Catastrophe* (New York: Oxford University Press, 2009), xxxv.

2. Bruguière gave a statement before the Committee on June 27, 2007.

3. Peter L. Bergen, *The Longest War: The Enduring Conflict between America and al-Qaeda* (New York: Free Press, 2011), 211.

4. Jeffrey Tayler, *Angry Wind: Through Muslim Black Africa by Truck, Bus, Boat, and Camel* (Boston: Houghton Mifflin, 2005), 235.

5. *Ibid.*, 249.

6. Robert R. Fowler, *A Season in Hell: My 130 Days in the Sahara with al Qaeda* (Toronto, ON: HarperCollins, 2011), 150.

7. Ibid., 153.

8. Eric Schmitt, "American Commander Details al Qaeda's Strength in Mali," *New York Times*, December 3, 2012.

9. Steven Erlenger, Adam Nossiter, and Alan Cowell, "French Say Airstrikes in Mali 'Blocked' Rebel Advance," *New York Times*, January 14, 2013.

10. Ibid.

11. "AQIM: The Threat to Western Interests in Africa and Beyond," *The Soufan Group IntelBrief*, October 10, 2012. http://soufangroup.com/briefs/details/?Article _Id=402.

12. Report from Agence France-Presse, October 17, 2011.

13. The revelation came in a letter to Congress, delivered in accordance with the disclosure requirements of the War Powers Act. Peter Baker, "Obama Acknowledges U.S. Is Fighting Groups Tied to al Qaeda in Somalia and Yemen," *New York Times*, June 16, 2012, A9.

14. Silas Apollo, "Eight Terror Suspects on the Loose," *Nation* (Kenya), September 14, 2012, http://www.nation.co.ke/News/Eight+terror+suspecto ı on ıtlıe+lo ose/-/1056/1507776/-/onde42/-/index.html.

15. Jean Herskovits, "In Nigeria, Boko Haram Is Not the Problem," *New York Times*, January 2, 2012.

16. Steve Coll, "Farouk Abdulmutallab," *New Yorker*, December 27, 2009, www .newyorker.com/online/blogs/stevecoll/2009/12/farouk-abdulmutallab.html

17. Personal interview with Pat D'Amuro, September 24, 2009.

18. Personal interview with Jean-Louis Bruguière, January 25, 2010.

19. "The Lion Kings," *Economist,* January 6, 2011, http://www.economist.com /node/17853324.

CONCLUSION

1. John Lukacs, *The Future of History* (New Haven, CT: Yale University Press, 2011), 55.

2. Gilles Kepel, *Jihad: The Trail of Political Islam* (Cambridge, MA: The Belknap Press of Harvard University Press), 2002, 4–5.

3. Ibid., 19.

4. Personal interview with Nelly Lahoud, September 21, 2011.

5. "Address to Joint Session of Congress (September 20, 2001)," in Barry Rubin and Judith Colp Rubin, eds., *Anti-American Terrorism and the Middle East: A Documentary Reader* (Oxford: Oxford University Press, 2002), 323.

6. Remarks by the President at the National Defense University, Fort McNair, Washington, May 23, 2013, www.whitehouse.gov/the-press-office/2013/05/23/remarks -president-national-defense-university.

7. Personal interview with Edward Wilford, September 25, 2009.

8. Quoted in Anthony Summers and Robbyn Swan, *The Eleventh Day: The Full Story of 9/11 and Osama bin Laden* (New York: Ballantine Books, 2011), 85.

9. Personal interview with Laura Gasiorowski, September 20, 2011.

10. Personal interview, September 22, 2010.

11. Daniel Benjamin and Steven Simon, *The Age of Sacred Terror* (New York: Random House, 2002), 160.

12. Michael Scheuer, *Through Our Enemies' Eyes: Osama bin Laden, Radical Islam, and the Future of America*, rev. ed. (Washington, DC, Potomac Books, 2006), 24–25.

APPENDIX

1. See Benjamin Weiser, "Al Qaeda member pleads guilty to 1990s conspiracy," *New York Times*, February 1, 2003, A13. Benjamin Weiser, "Terror Suspect Held Secretly for 4 Months," *New York Times*, March 22, 2002, B1. Benjamin Weiser, "10 Years for al Qaeda Operative," *New York Times*, February 2, 2003, B4.

FURTHER READING

All the sources employed in researching this book are appropriately cited in the notes. Individuals who were interviewed on the record are thanked in the acknowledgments. Listed below are especially noteworthy books recommended for readers seeking further information. I would be remiss if I didn't make mention of the court transcripts on which I relied so heavily, in particular the case of the United States of America v. Usama bin Laden et al., S(9) 98 Cr. 1023 (LBS). In addition, I wish to commend the exceptional reporting of the *New York Times*, which has provided—and continues to provide—comprehensive reportage of all aspects of this case.

Benjamin, Daniel, and Steven Simon. *The Age of Sacred Terror*. New York: Random House, 2002.

Bergen, Peter L. *Holy War, Inc.: Inside the Secret World of Osama bin Laden*. New York: Free Press, 2001.

————. *The Osama bin Laden I Know: An Oral History of al Qaeda's Leader*. New York: Free Press, 2006.

————. *The Longest War: The Enduring Conflict between America and al-Qaeda*. New York: Free Press, 2011.

————. *Manhunt: The Ten-Year Search for bin Laden from 9/11 to Abbottabad*. Toronto, ON: Doubleday Canada, 2012.

Berntsen, Gary, and Ralph Pezzullo. *Jawbreaker: The Attack on bin Laden and Al-Qaeda: A Personal Account by the CIA's Key Field Commander*. New York: Three Rivers Press, 2005.

Clarke, Richard A. *Against All Enemies: Inside America's War on Terror*. New York: Free Press, 2004.

Coll, Steve. *Ghost Wars: The Secret History of the CIA, Afghanistan, and Bin Laden, from the Soviet Invasion to September 10, 2001*. New York: Penguin Books, 2004.

————. *The Bin Ladens: An Arabian Family in the American Century*. New York: Penguin Press, 2008.

Hirsch, Susan F. *In the Moment of Greatest Calamity: Terrorism, Grief, and a Victim's Quest for Justice*. Princeton, NJ: Princeton University Press, 2006.

Kepel, Gilles. *Jihad: The Trail of Political Islam*. Cambridge, MA: The Belknap Press of Harvard University Press, 2002.

Lahoud, Nelly. *Beware of Imitators: Al-Qa'ida through the Lens of Its Confidential Secretary*. West Point, NY: The Combating Terrorism Center at West Point, June 4, 2012, http://www.ctc.usma.edu/wp-content/uploads/2012/06/CTC-Beware-of-Imitators-June2012.pdf.

Mayer, Jane. *The Dark Side: The Inside Story of How the War on Terror Turned into a War on American Ideals*. New York: Anchor Books, 2009.

McDermott, Terry, and Josh Meyer. *The Hunt for KSM: Inside the Pursuit and Takedown of the Real 9/11 Mastermind, Khalid Sheikh Mohammed*. New York: Little Brown, 2012.

Miller, John, Michael Stone, with Chris Mitchell. *The Cell: Inside the 9/11 Plot, and Why the FBI and CIA Failed to Stop It*. New York: Hyperion, 2002.

National Commission on Terrorist Attacks. *9/11 Commission Report*. New York: W.W. Norton, 2004.

Owen, Mark, with Kevin Maurer. *No Easy Day: The Firsthand Account of the Mission That Killed Osama bin Laden*. New York: Dutton, 2012.

Reeve, Simon. *The New Jackals: Ramzi Yousef, Osama bin Laden and the Future of Terrorism*. London: Carlton Books, 1999.

Report of the Accountability Review Boards: Bombings of the US Embassies in Nairobi, Kenya and Dar es Salaam, Tanzania on August 7, 1998, January 8, 1999. www.fas.org/irp/threat/arb/board_nairobi.html.

Rubin, Barry, and Judith Colp Rubin, eds. *Anti-American Terrorism and the Middle East: A Documentary Reader*. Oxford: Oxford University Press, 2002.

Scheuer, Michael. *Through Our Enemies' Eyes: Osama bin Laden, Radical Islam, and the Future of America*. Revised edition. Washington, DC: Potomac Books, 2006.

————. *Osama bin Laden*. New York: Oxford University Press, 2011.

Shawcross, William. *Justice and the Enemy: Nuremberg, 9/11, and the Trial of Khalid Sheikh Mohammed*. New York: PublicAffairs, 2011.

Soufan, Ali H., with Daniel Freedman. *The Black Banners: The Inside Story of 9/11 and the War against al-Qaeda*. New York: W.W. Norton, 2011.

Suskind, Ron. *The One Percent Doctrine: Deep Inside America's Pursuit of Its Enemies since 9/11*. New York: Simon & Schuster, 2006.

Wright, Lawrence. *The Looming Tower: Al-Qaeda and the Road to 9/11*. New York: Vintage Books, 2006.

INDEX